IN THE HIMALAYAS

Journeys Through Nepal, Tibet, and Bhutan

Jeremy Bernstein

A TOUCHSTONE BOOK

Published by Simon & Schuster Inc.
New York London Toronto Sydney Tokyo

Touchstone
Simon & Schuster Building
Rockefeller Center
1230 Avenue of the Americas
New York, New York 10020

Designed by Irving Perkins Associates
Manufactured in the United States of America

10   9   8   7   6   5   4   3   2   1

ISBN 0-671-68223-7

Portions were previously published in *The Wildest
Dreams of Kew.*

Contents

Acknowledgments

I owe a debt of gratitude to a great many people both for making our trip to Nepal possible and for helping me to gather the material presented in this book. In the former category, that our trip was possible at all is thanks to the editor of *The New Yorker*, William Shawn. Mr. Shawn encouraged us to make the trip and came to our rescue in financing it. Without the help of *The New Yorker* we simply would not have gotten to Nepal. In preparing the material for *The New Yorker* articles, which were based on the book, and in helping to edit the book itself I was very much aided by Gardner Botsford of *The New Yorker* editorial staff. I have been guided in my choice of material by his advice throughout. We are also indebted to Stanley Kubrick for some sage advice on photography. One of Kubrick's dicta was that one can never have too many light meters. Both of the ones that we *did* have broke while we were in the Nepalese back country, and it was only Jaccoux's expertise in mountain photography that saved us from a complete photographic catastrophe.

I spent a considerable amount of time with most of the people quoted in the book, and I am grateful collectively to them all and especially to Boris Lissanevitch, and his family, at the Hotel Royal. Boris took us under his generous wing and helped us to meet most of the people that we met in Kathmandu. There were, in addition to Boris, several people who have been enormously helpful to us, and who are not mentioned in the text. This is the place to thank them. In the first instance there is Elizabeth Ann Hawley, who, besides functioning as the éminence grise of the Tiger Tops Hotel, is also the Time-Life and Reuters correspondent in Nepal. Elizabeth knows as much about that fascinating country as anyone can know and she was, for us, a gold mine of information, both while we were there and by letter after we left. I am also grateful to Barbara Adams, another knowledgeable member of the American colony in Kathmandu, for her help and hospitality. I am also happy to thank Dr. John McKinnon and his wife, Diane, for their kindness when we visited their hospital in Khumjung, high up in the Sherpa country. Dr. Ray Fort of the United States AID mission in Kathmandu spent several days with me showing me how the AID program functions in Nepal. He also checked my manuscript for accuracy. I am very grateful to Ambassador Carol Laise for her help when we were in Nepal and for reading the manuscript of the articles, and for the kindness of the staff of the American embassy in Kathmandu and especially Gene Boster, who gave us every possible cooperation.

To these and the rest of the people, Nepalese and non-Nepalese, who made our trip such a rewarding experience, *namaste*—greetings—and many thanks.

—JEREMY BERNSTEIN, 1970

Preface

In the spring of 1968, upon returning from having spent the previous fall and part of the winter in Nepal, I wrote a profile of that country for *The New Yorker*. It became, a little later, the basis for the book I wrote about Nepal called *The Wildest Dreams of Kew*. The title, taken from the line in Kipling's poem "In the Neolithic Age"—"And the wildest dreams of Kew are the facts of Kathmandu"—was my idea and it was a bad one. When it was written the book was the first comprehensive modern accessible study of the country and it should have been presented as just that. Instead, with the odd title and its outré cover, bookstores had no idea where it belonged. I found it once in the gardening section of a local bookstore. Nonetheless it had a certain cult following—if that is the word—among the growing breed of adventure travelers. Several sent me letters and one kind soul even sent me a Pirandellesque photograph of himself—his feet really, on which my book was resting, opened to a picture taken at the very place where this photographer was taking the picture of my book. But, as is inevitable, the book became both out of print and out of date. (I was amused to see that it is offered now as a rarity in some book catalogues for several times its original price.) I had often thought of bringing out a new edition and, indeed, on my various trips back to Nepal I have collected data with that in mind.

In the spring of 1987, on my last trip to Nepal, I decided that it was not possible simply to update the book. The reason is that I had become a different person and Nepal had become a different country in the twenty years since I first visited it. *The Wildest Dreams of Kew* was, in its way, a very romantic book. My 1967 trip to Nepal was my first visit to Asia, to say nothing of the Himalayas. Since then I have traveled to the Indian subcontinent on an almost yearly basis. I felt a little like the late Wolfgang Pauli, who commented in middle age that he had lost his romantic feeling about physics because he knew too much. He had become, as he put it, a "quantum elder." I could see how dramatically Nepal had changed in twenty years, and some of it I did not like. Therefore to simply change a few facts and names and to reissue *Kew* in a revised edition would not work. On the other hand there was much that was valid in the original book. History is history and the history of Nepal I presented then is still its history. I decided that the thing to do was to revise *Kew*, dropping parts of it that did not seem to remain valid, but then to add new sections which complement the original book and bring things up to date. Furthermore, since the history of Nepal, Tibet, and Bhutan have been so closely intertwined I have brought them together in a single tale. I have traveled in all three countries since I wrote *Kew*.

I have preserved the original acknowledgments to *Kew* because in it I thanked a number of people, now old friends, who were so helpful. During my last trip to Kathmandu Jimmy Roberts—Colonel Roberts—pointed out to me that I hadn't thanked him for his help with *Kew*. He is right and I take this opportunity to thank him now. Ambassador Carol Laise is no longer in Nepal, but I want to thank Leon Weil, our ambassador to Nepal when I was there last, his wife, and the embassy people for their help and kindness, as well as William Dawson of USIS and his wife. I am grateful to Jim Edwards and Mountain Travel for arranging our Tibet trip and to my good traveling companions Sonam Gyalpo and Garry Daintry for their help as well. Elizabeth Hawley has been, for the last twenty years, a constant source of wisdom about this part of the world. To all of them—*dhanybad.*

Still the world is wondrous large—
Seven Seas from marge to marge—
And it holds a vast of various kinds of man,
And the wildest dreams of Kew
are the facts of Kathmandu
And the crimes of Clapham
chaste at Martaban.

—RUDYARD KIPLING,
"In the Neolithic Age"

PART I

Nepal

1

The Jewel and the Lotus

Once upon a time there was a lake called the Serpent's Lake, for Karkotak, the king of serpents, dwelt in it. It was a big, beautiful lake surrounded by lofty mountains. All water plants except the lotus grew in it, and one day Vipaswi Buddha came and threw a root of the lotus into the water.

"When this root shall produce a flower," declared the Buddha, "then Shoyambhu, the Self-Existent One, shall be revealed here in the form of a flame. Then the water in this lake shall go and there shall be a valley wherein shall flourish many towns and villages."

Years passed.

Lotus leaves were seen floating upon the water. And then the predicted flower bloomed in all its heavenly beauty, with a flame of five colors playing upon it.

Knowing that the Self-Existent One had been revealed in the lake, another Buddha, the Sikhi, made a pilgrimage to it with a large number of his followers. He went round the Serpent's Lake thrice and sat down to meditate at the top of a mountain; then he called his disciples together and told them of the future of the holy lake. He also informed them that it was time for him to leave the world, and amidst the lamentation of the men the Sikhi Buddha plunged into the lake and was absorbed in the spirit of the Self-Existent One.

Another long period elapsed, and the Visambhu Buddha arrived at the lake. Like his predecessors, he was accompanied by numerous followers to the Self-Existent One, and then he declared to his retinue, "The bodhisattva shall duly arrive here and let the water out of the lake." With that, the Buddha departed.

About this time in north China, the Bodhisattva Manjusri was meditating upon world events. When he knew that the Self-Existent One had been revealed in the Serpent's Lake, he called his followers, among whom was a person of high rank named Dharmakar, and he set out, accompanied by them, for the holy lake.

Arriving at the lake, Manjusri went around it until he came to a low hill in the south. Then he drew his scimitar and cut a passage through the hill, and the water gushed out. The bodhisattva then told his followers to settle down in the newly formed valley, and he departed, leaving Dharmarkar to become Nepal's first ruler.

This is the legend of the origin of the Kathmandu Valley. It is as close to an historical account of ancient Nepal as is available (archeology is, even now, in its infancy in the country), and like many Nepalese legends, there is a good deal about it that is true. Until about seven million years ago, according to the geologists, the Indian and Asiatic continents were separated by a sea, the Himalayan Sea, located about where the Himalayan chain is now. The Indian subcontinent drifted north, and when it collided with Asia the soft alluvial sea bottom was squeezed up. Gradually the Himalayan Sea was divided by the rising mountains into what are known as the Tibetan

Sea, now a high desertic plain north of the mountains, and
the Gangeatic Sea, now the flat plain of north India, to the
south. In the middle was left a fantastic land of high mountains, deep gorges and lakes. The Kathmandu Valley, which
lies slightly to the east of the middle of modern Nepal, was, as
is shown by fossils as well as by the alluvial character of the
rich soil in the valley, such a lake. (The only sizable lakes now
left in Nepal are in the midwestern region of the country, near
Pokhara, at the foothills of Annapurna.) The place near Kathmandu where Manjusri cut the mountains with his scimitar
to liberate the waters is well known to every Nepali. It is the
Chobar Gorge, three miles south of the city of Kathmandu. It
is a remarkably sharp gorge, through which the sacred
Bagamati River flows southward into the Ganges. The gorge
is spanned by a steel suspension bridge with wooden plank
flooring; and despite the fact that this is the oldest steel bridge
in the country, dating back about a half century, and that it
sways and creaks when one walks over it, it is one of the
better footbridges in Nepal.

The Kathmandu Valley floor ranges in altitude between
4,000 and 5,000 feet. The country as a whole exhibits the
widest altitude variation of any country on earth—from 150
feet above sea level in the south near India to 29,108 feet at the
summit of Mount Everest, which lies on the border between
Tibet and Nepal in the north. Since Nepal is at about the
latitude of Florida, the country is tropical wherever the altitude is low. In a general sort of way the average altitude
increases as one goes from the south to the Himalayas on the
northern frontier. The width of Nepal varies from 90 to 150
miles; it is, as a whole, a rectangularly shaped country
bounded by India on the west and Sikkim on the east, with
the long side of the rectangle stretching about 500 miles.

The south of Nepal is a flat region—an extension of the
Gangeatic plain—known as the Terai. It varies between 5 and
55 miles in width and consists of rice paddies, forests and
jungles. (The Terai jungle has been one of the most famous
big-game hunting grounds in the world and still contains its

share of tigers, cobras and pythons, crocodiles, and the one-horned Asian rhinoceros, whose horn, when ground up, produces a powder that is sold abroad as an aphrodisiac.) After the lower forests, the Himalayan foothills, which rise ten thousand feet or more, begin and extend up to the main Himalayan chain in the north. This part of the country is ribbed by gigantic gorges that have been created by the rivers running southward from the Himalayas. The geological forces that produced the mountains have twisted the rivers and the gorges and have left an occasional large valley—a former lake. The Kathmandu Valley, which has a population of about eight hundred thousand people (the total population of the country, which grows at a rate of somewhere between two and three percent a year and nearly six percent in the south, is now about seventeen million), is the largest valley. It is circular in shape and has an area of 218 square miles. Since the valley is neither very high nor very low, it has rather temperate weather, with temperatures that never exceed ninety degrees in the hot months of May and June and never get much below thirty-six degrees in the coldest month, January. Even in the winter months the sun warms the air during the day, it almost never snows, and it is rarely necessary to put on a sweater before evening.

Throughout the history of the country the Kathmandu Valley has been the cultural and political locus of Nepal. In fact, until the last forty years internal communication was so bad among the different communities in Nepal that a large fraction of the population was hardly aware that it belonged to any sort of nation at all. For most people in the hills or the Terai, Nepal meant the Kathmandu Valley, and in 1958 King Mahendra Bir Bikram Shah Deva, then ruler of Nepal, in an attempt to stimulate a national conscience, issued a decree asking the population to refrain from using Nepal in reference to the valley alone.

It is simply not known who the original settlers of the valley were. It is believed that the aboriginal population was overrun and absorbed during a series of migrations into the valley,

ending in the seventh century B.C., by an Indo-Mongoloid
race known as the Kirantis, from whom the present occupants
of the valley evolved. In 536 B.C. the Gautama Buddha was
born in the village of Lumbini in what is now the southern
part of Nepal—the Terai. Legend has it that the Buddha
visited the Kathmandu Valley. According to one account, he
and his party were warned before leaving, "In Nepal the
ground is nothing but rocks, and it is as humpy as the back of
a camel. Surely you are not going to enjoy your journey."
Whether because of the Buddha's visit or otherwise, the
Kirantis became Buddhists, and by the third century B.C.
some of the most famous Buddhist shrines in the valley—the
stupas at Swayambhunath, a hill near Kathmandu where the
first lotus took root and flowered, and at Bodnath, a small
town a few miles northeast of Kathmandu—had been built.
A stupa is a representation of the contemplating Buddha. In
form it has a hemispherical bottom, the *garbh*, representing
Buddha's body. At the top of the hemisphere is a cube—
Buddha's face. All the faces of the cube are painted to show
the Buddha's eyes. His nose is often represented by a curious
figure like a question mark that is usually interpreted as the
Sanskrit symbol for "one"—as in the "oneness" or "unique-
ness" of Buddha. In the middle of each of the four foreheads
there is a third eye. In Bodnath the four middle eyes have
been fitted with electric light bulbs which give the stupa an
uncanny appearance when viewed at night. During the day
the outstanding feature of the stupas is the eyes, which, as
one writer has remarked, have "a fascinating aspect of min-
gled meditation and detached watchfulness." They seem to
follow you as you go around the base. Above the face is a
series of coils, sometimes in metal and sometimes in stone,
that represent Buddha's hair. The legend has it that the Buddha was meditating one day when it occurred to him that he
was losing a certain amount of time away from his contemplation by the necessity of getting periodic haircuts. At once, the
story says, his hair became tightly coiled and turned blue,
and no further haircuts were required. In the countryside,

especially in the north, near Tibet, the landscape is dotted with stupas, many of which have, through age and neglect, lost their eyes but still retain a haunting suggestion of the original face.

The community of Bodnath is built in a circle surrounding the central stupa. It has long been a place of pilgrimage for Buddhists, especially from Tibet. Since the Chinese takeover of Tibet in the 1950s a certain number of Tibetan refugees have settled in Bodnath—there are about eight thousand Tibetan refugees left in Nepal out of the original group of fifteen thousand or so, the rest having re-migrated to India to join the Dalai Lama, spiritual leader of the Lamaistic Buddhists—and they ply their traditional trades such as farming and rug weaving. The Tibetans are extraordinarily persuasive salesmen, and any visitor to Nepal almost inevitably comes away with Tibetan statuary and *thanka*s, religious wall scrolls, which, he is assured, were brought down from the *ghompa*s—monasteries—in Lhasa. There is a thriving industry in the valley engaged in manufacturing imitation ancient Tibetan monastery art, and it may be just as well for the visitor that it is now all but impossible to find the real thing, since it is against the law in Nepal to export anything that is more than a hundred years old.

In Bodnath there was a man of Nepalese origin who claimed to be the Dalai Lama's "representative" in Nepal—the so-called Chini Lama, Chinese lama. Having met a few lamas and most especially the reincarnated head lama of the monastery in Thyangboche—a few miles from Mount Everest—and having been enormously impressed by the spiritual and human qualities of the ones I had met, I looked forward to meeting the Chini Lama on my first visit to Bodnath. I was somewhat shaken when the driver of the car that took me to Bodnath allowed that the Chini Lama had for sale a particularly fine collection of Tibetan rugs. The lama, a middle-aged man, lived in a small but elegant stone dwelling near the stupa. One climbed a wooden staircase to his quarters and removed one's shoes before entering the great man's presence.

His living room looked like a museum or the display room of an art gallery. When I walked in, there were several people with the lama, two of whom turned out to be art dealers from India. The lama himself was a spherical figure, shaped something like the stupa, which one can contemplate from his window. Unlike the Buddha, the Chini Lama had a totally bald round head. He motioned for me to sit down on a rug and, while drinking his morning tea, proceeded to study me with curiosity. After a few minutes of total silence, he held out an incredible statue, gold-plated, with dozens of arms, each arm holding a perfectly formed tiny gilded bird. His first words were, in English, "I'll bet that you have never seen one like this. It is worth fifteen hundred U.S. dollars." When it became clear that I was not going to buy his statue the lama lost interest in me and returned to bargaining with the art dealers. After inspecting a few rugs, I left. Later I was told that the Chini Lama also ran the only Tibetan distillery in the valley. He was completely untypical of the Buddhist religious leaders that I met, and the people in the Kathmandu Valley didn't have a great deal of use for him.

The main Buddhist sanctuary in the valley is Swayambhunath, situated on the top of a wooded hill just west of Kathmandu. It is best approached by climbing the three hundred steps that lead, rather steeply, to the summit. One first encounters a row of three very large, striking, and rather cruel-looking Buddhas that have been painted in bright colors. Everywhere one looks, there are small brown monkeys. (The monkey, like the cow, is a sacred, protected animal in Nepal, but this does not seem to stop the children who play near Swayambhunath from taking an occasional shot at them with small slingshots.) On the top of the hill there is a large cleared plateau, every square foot of which contains religious monuments. There is a huge stupa and dozens of small stupas; there is a large metal *dorje* (a symbolic lightning bolt); there are rows of prayer wheels that have *"Om mani padme hum"*—a sacred religious formula sometimes translated to mean "The jewel in the lotus" or "Hail to the jewel and the lotus"—engraved on the sides. The wheel, the wheel of life, representing the endless cycle of birth and rebirth, is one of the most important Buddhist symbols. To turn a prayer wheel adds to one's *sonam*—a measure of credit which a Buddhist hopes to accumulate in his present life in order to escape the pain of rebirth. In the mountainous countryside of Nepal, where the wheel for transportation is unknown, the only wheels one ever sees are wooden carousels that the Nepalis have constructed for their children to play on, water wheels for grinding corn or millet, prayer wheels, and potters' wheels. In the high mountain country near Tibet, one encounters prayer wheels that are turned by water in a stream; a bell rings each time a cycle is completed, and with the rushing stream it makes a lovely sound.

At the top of the hill one encounters a cross section from among all the races of Nepal: Sherpas and Tibetans from the north; Newars, the racial group that succeeded the Kirantis, in the valley; Gurungs, Magars, Sunwars, Rais, and Limbus— the hill peoples from whom the Gurkha soldiers are recruited; and a few Tharus, who have come north from the Terai to visit Kathmandu. (There are at least thirty separate local languages in Nepal and at least that many tribal groups. The official language of the country is Nepali, an Indo-Aryan language, derived from Sanskrit, which most of the population can now speak or understand. Most of the population is unable to read and write any language, and a number of the local languages, such as Sherpa, have no written counterparts.) Something like ninety percent of Nepalis are now Hindu or at least practice a religion which is a mixture of Buddhism, animism, and Hinduism, a mixture that is nearly pure Hinduism in the south near India and nearly pure Buddhism in the north near Tibet. However, almost all the great religious shrines in the Kathmandu Valley—there are more than twenty-seven hundred temples in the valley—contain icons that belong to both faiths. At Swayambhunath, for example, which is nominally a Buddhist shrine and indeed has an important monastery, also at the top of the hill, there is a shrine dedicated to Sitala, the Hindu goddess of smallpox, at which both Hindus and Buddhists used to pray for protection (smallpox was eradicated from Nepal in 1975). In all the complex and often bloody history of Nepal, there has never been a war fought along religious lines, and religious tolerance is both the law of the land and the practice of its people.

Buddhism was the religion of Nepal until about the fourth century A.D., when the valley fell under the influence of the Gupta kings of India, who were Hindus, and since that time the kings of Nepal have all been Hindu. Buddhism migrated north, through Nepal, into Tibet and China as increasing contacts developed among these countries in the seventh century. The first Chinese mission visited the Kathmandu Valley in A.D. 643. The leader of the second Chinese mission, in 647, Wang Huen Tse, recorded his mixed feelings about "Ni-Po-Lo"—Nepal—and its inhabitants:

> The kingdom of "Ni-Po-Lo" is about four thousand Li in circumference and the capital about twenty. It is situated in the middle of snowy mountains and, indeed, presents an uninterrupted series of hills and valleys. Its soil is suited to the cultivation of grain and abounds in flowers and fruits. One finds there red copper, yaks and birds of the name of ming ming. [Real yaks are never found below about thirteen thousand feet, so Wang Huen Tse was speaking either of yaks that he met while crossing the high passes leading from Tibet to Nepal or of one of the crossbreeds between yaks and buffalo such as the zopkio and zhum—the male and female offspring of such a union— which to the casual observer look like yaks, but which can and do live at lower altitudes.] Coins of red copper are used for exchange. The climate is very cold. The national character is stamped with falseness and perfidy, the inhabitants are all of a hard and savage nature: to them neither good faith nor justice nor literature appeal, but they are gifted with considerable skill in the arts. Their bodies are ugly and their faces are mean. Among them are both true believers [i.e., Buddhists] and heretics [i.e., Hindus]. Buddhist convents and the temples of the Hindu gods touch each other. It is reckoned that there are about two thousand religious who study both the Greater and Lesser

Vehicle. The number of Brahmans and of the nonconformists has never been ascertained exactly.

Curiously, Buddhism was, at the time of Wang Huen Tse's visit to Ni-Po-Lo, a relatively new export from Nepal to Tibet and China. Indeed, the ruler of Nepal, Amshuvarma, had only recently given his daughter Bhirkuti in marriage to the Tibetan King Songsten Gampo. The king also took a Chinese princess in marriage. (The two brides have become canonized in the Buddhist tradition and are now worshiped in Nepal as the Green and White Taras, the goddesses of compassion. Some of the most beautiful Nepalese statuary shows a tara traditionally with her hand held out in a gesture of offering.) Bhirkuti transmitted the Buddhist tradition to Tibet and hence to China. In addition, at this time the greatest architectural innovation that has ever been produced by the Nepalese, the pagoda, also moved north. According to Nepalese scholars, the pagoda can be traced back four thousand years in Nepal. It is said to have its origins in the practice of animal sacrifice.

There is still a great deal of ritual animal sacrifice in Nepal. On Saturdays one can drive past the Chobar Gorge to Dashinkali, a temple dedicated to Kali, the Hindu goddess of destruction, located about ten miles south of the city. Here hundreds of Nepalese come on foot and by truck with ducks, chickens, and goats that are to be sacrificed on the altar of Kali. The animals, which are led to the altar in a strangely silent procession, are killed with a single stroke of a kukri, the traditional Nepalese scimitar. Almost every Nepalese boy— not the Buddhists, who abhor the killing of animals— acquires a kukri as a sign of his manhood. The knives, kept razor-sharp, are worn in the belt and are used for everything from felling small trees to killing buffalo. The Gurkha soldiers often use kukris in hand-to-hand combat with devastating effect. After an animal sacrifice, the blood of the animal is used as a religious ornament and the animal is eaten. (Once, in the hills, I came across a small village all of whose inhabitants were gathered around a buffalo which had been hit in the neck with an ax, another weapon of sacrifice, and was slowly dying while the fresh blood was being collected in a copper vessel.) In these ancient rites the animals were often burned after being killed. It was necessary to design an altar that was sheltered to keep the rain from extinguishing the fire. It was also necessary, however, to cut a hole in the roof in order to let out the smoke. Hence to keep the rain from entering the hole a second roof was put on top of the first one—thus, the pagoda. The Kathmandu Valley is dotted with pagodas, often with three or four gilded roofs, resting lightly one on top of the other. At sunrise and sunset they glitter like jewels.

The city of Kathmandu is thought to have been founded in the eighth century. Its name, until the beginning of the sixteenth century, was Kantipur. At that time, according to legend, during a religious procession a sacred tree of Paradise took on human form and wandered among the spectators. The tree was recognized and held prisoner until it promised to give itself up and to allow its wood to be used in the construction of a single pagoda. Thus, in the center of the town there is a pagoda that is said to have been built from the wood of the sacred tree. In Nepali *kath* means "wood" and *mandu* means "house."

The real history of modern Nepal begins in the thirteenth century, with the advent of the Malla kings. The Mallas, assumed to be of Indian origin, acquired control over a part of what is now western Nepal and over the numerous feudal principalities in the Kathmandu Valley. (In addition to Kathmandu itself, and the small community of Bodnath, where the Chini Lama lived, there are two more major communities in the valley: Patan, which has structures that date back to at least the third century B.C.; about three miles southeast of Kathmandu and the oldest city in the valley, with a population now of about eighty thousand, and Bhadgaon, which is about eight miles east of Kathmandu and has a population of about fifty thousand.) At one point, before the advent of the

Mallas, each ward of Patan had its own king, while twelve kings ruled over Kathmandu and Bhadgaon. It appears that the Mallas were of Buddhist origin but adopted the Hinduism of the Newars, the race that succeeded the Kirantis in the valley. (Again, it is not well known what the exact origins of the Newars are and, indeed, when they came to the valley. Many of them have Mongolian features, indicating that they may have come down from the north. But they now practice Hinduism and their social lives are governed by a caste system similar to but somewhat less rigid than the Indian system. *Nava* means "valley" in Newari, and it is sometimes thought that *Nepal* is derived from *nava*. The Newars have some especially interesting matrimonial customs. Sometime between the ages of seven and nine a Newar girl is symbolically married to a tree, so that in the event that she is later divorced or widowed she still retains her status as a married woman. At the time of her marriage, her husband presents her a gift of areca nuts, and if, later, she decides to divorce him, she merely has to leave an areca nut on his bed and the marriage is terminated.) The Malla kings were great patrons of the arts, and under their reign most of the pagoda temples and gilded statues that are now the glory of the valley were constructed by Newar craftsmen. The Newars excelled in both metal- and woodwork. A typical Newar house—and many that are now occupied in the valley date back to the time of the Mallas—is made of red brick, but the windows and roofs are decorated with marvelously intricate wood carvings. It is one of the sadder aspects of modern Nepal that the Newar arts are disappearing. The brass workers have become plumbers, the woodworkers carpenters, and the wonderful old brick Newar houses are being plastered over with cement whenever their occupants can afford it.

The Malla dynasty reached its political apex under the rule of Yaksha Malla, which began in 1417 and lasted for forty-two years. He extended his domain into the west of Nepal and into present-day Tibet. At Yaksha Malla's death his kingdom broke up again into lesser principalities, and it was not until

the eighteenth century that Nepal was reunited. The three
sons of Yaksha Malla each ruled over a part of his empire,
with a resultant chaos of internecine warfare among their
descendants that lasted three centuries. The greatest achievements of this period were in the proliferation of Newar mas-
terpieces as each Malla king vied with the others in building
palaces and pagoda temples. In the beginning of the eighteenth century Bhupatindra Malla had built, in Bhadgaon,
the Nyatpola, a giant wooden pagoda temple with five roofs,
which despite the earthquakes that strike Nepal about once
in thirty-five years—the last severe earthquake in Kathmandu was in 1934, and it caused the destruction of entire
villages as well as a great many of the buildings in the city—
remains intact as one of the architectural marvels of the country. The entrance is guarded by a pair of legendary heroes ten
times as strong as an ordinary man. Above them is a pair of
elephants ten times stronger than they and above the elephants are two lions ten times stronger than the elephants
and above the lions are two dragons ten times stronger than
the lions. Finally, above the lions are two goddesses said to be
ten times more powerful than the lions and so one hundred
thousand times more powerful than an ordinary man.

While the Mallas were fighting among each other and
building statues of elephants and lions, another family dynasty was building its power in western Nepal. This was the
Shah family, whose dynastic capital was Gorkha, now a fairly
modest town some forty miles west of Kathmandu. The hill
tribes who became the subjects of the Shah kings of Gorkha
were, and are, superb fighters, and it is from among them
that the so-called Gurkha soldiers are recruited. It was not
until the middle of the nineteenth century that the British
army in India began employing the Gurkhas as military mer-
cenaries. (There are now four regiments—about ten thousand men—of Gurkhas in the British army and, while the
exact figure has not been made public, it is estimated that
there are about forty-five thousand Gurkhas in six regiments
in the Indian army.) Until that time they formed the army of

the kings of Gorkha and were used by them in the conquest of the Mallas. In 1736 the ninth king of the house of Gorkha, Marbhupal Shah, made the first invasion of the Kathmandu Valley. He was badly beaten by the Malla king and died in 1742. But his son Prithwi Narayan Shah, who became king at the age of twelve, took up where his father had failed, and by the time of his death, in 1775, he had succeeded in subjugating all of Nepal and establishing its borders pretty much as they are at the present time.

Prithwi Narayan was a ruthless soldier. He began his conquest of the valley by laying siege, three times, to the town of Kirtipur, a small medieval village on top of a hill a few miles south of Kathmandu. Its inhabitants were firmly entrenched in their fortifications, but Prithwi Narayan offered a general amnesty if they surrendered. They did, and he promptly gave orders that the lips and noses of all males twelve and over be cut off and that the name of the town be changed to Naskatipur—the City of Cut Noses. Only the players of wind instruments were spared mutilation. The rest of the towns surrendered to the Gurkhas one after the other, and by 1768 Prithwi Narayan had conquered the entire valley and had established the national capital of Nepal at Kathmandu. The present king, Birendra, is the tenth Shah king to rule Nepal.

It was with Prithwi Narayan that the systematic exclusion of Europeans began in Nepal, a policy that was followed, with rare exceptions, until 1950. Before the rise of the Shahs Nepal had been visited, more or less freely, by Europeans and especially by Christian missionaries. In 1661 a German Jesuit, Father Greuber, made a celebrated exodus from Peking, from which he had been expelled, south through Tibet and into Nepal. His journal is a fascinating record of how the country appeared in the mid-seventeenth century. Like all travelers from Nepal to Tibet he had to cross the high mountain passes that traverse the Himalayan range, which forms the common boundary of the two countries. Some of these passes are more than nineteen thousand feet, and the unacclimated traveler experiences serious effects from the lack of oxygen. As Father Greuber wrote upon crossing such a pass, "This hill is of unsurpassed altitude, so high that travelers can scarcely breathe when they reach the top, so attenuated is the air. In summer no one can cross it without gravely risking his life because of the poisonous exhalations of certain herbs." After a month's journey he reached the Nepalese town of Nesti, where he found that the inhabitants "live in the darkness of idolatry. There was no sign of the Christian faith. However, all things which are necessary for human life were abundant and one could there, as a matter of course, buy thirty or forty chickens for a crown." Six days later Father Greuber reached "Cadmendu," whose inhabitants, especially the women, offended his sensibilities even more than the residents of Nesti. "The women of this country are so ugly," he wrote, "that they resemble rather devils than human beings. It is actually true that from a religious scruple they never wash themselves with water but with an oil of a very unpleasant smell. Let us add that they themselves are no pleasanter and with the addition of this oil one would not say that they were human beings but ghouls." Prithwi Narayan summarized his attitude toward missionaries in the formula "First the Bible; then the trading stations; then the cannon." Even now all religious missionary activity in Nepal is forbidden by law, although there are missionary hospitals and schools that are allowed to function so long as they do not make any attempt at conversion.

After the death of Prithwi Narayan, Nepal entered a period of internal political disorder and external expansion. The sons of Prithwi Narayan plotted against each other until finally, in 1786, Bahadur Shah, the youngest son, removed the legitimate heir and became the de facto ruler until 1795. It was under Bahadur Shah that Nepal had its first confrontation with Chinese power. The Nepalis invaded Tibet in 1788 and 1791. Tibet was at that time a domain of the Manchu emperors of China. In 1791 a Chinese army of seventy thousand expelled the Nepalese from Tibet and marched over the high Himalayan passes to within a short distance of Kathmandu.

Undoubtedly the Chinese then, and the British in the next century, could have annexed Nepal. But for one reason or another, perhaps the stubborn fighting qualities of the inhabitants, both powers chose to administer military lessons and then withdraw. In this case, in 1792, the Nepalese agreed to leave Tibet and to send a tribute mission to Beijing every five years, a practice that continued until 1908.

Bahadur Shah was the first *mukhtiyar,* or prime minister, to assume executive powers in the name of the king. From his reign, and indeed until that of the present king, who reestablished the absolute authority of the monarch, the prime minister became, in Nepalese politics, an important and often the dominant figure. Such were the rivalries between the king and his executive officer that none of the *mukhtiyars,* from Bahadur Shah who began his office in 1769, until the rise of the first of the Ranas, the family that ruled Nepal with an iron hand as *hereditary* prime ministers from 1846 until 1951, died a natural death. All were assassinated or committed suicide. A British commentator, Laurence Oliphant, who made a rare visit to Nepal in the 1850s, observed that "the power of the prime minister is absolute till he is shot, when it becomes unnecessary to question the expediency of his measures," and he added that a man's chance of filling the office did not depend on his ability to form a ministry "so much as upon his accuracy in taking aim and his skill in seizing any opportunity offered by his rival of showing his dexterity in a manner more personal than pleasant."

The Shah kings adopted the practice, maintained up to the present king's grandfather, of marrying two queens at once. This introduced another source of confusion and intrigue into the government, with the queens and their assorted offspring vying for political power. In their fascinating book *Democratic Innovations in Nepal,* Leo Rose and Bhuwan Joshi describe the court scene as it was in the early 1840s, when the power struggle produced a state of almost total chaos: "The royal household was at this time badly split between the King, the Junior Queen, and the Crown Prince. The King was anxious to fix the succession on the Crown Prince, but without his own abdication; the Junior Queen was conspiring to put her son on the throne in place of the son of the late Senior Queen; the Crown Prince was conspiring against both his father and his stepmother in his eagerness to be seated on the throne at the earliest opportunity." To make matters worse, during this period the Nepalese attempted to penetrate south into India, an effort which led to an inevitable confrontation with the British.

The first British entry into Nepal came at the time of Prithwi Narayan. In 1767 the Malla king of Patan asked the Honourable East India Company to send troops to help lift the siege that Prithwi Narayan had laid upon the city. A force under the command of one Captain Kinloch was sent north. Before they even made contact with the Gurkhas, however, they were stopped in the Terai by an impassable natural barrier that the jungle and swamp country interposed—malaria. In Captain Kinloch's day the malaria-carrying mosquito was more than a match for any European army. As a British historian of Nepal put it, "Throughout the hours of daylight the Terai is safe enough. It is the evening that man may not spend in his most beautiful park. Sundown in the Terai has brought to an end more attempted raids into Nepal and has buried more political hopes than will ever be known."

In 1800 the Shah king, Girvana Jadha Bikram Shah, was deposed by his prime minister and fled to British India to organize, with the aid of the British, an attempt to regain the throne. But the new government, in order to avoid a direct confrontation with the British, signed a treaty in 1801 with the East India Company, which gave the company special trade rights and, most significantly, permitted the British to establish a residency in Kathmandu. This residency, which in 1947 became the British embassy, has functioned, with a few interruptions, since 1801. It was the only real contact that the Nepalese government had with Europe and the West until 1951. The first Resident, however, lasted only a year— the Nepalese government made it impossible for him to function—and shortly after he was withdrawn the Nepalese began raiding northern India from the Terai. The border situation deteriorated to such an extent that in November of 1814 Great Britain declared war on Nepal. After several setbacks, a British army under General Ochterlony defeated the Gurkhas in 1815 in the Garhwal hills. The Nepalese delayed in ratifying the treaty of armistice, and in 1816 General Ochterlony was ordered to take the capital, Kathmandu. There is little doubt that he could have done so, but in March of 1816 the Nepalese signed the Treaty of Segauli, which conceded portions of the Terai to the East India Company and which established the British Resident in Kathmandu once and for all. One of the most extraordinary provisions of the treaty, Article 7, gave the British a veto right over any future employment of Westerners in Nepal: "The Rajah of Nepal hereby engages never to take or retain in his service any British subject, nor the subject of any European or American State, without the consent of the British Government."

General Ochterlony, through his bitter struggles with the Gurkhas, had come to appreciate their exceptional qualities as soldiers, and he conceived the idea of recruiting them into the British army—if for no other reason than to keep them from making trouble in India. This was not done at once, on the grounds that the Gurkhas might have divided loyalties. But in 1832 Sir Brian Hodgson, the second British Resident, again urged their recruitment, and in a communication to his government he wrote:

> These Highland soldiers, who dispatch their meal in half an hour, and satisfy the ceremonial law by merely washing their hands and face and taking off their turbans before cooking, laugh at the pharisaical rigour of our sepoys, who must bathe from head to foot and make puja ere they begin to address their dinner, must eat nearly naked in the coldest weather, and cannot be marching trim again in less than three hours—the best part of the day. In war, the former carry several days' provisions on their backs, the latter would deem such an act intolerably degrading. The former see in foreign service nothing but the

prospect of gain and glory, the latter can discover in it nothing but pollution and peril from unclean men and terrible wizards and goblins and evil spirits. . . .

I calculate that there are at this time in Nepal no less than 30,000 dhakeries, or soldiers off the roll by rotation, belonging to the Khas, Muggars and Gurung tribes. I am not sure that there exists any insuperable obstacle to our obtaining, in one form or another, the services of a large body of these men, and such are their energy of character, love of enterprise, and freedom from the shackles of caste, that I am well assured their services, if obtained, would soon come to be most highly prized.

In 1857, when the Sepoy Mutiny broke out in India, the Nepalese offered to send Gurkha troops to the aid of the British, and the offer was accepted. Four thousand men were sent. From that time on the recruitment of Gurkha soldiers, which the British had been practicing clandestinely in Nepal for some time, became officially accepted by both governments. By 1908 the first Gurkha brigade in the British army was formed. It numbered about twelve thousand men organized into ten regiments. In the First World War the Nepalese government placed the whole of its military resources at the service of the British, and more than two hundred thousand Gurkhas fought in the war and suffered twenty thousand casualties. (Just before the war the Nepalese prime minister complained to the British Resident, "We have forty thousand soldiers ready in Nepal and there is nothing to fight.") After the war, Colonel Kennion, the British Resident, made a speech of appreciation to the prime minister in which he said, "I cannot attempt to enumerate all that His Highness did during the four years of war and after. Let it suffice to say that in this great war, if the expression may be allowed, Nepal pulled her weight, and more than pulled her weight." The British historian and journalist Percival Landon, in his book *Nepal*, written in 1928, commented in a footnote to Colonel Kennion's speech: "It would be interesting to know what meaning this expression, so full of significance to any Englishman, actually conveyed to the minds of the Resident's hearers; for there is scarcely a country in the world in which there are so few pieces of water and boat racing is entirely unknown." In the Second World War, the Gurkhas served with the British on every front, and most recently they were responsible for eliminating Communist guerrillas in Malaya and keeping order in Hong Kong. At the present time the British recruit about three hundred Gurkhas a year, a number that is steadily declining as the British cut back their military establishment. Pensions and salaries paid to the Gurkhas, plus the funds spent to maintain the recruiting depots, come to about fifteen million dollars a year and are after tourism the largest source of foreign exchange in Nepal exclusive of the Indian rupees that the Nepalese earn by exporting surplus rice to India.

By 1843 the political situation in Nepal had decayed into a state of nearly total chaos. There were three principal contending centers of power. There was the king, Rajendra Bir Bikram Shah, who has been described at best as weak and vacillating. There was the crown prince, Surendra Bikram Shah, the late senior queen's son, who was anxious to replace his father on the throne as soon as possible. And there was the junior queen, Lakshmi Devi, who, in a secret collaboration with General Mahatabar Singh Thapa, commander in chief of the army and prime minister, was attempting to put *her* son on the throne. The king sided alternately with the queen and the crown prince. In 1843 he made a formal declaration investing the junior queen with what amounted to the power to govern the country, and in December of 1844 the crown prince left Kathmandu for the Terai, vowing not to return until his father had turned over the throne to him. The king followed his son to the Terai and persuaded him to come back to Kathmandu by transferring some of his royal prerogatives to the crown prince. In addition, but still in the background, there was a young army officer, Jang Bahadur Kunwar, who later added the title *Rana* to his name, claiming descent from the Rajput ranas of Rajasthan, in India, a famous Indian royal house. During the next three years Jang Bahadur unleashed or profited from a series of events that catapulted him into absolute power in Nepal and have shaped the destiny of the country to the present day.

The first act of the drama occurred in May of 1845. Both the king and the junior queen had become apprehensive about the growing power of the prime minister, Mahatabar Singh, and they decided, in a rare collaborative effort, that he should be done away with. For this purpose they selected as executioner Jang Bahadur, who was Mahatabar Singh's nephew. It is not entirely clear whether, as Jang later claimed, he was ordered to shoot his uncle or be shot himself, or whether he realized that shooting his uncle would give him a new status with the royal family, and so accepted the job willingly. In any event, one night in May, Mahatabar was summoned to the palace on the pretext that the queen was ill, and when he arrived in her room he was shot dead by his nephew. For this act Jang was given command of a quarter of the Nepalese army. This was only the beginning. The queen had a lover in court, one Gagan Singh, who, through his liaison with her, had become the commander of seven Nepalese regiments and was in charge of supervising all of the arsenals and magazines in the country. The queen's love affair became known to the king, who decided that Gagan Singh was to be assassinated. At ten P.M. on the fourteenth of September of 1846 Gagan Singh was shot while kneeling in his room in prayer. It is not clear what role, if any, Jang Bahadur had in this assassination, but he took full advantage of it to precipitate the next act. The queen, upon hearing of the murder, was beside herself with rage and, on Jang's advice, summoned all the civil and military officials in the capital to the Kot, or courtyard, of the Royal palace. She proceeded to the Kot herself, armed with a sword, which she intended to use or to have used to behead her lover's murderer. As the courtiers assembled, unarmed and unsuspecting, Jang Bahadur surrounded the Kot with his own troops. At one A.M. the Kot was full. What happened next is subject to a great deal of controversy among historians of Nepal, and the different accounts tend to be flavored by a given historian's feelings toward the Ranas in general. In sifting through the different versions, one gets the impression that the queen, for reasons of her own, had fixed the guilt on a government minister, one of those assembled in the Kot, named Birkishore Pande, who at once proclaimed his innocence. The queen nevertheless demanded that he be beheaded immediately and without trial. General Abhiman Singh, whom the queen commanded to carry out the execution, refused, and Jang Bahadur, taking advantage of the general confusion, advised the queen to arrest General Singh, telling her, probably falsely, that Singh's troops were even then moving on the palace and that there was no time to lose. Singh resisted arrest and was stabbed to death by one of Jang's soldiers. (One account says that he was cut in two by a single stroke of a sword at the hand of one of Jang's brothers.) At this juncture the situation got out of control, and in the next few hours Jang's soldiers slaughtered most of the nobility in Nepal. This event, known as the Kot Massacre, eliminated in one swoop most of Jang's rivals for power. The king himself sought refuge in the British residency, and the next day the queen conferred the title of prime minister on Jang Bahadur. Most of those government officials not already under Jang's control fled the country. Jang had seven brothers and within a few days they held essentially all of the important government posts in Nepal. Indeed, for the next century Jang Bahadur and his descendants, the Ranas, controlled *everything* in Nepal as a sort of private family preserve.

Jang Bahadur became, in the thirty years that he ruled Nepal, that country's first really international political figure. The Rana regimes—the "Ranacracy," as it is usually referred to now in Nepal—left so many scars and bitter memories that even now, although four decades have passed since the Ranas were overthrown and the monarchy restored, Nepalese historians find it all but impossible to give an objective account of Jang Bahadur's life and career. There is no question, though, that he was a man of extraordinary physical courage, and while illiterate and uneducated, a man of immense native intelligence, political shrewdness, and wit. Very soon after he seized power, the British realized that Jang was potentially an invaluable ally who, if cultivated, could guarantee stability on the northern frontier with India. Thus, in 1850, Jang was invited to make a state visit to Great Britain to meet Queen Victoria. It is quite likely that Jang's party, which included four cooks and twenty-two domestic servants and which arrived in Britain in May of 1850, was the first group of Nepalese to cross the ocean and visit the West. The visit included a tour of the arsenals and munitions factories in Britain and a review of the troops—both of which were intended to, and did, convince Jang that it was hopeless to fight the British—as well as a night at the opera. The last, according to Percival Landon, produced an exchange with Queen Victoria that became the talk of London. As Landon tells it, "A distinguished prima donna had just given an exhibition of her powers and Jang Bahadur applauded. The Queen, turning to him, said, 'But you have not understood what she was singing.' Jang Bahadur at once replied, 'No, Madam, nor do I understand what the Nightingales are saying.' "

After returning home—through France, where he demanded a review of a hundred thousand French troops, and through India, where he visited a number of Hindu shrines in order to obtain ritual purification for having crossed the waters to the lands of the infidel—Jang, inspired by the British example, made at least some attempt to reform the legal code of Nepal. Nepalese law had evolved from Hindu religious practices and local tribal customs. Mutilation was a common punishment for thievery—the thief was given his choice of having what was left of his arm bound or of bleeding to death—and executions were often carried out on the spot by the prosecutor. (Brahmans were, under all circumstances, exempt from capital punishment.) Slavery was legal, and in order to pay a debt an individual could sell either himself or some member of his family into slavery. Civil disputes were frequently settled by a remarkable procedure involving a "water test" that took place in the Rani Pokhari, the Queen's Tank, in Kathmandu. If the disputants were unable otherwise to settle their quarrel, the name of each was inscribed on a slip of paper, which was rolled into a ball. Each ball, with the name hidden, was then attached to a reed, which was immersed in the deep end of the pool. Two members of the *chamkhalak* caste (the leather workers) were selected, one for each party to the dispute. They entered the tank and, at a signal, immersed themselves simultaneously, head down, in the water. The first man to rise was declared the loser, and the paper ball attached to his reed was opened to see who had lost the case. Adultery was punishable by the summary execution of the adulterer at the hand of the offended husband; sati, the practice among Hindu widows of offering themselves for burning on their husbands' funeral pyres, was common. Jang abolished the mutilation penalty and the water test: he made it illegal for a man to sell himself or his children into slavery, although it was not until 1924 that slavery as an institution was abolished in Nepal, and he discouraged the practice of sati. (Nevertheless, when he died, in 1877, his three senior wives committed themselves to the pyre.) The method of punishing an adulterer was subtly modified—the adulterer was allowed a moment's head start to flee for his life, an advantage that was, in general, of small value, since friends of the husband were allowed to trip the adulterer as he tried to get away. There was a system of lower and higher courts, with Jang exercising the ultimate judicial power, an intriguing feature of which was that a lower-court magistrate whose ruling was overturned was liable to fine, corporal punishment, and even decapitation.

On his return trip from England to Nepal, Jang encountered in Ceylon the English hunter and sportsman Laurence Oliphant, whose observations on the vulnerability of the prime ministers to gunshot were cited earlier. Oliphant was invited to accompany Jang on a hunting trip to the Terai and, ultimately, to Kathmandu, and his account of the voyage, *A*

Journey to Kathmandu, published in 1852,* is one of the delights of Himalayan literature. Oliphant and his host did some fine tiger hunting in the Terai. The method used to hunt tiger and other big game in the Terai did not appear to the casual observer to give the beasts much of a chance. For weeks in advance of the shoot the animals were "beaten"— essentially, herded—by a ring of native "beaters" into a small area in the jungle, which was surrounded by men and tame elephants in order to keep the game inside. The animals were then allowed a few weeks before the shoot to calm down and become accustomed to their new home. At the time of the shoot, bait, which for tiger was a live buffalo, was staked out; the buffalo was literally staked to a post or a tree. When the tiger came to kill and eat the buffalo the stake was surrounded by a ring of trained elephants, which kept the tiger trapped until the hunter, on the back of one of the elephants, could shoot him. About the only chance the tiger had was to panic and stampede an elephant. This was not too common, since a

---

* The book is long out of print, but I had the good fortune to find it and several other out-of-print classics on Nepal in a remarkable private library in Kathmandu belonging to one of Jang's descendants, Field Marshal Kaiser Shamsher Rana. (Keshar is a fairly common Nepalese first name, but the field marshal, who was the commander in chief of the Nepalese army and an admirer of Kaiser Wilhelm, preferred the Western spelling.) The library, reputed to have been the largest private library in Asia, is housed in several rooms in the field marshal's mansion. People who knew him said that the old gentleman—he died in 1964 at the age of seventy-two— delighted in working a conversation around to the point where he could say, "On page thus-and-so of the first volume of thus-and-so the author says . . . ," and then quoting verbatim from one of his books, which he would then produce from the depths of his library to clinch the point. In addition to being a book collector, the field marshal was an avid hunter, and a visitor to the largest of the rooms in which the books are housed, on the first floor of the mansion, is stunned by the sight of an extremely lifelike stuffed tiger evidently ready to pounce. On one of my visits, arranged by writing a note of request to the field marshal's widow, who then lived in the house, I came upon a live spotted deer in the library chewing on the fur of the tiger. The book collection is incredibly eclectic, ranging from *The Wizard of Oz* to an entire cabinet devoted to works on sex. In addition to an enormous ensemble of rare, handwritten ancient Tibetan manuscripts, the field marshal had probably every book on Nepal and Tibet ever written in any language. The library has now been turned over to the Nepalese government by his widow, and on my last visit it had been cataloged, and several other visitors seemed to be making use of the books that are now available to the general community.

tiger is no match for an elephant, who, when attacked, simply lifts the tiger with his trunk and pounds him several times on the ground until he is dead. (On a visit to the Terai I had occasion to take an elephant ride in the jungle. At one point the beast suddenly knelt on its forefeet as if in prayer. Later, when I asked why, I was told that this was the elephant's defensive fighting position and that it had probably scented a tiger, which, happily, had been scared off by the noise of our party.)

After the hunt Oliphant and his host started the long trek over the mountains to Kathmandu. Oliphant describes the trek in terms that strike a chord of sympathy in anyone who has traveled in the Himalayas of Nepal on foot: "It was with no little regret then that we made the almost interminable descent, apparently for the mere purpose of starting fair from the bottom of the valley, before we commenced the arduous climb in store for us over a range still higher than the one we had just traversed." Finally they came upon the Kathmandu Valley and, like so many travelers before and since, he was overwhelmed by its sheer beauty. He writes:

> A tradition is current in Nepaul [Oliphant's spelling] that the valley of Kathmandu was at some former period a lake, and it is difficult to say in which character it would have appeared the most beautiful. The knolls, wooded or terraced, with romantic old Newar towns crowning their summits—the five rivers of the valley winding amongst verdant meadows—the banks here and there precipitous where the soft clayey soil had yielded to the action of the torrent in the rains—the glittering city itself—the narrow paved ways leading between high hedges of prickly pear—the pagodas and temples studded in all directions, presented a scene as picturesque and perhaps more interesting than would have been afforded by the still lake embedded in wild mountains and frowned upon by snow-capped peaks.

As Jang's guest in Kathmandu, Oliphant developed a thoroughgoing admiration for the foresight of his host when it came to dealing with potential conspiracies against his life. In particular he writes, "It is by no means an uncommon mode of execution in Nepaul to throw the unfortunate victim down a well: Jang had often thought that it was entirely the fault of the aforesaid victim if he did not come up again alive and unhurt. In order to prove the matter satisfactorily, and also to be prepared for any case of future emergency, he practiced the art of jumping down wells and finally perfected himself therein." Indeed, Jang claimed to have been thrown down a well at one point in his career before becoming prime minister, in an attempted assassination organized by the crown prince. By a prearranged plan he clung to the side until midnight, when he was rescued by some friends. (In Field Marshal Kaiser Shamsher Rana's copy of Oliphant the word "dexterously," used to describe Jang's acrobatics in the well, is printed upside down and backward; in a careful script, with red ink, the field marshal, who evidently thought well of his ancestor's feat, had crossed out the offending misprint and rewritten it.) On a tour of Jang's residence, Oliphant happened on a portrait of Queen Victoria and also of a gentleman with "keen eyes and high forehead" whom he did not recognize. Jang was helpful. "See," said Jang enthusiastically, "here is the Queen of England and she has not got a more loyal subject than I am." Then turning to the picture of the man with the keen eyes and high forehead, he remarked, "That is my poor uncle Mahatabar Singh, whom I shot; it is very like him." (This portrait, or one like it, is in the Nepal National Museum in Kathmandu. It is difficult to be sure of the origin of *anything* in the museum, because almost none of the objects are labeled with their dates and histories. Most of the labels are in Nepali, which is fair enough, but even these when translated do not say much more than "Shiva" or "Tara" or whatever. The collection is an odd mixture of old weapons, including a "Tibetan leather gun," magnificent pieces of Newar and Tibetan art, and a random assortment of portraits of Victorian figures such as Prince Albert. It seems to be a collection in search of a curator.)

Jang Bahadur regarded the law of succession of the prime

ministry—as established by the Sanad of 1856—which King Surendra, the former crown prince, signed, and which reduced the royal family to political impotence, as the master stroke of his political career. In order to understand the circumstances under which the king issued a decree eliminating himself and his family, in perpetuity, from playing any sort of active role in the government of his country, one must recapitulate a bit as to what happened to the junior queen, King Rajendra, and Crown Prince Surendra after the Kot Massacre. No sooner had the queen proclaimed Jang Bahadur prime minister than she entered into a conspiracy with one of the few remaining noble families not decimated in the massacre—a conspiracy in which she intended to murder Jang, the king, *and* the crown prince. But one of the plotters gave away the show, and Jang had thirteen members of the family killed on the night of October 31, less than a month after the affair at the Kot. The queen was banished to Benares, in India, and King Rajendra, apparently reasoning that, despite everything, he was safer with the queen than with Jang, went with her. The king organized a naïve and futile attempt to regain his throne, and in May of 1847 Jang deposed him and elevated the crown prince to the throne, an arrangement that was endorsed by the British, giving it international status. Shortly thereafter the old king was arrested and brought back to Kathmandu, where he lived out the remainder of his life as a prisoner. The queen died in exile and Jang maintained the new king, Surendra, as a puppet. During this period a member of the staff of the British residency wrote that "one may live for years in Nepal, without either seeing or hearing of the King." One may, indeed, wonder why Jang did not simply eliminate the monarchy once and for all rather than preserve at least its symbolic status. The answer is that in Nepal the monarch was—and, by a considerable fraction of the population, still is—regarded as a direct descendant of the god Vishnu, so to have done away with the king altogether would have aroused considerable hostility and perhaps open rebellion among the populace. So Jang was content to keep him out of sight, but alive, in Kathmandu.

The law of succession, introduced by Jang, passed the office of prime minister, not from father to son as was the case with the royal house, but from brother to brother. The first to succeed was, therefore, the eldest surviving brother of the prime minister, then the next oldest, and so on, and when these had been exhausted the job was to pass to the sons of Jang, then the sons of his oldest brother, and so on. The system was designed to ensure that Nepal would have a mature ruler at all times. Indeed, one of the problems that had plagued the Shah dynasty was that, since many of the kings died young, their offspring were often infants when they inherited the crown, which meant that the country was ruled by the prime minister or the queen or one of the brothers of the king—whoever succeeded in eliminating the others, usu- ally by assassination, from the race for power. As far as it went, Jang's scheme did at least ensure that there were no infant prime ministers. But Jang failed to anticipate the prob- lems that arose from the fact that all of the Ranas had enormous numbers of children, legitimate and illegitimate. According to Dr. Daniel Wright, who was the surgeon at- tached to the British residency during Jang's lifetime, Jang fathered at least a hundred children, including ten legitimate sons, while his youngest brother, Dhir Shamsher, had seven- teen legitimate sons. A later-day British commentator who was shown a picture of a typical Rana general and his family remarked, "He is surrounded by so many children that the picture looks more like a photograph of a school than a family group." The situation reached such proportions that Chandra Shamsher Rana, who ruled as prime minister from 1901 to 1929, made a formal division of Rana offspring into three classes. The "A" class Ranas were children of Ranas and wives of equally high-caste families. These families were allowed by the caste system to dine with the Ranas, and male "A" Ranas automatically became major generals at the age of twenty-one and could advance—at least in principle—to commander in chief. The "B" class Ranas had mothers who were also legitimate wives but whose families were of lower, though good, caste. These families were allowed to take part in Rana social occasions but were not allowed to eat boiled rice with the Ranas of higher caste. The "B" male offspring became, at the age of twenty-one, lieutenant colonels, but could never rise above the rank of full colonel. Finally there were the "C" class Ranas, born of mistresses, whose families, being of lower caste, were not allowed to eat with the Ranas at all. Various influential Ranas after Chandra Shamsher, however, made special exemptions for certain of their offspring of whom they were especially fond. Until the end of the Second World War the Rana regime was so powerful that there was very little, and certainly no successful, resistance to it, but such resistance as there was came, in most cases, from lower-class Ranas who felt frustrated by their inability to rise within the succession and hence made attempts to overthrow the system.

Jang was immensely pleased with the Sanad, which enunciated the law of succession, and he commented to his sons and brothers, "I have established a constitution unknown in the annals of gods or emperors by setting up a covenant, and you should not think of acting in contravention of the order of succession. Even if your superior and master takes to tying up goats to elephants' posts or vice versa or to paying no heed to merit, do not oppose him, but rather forsake the country and retire to a sacred place." Needless to say, no sooner had Jang died than his ten sons and the seventeen sons of Dhir Shamsher, along with various surviving members of Jang's family, began conspiring against each other for power. In 1885 Bir Shamsher, the oldest son of Dhir Shamsher, who had in the meanwhile died, organized a coup in which Jang's eldest and only surviving brother, the prime minister at the time, was shot, along with most of Jang's sons and their families. Bir Shamsher elevated himself to the prime ministry in a ceremony that was presided over by the then king, Prithi Vir

Bikram Shah, who was five years old. From that time until the overthrow of the Ranas in 1951, all of the prime ministers came from the Shamsher branch of the family. (In Urdu *sham* means "equal" and *sher* means "lion.") Jang was not only concerned about arranging the succession, but also he set about to interlock his family with the royal house through marriage. Indeed, three of his daughters were married to the king's oldest son, and *his* oldest son married the king's daughter. It became the practice of the Ranas to arrange marriages for the young kings as early as possible and very often with Rana girls. Thus, for example, the present king's grandfather, King Tribhuvan, was married to two young girls when he was thirteen, and his father, Mahendra, was only fourteen years younger than his late father. (Tribhuvan had fathered three sons by the time he reached sixteen.) King Mahendra, defying tradition, married only one wife in 1940; when she died he married her sister. They were Rana noblewomen. The present queen, Aishwarya Rajya Laxmi Davi Shah, is the oldest daughter of the late Lieutenant General Tandra Shumshare J.B. Rana. She married King Birendra, who was born in 1945, in 1970.

In 1854, the Nepalese, under Jang, invaded Tibet, and after a certain number of indecisive battles the Chinese mediated an armistice, the Treaty of Thapathali, in which both governments pledged "respect" for the emperor of China. The treaty went on to say, "Tibet being merely a country of Monasteries of Lamas and a place for recitation of prayers and practice of religious austerities, should any foreign country invade Tibet in the future, Gorkha [i.e., Nepal] will afford such assistance and protection as it can." In fact in 1903 when the British invaded Tibet the Nepalese supplied them with yaks and porters despite the treaty. One of Jang's more ingenious maneuvers in the war of 1854 was to obtain a declaration from the rajguru, the highest Hindu religious authority then in Nepal, that yaks were a species of deer, so that the Gurkha soldiers could eat them without breaking the Hindu law against consuming beef. It was Jang who, in 1857, sent the

Gurkhas to India to help suppress the mutiny; in recognition for this he was decorated by the British and, more important, Nepal received back the portions of the Terai which had been given to the British in 1816. Since the agricultural produce of the Terai is now the most important export from Nepal, it is quite possible that the return of these territories was the most significant act of foreign policy during the century of Rana rule.

In 1901 Bir Shamsher, the prime minister who had come to power after the assassination of Jang's older brother, died and was succeeded by Deva Shamsher. If Deva had been allowed to rule, the subsequent history of Nepal might well have been entirely different and the country could have been a half century further along in its development than it is today. Deva Shamsher was a progressive. He opened a network of primary schools in the Kathmandu Valley, favored judicial reforms, and even hinted at the beginnings of some sort of popular democracy. He lasted four months in office and, because of his ideas, was deposed by his younger half-brother Chandra at gunpoint and sent into exile. The only tangible result of Deva's ministry that has endured is the custom, initiated by him, of having cannons fired in Kathmandu to indicate high noon.

Chandra Shamsher was the first Rana prime minister to have a formal education. He studied at Calcutta University, where he learned English. (According to a contemporary account, Jang made a few attempts to learn English during his lifetime and had a fondness throughout his life for having the English and Indian newspapers read and explained to him. There were no newspapers in Nepal.) Perhaps because he had been educated, Chandra Shamsher understood the dangers that an educated population would pose to an authoritarian government, and one of his first acts as prime minister was to close his brother's primary schools. Chandra also maintained the Rana tradition of excluding nearly all foreigners from Nepal. The rare exceptions were either guests of the British Resident or journalists and scholars such as

Percival Landon and the great French Orientalist Sylvain Levi, who wrote favorably about the regime. In Percival Landon's book *Nepal* he gives a list of all the Europeans who visited Nepal, officially, from 1881 to 1923; there were exactly 153. Even these visitors were not allowed to leave the Kathmandu Valley, except for hunting in the Terai. Indeed, the second volume of Landon's monumental work begins with a sort of illustrated tour of the countryside, complete with photographs, which he received from the government, along with a text, written in travelogue style, which he appears to have invented partly from his imagination and partly from what he was told to write. At one point he asked Chandra why none of the English visitors to Nepal, including the Resident, were allowed to leave the valley and why so few Englishmen were allowed to come to Nepal at all. He was told, "My friend, the English have at times difficulty in the government of India. These difficulties arise in no small measure from the fact that in these days of easy travel all English sahibs are not sahibs. Now, I am convinced that the prosperity of Nepal is bound up with the maintenance of British predominance in India, and I am determined that the sahib who is no sahib shall never enter Nepal and weaken my people's belief that every Englishman is a gentleman." As late as 1960, after a decade of intense effort by the post-Rana governments to improve conditions in the villages in the countryside of Nepal (following a century of total neglect under the Ranas), the life expectancy of a rural Nepali was twenty-six years, and two out of three children failed to survive infancy. It is small wonder that Chandra was not inclined to allow European journalists to learn firsthand about the life of the Nepalese people.

Despite everything, it must be said that Chandra Shamsher brought the beginnings of Western technology to Nepal, or, at least, to the Kathmandu Valley. In 1904 Kathmandu was electrified, and in 1906 Lord Kitchener, the commander in chief of the British forces in India, who visited the valley, could write, "There I found marble palaces lighted by electricity and full of

Nepalese officers who are . . . always in uniform like a conti-
nental nation." During Chandra's regime the Ranas began the
construction of fantastic mansions modeled after French châ-
teaux. Fixtures like the crystal clock, chandeliers, and illumi-
nated fountain that decorated Chandra's own dining room,
which is now used for state dinners, were carried across the
mountains from India on the backs of coolies. Chandra's palace, the Singha Durbar, constructed in 1905 and modeled
after the Palace of Versailles, contains more than fourteen
hundred rooms. It now houses the offices of nearly the entire
Nepalese government.*

The ruling elite were vaccinated against smallpox. A
narrow-gauge railroad was constructed from the Indian border through part of the Terai, and a road was built from
Birganj on the Indian border to Bhimphedi at the foothills
leading to Kathmandu, and then a ropeway was constructed
for transporting small amounts of freight over the hills to the
capital. In 1918 Chandra built the English College in Kathmandu, but it trained only a few members of elite families.
(Dr. T. N. Upraity, the former vice chancellor of Tribhuvan
University, which is the only university in Nepal and which
graduated its first PhD in 1968, told me, when I went to visit
the school, that in his class at the English College, the class of
1945, there had been eleven students.)

All of the Rana prime ministers, Chandra included, ran
Nepal as if it were a private business corporation. Any income
from taxes in excess of the meager expenditures that the
government made for public works and administrative expenses was kept by the Rana family, who banked it in Europe
and India. The only connection that the government had with
most people, who lived in isolation, often several weeks'
march by foot from Kathmandu, was the tax collector. Within

---

* There is one curiosity in the palace that must have reflected an odd quirk in
Chandra's character. Between the main dining room and a rather charming smaller
room, used now by the king for receiving state guests, there is a connecting ante-
chamber lined with amusement-park mirrors that distort and distend the image of
the passing visitor.

the country there were private principalities, like Mustang, in the west near the Tibetan border, that were allowed to function autonomously so long as the tax was collected. All opposition, or even potential opposition, was ruthlessly suppressed. Radios were forbidden to the Nepalese until 1946. Most foreign newspapers and periodicals were not allowed into the country, and when a group petitioned the government for a public library in Kathmandu in 1930, the petitioners were prosecuted for contemplating an unlawful action and fined. There was an eight-o'clock curfew in Kathmandu and a similar curfew in every substantial town in the country. Any sort of native talent in the arts or literature was discouraged and, indeed, most of the older generation of writers and poets now in Nepal have spent time either in jail or in exile. Land was held in a system of tenure and debt designed to keep the Nepalese farmer in perpetual servitude to a few large landowners—a system so intricate that even now, forty years after the fall of the Rana regime, the government is just beginning to make successful inroads in the redistribution of land. A few wealthy families in Kathmandu had telephones and automobiles, but the rest of the country lived in towns and villages that had remained, and to some measure still do remain, as they were in the fifteenth century.

From Chandra Shamsher's death in 1929 until the revolution of 1950, two of his brothers, one of his sons, and a nephew became prime minister in succession. In the 1930s secret opposition groups, including the People's Party (Praja Parishad), began forming, aided, both morally and financially, by King Tribhuvan, whose reign began in 1911. In 1941 the then prime minister, Juddah Shamsher, tried to depose the king and put Crown Prince Mahendra—the present king's father—on the throne. The crown prince, who was then twenty-one, refused, in an act of great courage. After the war, serious agitation against the regime began. In 1946 the Nepali Congress Party, modeled after the Indian Congress Party, was formed in India by exiles from Nepal, and in 1947 the first of a series of strikes organized by the party began. In 1948 the

Rana prime minister, Padma Shamsher, attempted some reforms, but was quickly forced to resign by his cousin Mohan
Shamsher, who preferred the status quo.

In 1947 the British left India, and with their departure the
traditional bond between the Rana governments and the British raj was broken. The new government of India, under
Nehru, was extremely eager to promote change in Nepal.
After the Communists came to power in China in 1949, it
became clear that Tibet was going to be invaded. Clearly
understanding the implications of having Chinese power on
the borders of an unstable Nepal—after the Himalayan foothills of Nepal are crossed, going south, the terrain is completely open and merges into northern India with no natural
barriers whatever—the Indians put strong pressure on the
Ranas to modernize their government. In fact, in early 1950
Nehru stated, "If [freedom] does not come [to Nepal] forces
that will ultimately disrupt freedom itself will be created and
encouraged. We have accordingly advised the Government of
Nepal, in all earnestness, to bring themselves into line with
democratic forces that are stirring in the world today. Not to
do so is not only wrong but also unwise."

In November of 1950, King Tribhuvan precipitated the
events that led to the fall of the Ranas. All of the king's
movements were closely guarded and any trip outside the
capital could be made only with the permission of the prime
minister, and then never unescorted. On November 5, the
king saw the prime minister to arrange for permission to leave
Kathmandu on a hunting trip. What happened next is graphically described by Joshi and Rose in their book *Democratic
Innovations in Nepal.*

The Rana ruler agreed and provided the necessary military
escort, unaware that among the escort were several whom
King Tribhuvan had already won over to his side. On the
morning of November 6, King Tribhuvan and his entire family, with the exception of his four-year-old grandson Gyamendra, departed by automobile from the Royal Palace on
what was ostensibly a hunting trip. The Indian embassy was

on the road the royal party was supposed to follow. On reaching the gates of the embassy, the king and his sons, who were all driving their own cars, suddenly swung through the gates and into the grounds, to the surprise and consternation of those Rana guards who had not been apprised of the king's plan. Thus the royal family took sanctuary and escaped from the Rana ruler's control. It seems probable that Prince Gyamendra was left behind to avoid suspicion about the hunting trip and to provide protection for him and the royal line in the event of mishap to the others if the plan should fail.

The Ranas attempted to entice the king out of the embassy, and when that failed they crowned his four-year-old grandson as the new king. On November 10, King Tribhuvan was flown in an Indian air force plane to New Delhi, and shortly thereafter armed rebellions broke out at several points in the Terai. In December, when the rebellion had not been contained and it became clear that the new king was not going to be recognized by foreign governments, the Indians proposed a settlement in which King Tribhuvan was to be restored, a constituent assembly was to be brought into being for the purpose of writing a new constitution for the country, and a Rana would continue as prime minister but with greatly reduced powers. In early February King Tribhuvan and the leaders of the Nepali Congress Party returned in triumph to Kathmandu, where they were met at the airport by Mohan Shamsher, the last of the old-style Rana prime ministers. With this meeting the Rana regime was ended and Nepal began its struggle to reenter the modern world.

For the next four years the king attempted to create a stable government. The coalition with the Rana prime minister failed to work and was dissolved in a few months; a chaotic period followed, during which the political power shifted back and forth between the king and the Congress Party. By March of 1955, when King Tribhuvan died in Switzerland, where he had gone for treatment of a chronic heart condition, there was a general deterioration of the situation in the country. Inflation had decreased the value of the Nepalese rupee, and floods and droughts had brought famine to parts of the country. There were uprisings and disorders and indications of a growing Communist movement with links to the Chinese in Tibet. King Tribhuvan had been immensely popular with the Nepalese people, who revered him for the courageous stand that he had taken during the Rana regimes and for his genuinely democratic instincts. But ill health and, no doubt, personal temperament prevented him from becoming a strong central figure around whom the diverse and usually bitterly opposed political factions in the country could rally.

Churchill once said, "Democracy is the worst form of government except for all of the others." But in a country like Nepal, where most of the inhabitants cannot read or write and it is a constant struggle for a family to find enough to eat, it is not clear what "democracy" is supposed to mean. It is as easy for a demagogic politician, acting on behalf of a political party whose aims and purposes are beyond the comprehension of the average citizen, to exploit popular discontent to further his own ambitions as it is for a dictator to take command by force. The present government, under King Birendra, is not a democracy as the term is understood in the West. But a Westerner who looks at Nepal out of a background of centuries of democratic tradition and from a position of great material comfort and wealth should think twice before criticizing the Nepalese in terms that may not be relevant to the problems and conditions of their country.

Birendra's father, King Mahendra, who died in 1972, made it clear from the beginning that he was a strong personality to be reckoned with. Despite the disapproval of his father and the possibility that he might be jeopardizing his own chances of succession, he married a Rana noblewoman in 1952, just after the revolution, when the feelings against the Ranas ran extremely high. In 1955, after he had become king, he issued a statement in which he said, "Today marks the completion of four years of democracy in the country, but it is a matter of great shame that we cannot point to even four important achievements that we have made during this period. If we say

that democracy is still in its infancy, we have seen such qualities as selfishness, greed and jealousy which are not found in
an infant. If we say that it has matured, unfortunately we do
not see it flourishing anywhere, and, I presume, this is not
hidden from anyone in the country."

The four-year period from the beginning of Mahendra's
rule to the installation of the first elected ministerial government on May 27, 1959, was one of political chaos. There were
ten different regimes, which oscillated in tone from conservative to liberal, but in which the king played an increasingly
important role. General elections and a new constitution had
been promised to the Nepalese since the revolution of 1951,
and when the constitution was finally presented in 1959 it
provided for a bicameral parliament, with an elected prime
minister, but it reserved for the king a wide variety of fundamental powers. Despite the political inexperience of the Nepalese, and the fact that the country appeared to have so much
political division, the 1959 elections were both extremely orderly and remarkably unanimous. The Nepali Congress
Party, which had been so active in fomenting the overthrow of
the Ranas, won a stunning and nearly total victory. The new
prime minister, B. P. Koirala, was a thirty-nine-year-old char-
ismatic revolutionary, an intellectual (he was widely known as
a short-story writer) and, in the spirit of the Congress Party, a
socialist. Despite some sporadic unrest in some of the western districts of the country and a few border incidents with
China,* it seemed to many observers within and without
Nepal that the Congress government was making slow but
steady progress with the grave problems of the country.
Therefore it came as a great surprise when, in December of
1960, King Mahendra suddenly, with essentially no warning,
dismissed the Congress government and arrested Prime Min-

---

* At one point during 1960 it appeared as if the Chinese were going to make a
serious territorial claim to Mount Everest, but this was settled in April of 1960 when
Chou En-lai stated in a press conference in Kathmandu that the Chinese acknowledged the Nepalese sovereignty over all of the approaches to the summit from the
south.

ister Koirala. (Koirala was held in detention a few miles from Kathmandu until his release in October of 1968 by the king.) The reasons for the king's action have never been explained fully, but it may well be that in Koirala the king saw a growing political force that could, if not checked, erode the power of the monarchy. It appears as if some of the younger Congress politicians had made it known that they regarded the monarchy as an outmoded institution. King Mahendra, unlike his predecessors under the Ranas, was a strong activist, and it is quite possible that he found it intolerable to play a role almost secondary to his prime minister.

Since 1963 Nepal has been experimenting with a political innovation known as the *panchayat* system. For administrative purposes the country is divided into seventy-five districts, comparable to counties, and fourteen zones, comparable to states. Each village, or village unit, with a population of at least two thousand, elects a local *panchayat* (literally a "committee of five," although none of the *panchayat*s as presently constituted have as few as five members) of eleven members who are, in principle, responsible for such affairs of the village as schools, roads, and local taxes. There are now something over four thousand village *panchayat*s. There are, in addition, fourteen "town" *panchayat*s, one for each of the towns in Nepal with a population of ten thousand or more. The town *panchayat*s also have eleven members. Each of the local *panchayat*s chooses a representative to elect the eleven members of the district *panchayat* which governs the district in which the various towns and villages of the constituency are located. The districts, in turn, elect representatives to the zonal *panchayat*s. At the apex of the system is the National Panchayat, which is located in Kathmandu. It contains seventy-five members, one from each district, as well as fifteen additional members, one from each of the fifteen districts that contain a population of over one hundred thousand. This group of ninety is elected by the zonal *panchayat*. In addition there are sixteen members appointed directly by the king, as well as nineteen members who represent special groups such as labor, youth, and service veterans. The National Panchayat can propose legislation and debate legislation proposed by the king, but, in the last analysis, it is the king who has the ultimate power to decide whether or not any given legislative proposal becomes the law of the land.

In December of 1960 King Mahendra made political parties illegal in Nepal, and several party leaders were subsequently arrested. Most have now been released on the condition that they refrain from political activities, at least in the sense of party politics; some are in India, and there is a certain amount of underground party activity in Nepal, some Communist and some Congress, which could be a potential source of difficulty for the future. During the two years after the coup of 1960 there was a good deal of division in the country over both domestic and foreign affairs. But in October of 1962 the Chinese and the Indians had a serious border war which served to emphasize to the Nepalese the precariousness of their own national existence. "Nepal," it has been said, "is like a fragile clay vessel wedged between two giant copper cauldrons." (This was made only too evident in April of 1989 when India closed nineteen of its twenty-one borders to Nepal. This had partly to do with a trade pact the Indians wanted changed and partly to do with the fact that in August of 1988 the Nepalese bought antiaircraft guns from China. The Nepalese have shown no signs of backing down and have accepted gasoline and oil shortages caused by the embargo as a price for their independence.) Since the Sino-Indian border incidents there has been a growing national conscience in Nepal and a sense that the only way the country can preserve its national identity, immensely important to the average Nepalese, is to have a strong, internally stable government, and this hope has crystallized around the personality of the king. Whatever one may think about the loss of democracy in Nepal in the abstract, the fact of the matter is that the average Nepalese, who is a poor farmer living in a small village, has more to say about governing his own affairs than he ever did before in the entire history of the country. While there is some discontent about the power of the monarchy among students, intellectuals, and former political leaders in the large towns, where three percent of the people live, it is probably fair to say that the feelings of the other ninety-seven percent, at least at the moment, can be roughly summarized by what a young Sherpa living high in the Himalayas said to me in all simplicity: "We love our King."

Nevertheless there has been sporadic political unrest in the country, some of it leading to violence. In 1979 King Birendra proclaimed a referendum to decide between the *panchayat* system and a return to political parties. The vote was a virtual tie and the *panchayat* system was retained, at least for the present.

Since Nepal has had so little chance to modernize, it is not surprising that one finds so much of the country's history preserved, almost intact, everywhere one travels. Kathmandu, for example, is a living epitome of its past. Every era is represented in a tumbling chaos of palaces, pagodas, gilded temples, and concrete buildings—an archeological museum come to life. Some of the impression that Kathmandu makes upon the visitor was captured in a series of articles by Kamal P. Malla that were published in *The Rising Nepal,* the leading English-language daily in the country. Entitled "Kathmandu Your Kathmandu," they had something of the bittersweet quality of letters in a lovers' quarrel, and they aroused a good deal of comment in the city. Malla wrote:

. . . Kathmandu was never built, it just grew up like weeds. That is why the city takes the knowledgeable tourist perpetually by surprise. He can never tell what next he may bump into after drifting along for a five minute distance from a golden pagoda. The old city abounds in the deposits of time, groaning buildings with beautifully carved but rotting verandas, temples and pagodas in disrepair, cracking door-frames with exquisite details, places of worship with obscene terracotta. It is the art in ruins and disarray, the islands of symmetry in the thick of fuming slums and green gutters, the harmony in bronze and stone thick with pious scum that unnerve every outsider in Kathmandu. Amidst such a mighty confusion of holy cows and mangy dogs, elusive men and markets, suffocating traffic and pedestrians, stubborn street vendors and obscure holes, suddenly there is an island of calm and order, repose and harmony, the work of an unknown artist or artists who betrayed their disdain everywhere in stone, wood and metals.

To the Western eye, accustomed to cities with a kind of rectangular order, Kathmandu presents the aspect of a perpetual bazaar. Shops with open fronts crowd each other, and vendors selling at the top of their lungs everything from shoelaces to mandarins line the sidewalks. The tiny streets are now thick with bicycles and rickshas. The automobile is a relatively recent Nepalese discovery and to add to the general confusion the typical Nepalese driver has implicit faith in the power of the horn. Pedestrians, cows, chickens, and dogs scurry in all directions to escape jeeps, buses, government limousines, and taxis, all honking at each other like angry geese. Moreover, the Nepalese are physically a small people (their average height is about five feet three inches) and the houses of Kathmandu are also small—dimensions that sometimes give the Western visitor the odd sense that the whole city is somehow a figment of his imagination. The Nepalese are fond of singing, and in the middle of the street there are often knots of people gathered around groups of singers who have come together for the pleasure of it. Above everything else and permeating the entire fabric of Nepalese life is a sense of religion. Religion is the central and sustaining force in the life of the average Nepalese. The city exudes temples and religious statues, some magnificent and some in decay. Religious festivals occur almost continually, and the streets are often crowded with parades in which masked deities are carried along on the shoulders of the crowd. In the early evening, when the city is quiet, people often gather in the temples to sing or pray. Sometimes a holy man, his face distant with rapture, plays a harmonium and chants songs that must be as old as the country itself.

In all of the history of Nepal there has never been a scientific tradition, although one is now being created, and the affairs of men and nature have always been seen as reflections of the activities of the gods. Nepal is now entering the modern world; science will play its role and perhaps the religious traditions will alter and, in some cases, disappear. In 1884 a French visitor to Kathmandu, Gustave Le Bon, was struck, even then, by a sense of a culture in transition, and what he wrote seems even truer now:

Before the sparkling but cold illuminations of modern science, the giant epochs of Gods and Heroes that unfold in all these mysterious sanctuaries are becoming pale phantoms, and the world out of which they came, a vain mirage. It is, however, from this world, so poetically strange, that our modern world was born. The pitiless hand of time, and the still more pitiless hand of man, destroys every day the last debris of monuments accumulated out of centuries of belief. One must hurry to study these vestiges of ages that humanity has passed forever. This debris of a world forgotten, whose contours dissolve and disappear in the mists of time, speaks to us of ideas and beliefs of the races that have civilized our own, and they speak in a language that soon man will understand no longer.

2

Fortune Has Wings

As nearly as one could determine, there were in 1970 twenty-four aircraft based in Nepal, of which eighteen were owned and operated by the Nepalese. The international flavor of the list of planes, many of which were given to the Nepalese by various countries, is an illustration of the fact that Nepal is one of the few countries (if not the only country) in the world where *all* the major powers, and many of the minor ones as well, are actively engaged, for whatever reasons, in constructive, helpful development. Among the aircraft were seven DC-3s of American origin. Five were owned by the Royal Nepal Airlines Corporation—a government-controlled outfit—for the commercial transport of freight and passengers; one belonged to the king's own Royal Air Flight, and one belonged to the Nepalese army. There was a forty-passenger Dutch Fokker Friendship turboprop used by the RNAC for its international flights. There were two Pilatus Porters; one belonged to the United Nations mission in Nepal and was used for official business, and the other belonged to the Swiss Association for Technical Assistance. (The Swiss pilot who flew this plane had been in Nepal for several years and estimated that he had over three thousand hours of flying time in that country, which may well be some sort of record.) These are STOL—short takeoff and landing—planes, adaptable to extremely short fields. In fact, most of the "fields" they use are just that—grassy pastures on which buffalo, yaks, and goats graze until the plane comes in. There were two Bell helicopters and one STOL Heliocourier (made in Bedford, Massachusetts) used by United States AID. These were employed on all sorts of AID missions, including flying animals and fruit trees to remote farms, and keeping Peace Corps volunteers supplied with medicines. In addition to the DC-3 the king has had presented to him as gifts one Russian Ilyushin-14 transport (something like a DC-3), one French Alouette helicopter, one Twin Otter, and three Chinese Harvesters. Most of these planes saw rather little service, mainly because they cost too much to run. To complete the list, the army had three British twin-engine Pioneers, also STOLs, of which two had been more or less cannibalized to provide parts for the third, and one Russian MI-4 helicopter. An odd addition to the local aerial scene was a Cessna owned by an outfit called the Summer Institute of Linguistics, people who apparently came to Nepal to try to translate the Bible into Nepali. The Cessna was occasionally available for charter to climbers and hikers. Since 1970 the fleet has been expanded to include forty-four-seat Avro 748s and a Boeing 727 jet.

Kathmandu's airport, now known as the Tribhuvan Airport, was originally known as Gaucher Field. Since *gaucher* means "cow pasture" in Nepali, one may imagine what the state of the art was. The field is now long enough to accommodate jets and recently Lufthansa inaugurated direct flights from Germany to Nepal, eliminating the necessity to pass through New Delhi or Bangkok. So far as anyone knows, an Englishman by the name of Mickey Weatherall in 1947 made the first landing of *any* plane in Nepal. At that time the country was still under the rule of the Rana family and hermetically sealed to foreigners, but some hunting parties were allowed in the Terai, and Weatherall flew into Simra, in the south, for hunting. By 1949 DC-3s were landing on the pasture near Kathmandu that is now the modern Tribhuvan Field. In 1951 Indian National Airways—a now defunct company that, despite its name, was owned by a Rana in India—inaugurated a weekly service to Kathmandu from Patna and Calcutta in northern India. In 1953, the first concrete airstrip was built at Tribhuvan by the Indian army at a cost of $147,000. At the same time the Indians built a remarkable road from Kathmandu to Rauxaul on their northern border—called the Tribhuvan Rajpath, in honor of the late Nepalese king—and completed it in 1956. While the road is not as well engineered as the Chinese highway built in 1967 which links Kathmandu to Tibet, it is, considering the extraordinarily tortuous mountain terrain that it crosses, a more remarkable achievement. The sixty miles or so of the road that pass through the mountains just to the south of Kathmandu are composed of an endless series of hairpin turns over steep ravines. In the monsoon, many parts of the road tend to be washed away by landslides, and whenever I have traveled over it there are small groups of Nepalese every few miles, chopping up large rocks with hammers in order to get small stones with which to fill in some of the weak spots. Despite the imperfections, the road is in constant and very heavy use by cars, buses, and trucks and is the main supply line connecting Kathmandu, and the adjoining territory, to India. That the two roads, taken together, link India to Chinese-controlled Tibet is a fact the geopolitical significance of which is lost on no one.

In May of 1958, the Royal Nepal Airlines Corporation was formed, with fifty-one percent of the shares under the permanent control of the government. Until 1963, when RNAC acquired the Fokker Friendship, which is pressurized, all of the commercial flights were made with the DC-3s, which are not.

The DC-3s provided the brunt of the air service in Nepal, and there was a sort of homespun quality to the way in which they were operated. I had occasion to witness this myself. I had made a nine-day trek into the mountains around Annapurna, along with a small group of friends and the usual retinue of Sherpas, who function as guides on these treks, and porters. The airfield nearest to Annapurna is at Pokhara, a large market town forty miles southeast of the celebrated peak, and is literally a field, a grassy sward, but one that will accommodate the DC-3s. (Pokhara itself is one of the principal tourist spots in Nepal, with many hotels of all categories—and a magnificent view of the mountains.) Getting to Pokhara from Kathmandu is no problem at all, since the RNAC operates a regular morning flight, leaving more or less on time, that makes the ninety-mile trip in something less than an hour. The return flight, at least as we experienced it, was something else again. After our nine days in the brush, we arrived at the field hot and tired but promptly at one in the afternoon, as instructed. Around two, a siren sounded at the other end of the field and a large number of assorted animals were driven off what they had come to assume was their pasture. At the same time, a great variety of the local citizenry appeared, as if out of nowhere, to watch the plane land. (In many areas of Nepal people have seen airplanes but no cars—or, indeed, any wheeled transportation at all.) When it did land, a huge ground crew proceeded to unload freight, which I noted included several wooden crates of Lux toilet soap. It was not clear to me how the passengers were meant to accommodate themselves in what appeared to be a cargo plane, but this consideration turned out to be not immediately relevant. Our plane was reloaded with freight, and it took off without us. For the next hour and a half it shuttled back and forth between Pokhara and some destination in the south, carrying freight. At about four o'clock the pilot decided that he had handled enough freight for the day and, after landing his plane in Pokhara, went off to tea. Meanwhile there was a scrupulous brushing of the interior of the plane, and we were told that we could board as soon as the pilot came back, which he did in a half hour or so. We were then strapped into bucket seats along the sides of the plane, given a little hard candy, and flown off to Kathmandu, where we landed just before sundown.

The most obvious application of Nepalese air travel, at least international air travel, is, of course, to tourism. Most tourists to Nepal come from the Indian cities via RNAC or Air India, or from Bangkok. (The introduction of the service from Dacca, then in East Pakistan, in March of 1963 was very important to Nepal's development—which is always guided by a preoccupation with political independence—because it made it possible, for the first time since the closing of Tibet, for foreigners to travel out of Nepal without passing through India. Of equal importance was the inauguration of the Thai Caravelle service from Bangkok via Calcutta in December of 1968, to be followed by DC-9 service by the same airline in February of 1970. These new jet routes mean that Nepal is now directly connected to countries outside the Indian sub-continent by air. Since Bangkok is on most of the "around-the-world" tourist itineraries, the new air routes have been at least partly responsible for the all but incredible increase in the tourist trade in the last several years.) Until 1950 essentially no foreigners of *any* description, let alone tourists, were allowed in Nepal. With the overthrow of the Ranas and the return of power to the monarchy, there came an almost feverish desire to make up for the isolation of a hundred years and to become part of the international community. (By now, Nepal has diplomatic relations with nearly fifty countries, and in 1955, after a six-year dispute between the Communist and non-Communist blocs as to whether countries should be voted on individually or in groups for admission, Nepal was admitted to the United Nations. It now has a seat on the Security Council.) The first visitors to the country, in the early 1950s, were mainly alpinists. In 1950 the French climbed Annapurna, the highest mountain ever climbed to its summit at that time; the French were the first Europeans ever to visit this Himalayan region, and maps, where any existed at all, were so poor that the climbers spent most of their time actually looking for the mountain. In 1955 Thomas Cook & Son booked the first real tourists into Nepal, a group that flew in from India while on an around-the-world tour on the steamship *Caronia*.

That tourism got started in Nepal is due, as much as to anyone, to an extraordinary and delightful White Russian named Boris Nikolaevich Lissanevitch, known ubiquitously in Kathmandu simply as Boris, who died at the age of eighty in 1985. Before the Russian revolution, the Lissanevitch family were horse breeders for the nobility, an occupation that went rapidly out of fashion when Odessa, the family seat, was taken over by the Reds. At this time, Boris, who was in his early teens, was training to be a naval officer, a career often favored by the aristocracy; indeed, both of his brothers were naval officers. When it appeared that Odessa was going to be permanently occupied, the Lissanevitch family fled, on horseback, to Warsaw. The situation in Odessa, however, remained fluid for a considerable time during the revolution, and in one of the periods in which the Whites seemed to have regained control the family returned. The White occupation was short-lived, and it became necessary to find some sort of cover for Boris to keep him from being interned as a former tsarist military functionary. As it happened, he and his mother were staying with an aunt who was the ballet mistress of the Odessa Opera House and a noted teacher of ballet. She arranged for Boris to become registered as a member of the corps de ballet, and to make matters more convincing he began actually studying ballet, which he found, to his surprise, he both liked and was gifted at. He remained in the Odessa company until 1924, when he fled to France. After some desultory employment, he joined Diaghilev's Ballet Russe. For the next four years Boris toured Europe with the Ballet Russe, but when Diaghilev died, in 1929, the company disbanded and Boris was once again on his own. For the next four years he danced with several companies in Europe, performed in a celebrated production of *The Miracle* in London with Léonide Massine—a reviewer called Boris "the personification of lithe, sinuous evil"—and married his first wife, the dancer Kira Stcherbatcheva. Kira and Boris became a well-known theatrical dance duo, and in 1933 they were invited to tour the Far East. Their tour lasted three years and took them to India, China, Bali, Ceylon, and French Indochina. During this time Boris developed a special fondness for Calcutta, whose clubs, racetracks, and cafés during the era of the British raj were among the most elegant in the Far East. But as Boris saw it, there were two serious defects in the city's social life: there was no place to get a drink after two A.M. and there was no private club that admitted both Indians and Europeans. In December of 1936, with the aid of some wealthy Calcutta friends, Boris opened the "300" Club in a palace built and abandoned by an eccentric Armenian millionaire. It was limited to exactly three hundred members, Indian and European, and the bar remained open twenty-four hours a day. In addition, he imported a Russian chef, Vladimir Haletzki, from Nice to provide the cuisine. Boris once remarked that whenever one finds Boeuf Stroganoff on the menu in a restaurant in India one can be sure that the chef is someone that he or Haletzki trained at the "300." Of course most of the Indians who belonged to the "300" were wealthy aristocrats, maharajas and the like, who could afford it, and through the club members Boris came to know the Indian establishment that functioned under the raj. In particular, he got to know those members of the Nepalese Rana family who had built homes in India, often because they had been exiled by the Rana rulers for holding antagonistic political views. He became an especially close friend of a Nepalese general, Mahabir Shamsher Jang Bahadur Rana, who had left Nepal with a considerable fortune and taken residence in India. It was through General Mahabir that Boris met King Tribhuvan, then nominally the ruler of Nepal but in fact essentially a prisoner of the Ranas. Their first meeting occurred in 1944.

(During the war the "300" had been used in part as a recreation center by military personnel, pilots and others, stationed in India.) By this time it was already clear to many observers, Boris included, that the days of the British in India were numbered and that, with their departure, a number of institutions, including social clubs for the elite, would disappear. More significantly, since it was the British presence in India and its tacit, or explicit, acceptance of the Ranas that had helped stabilize the regime, it became evident that in the absence of the British a revolution might be expected in Nepal. Indeed, while the king's nominal reason for his presence in Calcutta in 1944 was to seek medical help for a chronic heart condition, he was, in fact, using these visits to make contact with exiled Nepalese like General Mahabir and with the Indian Congress Party, which favored a change of regime in Nepal. The "300" Club became the medium through which these meetings were arranged, and Boris became a very close friend of the king. In 1947 India gained its independence and by 1951 the Ranas had been overthrown and the king restored to power.

Boris had become an avid big-game hunter since first coming to Asia, and it had long been his ambition to visit Nepal and to hunt in the jungles of the Terai. Under the Ranas, though, he had not been permitted to do so, and thus when King Tribhuvan invited Boris to come to Kathmandu he readily accepted. In September of 1951 he flew to Kathmandu in the king's plane. Boris vividly recalled his first night in Kathmandu, when he was taken for an automobile ride in the city by the king and two of his sons. No sooner had they started driving than a leopard jumped across the path of the car and, after staring at its occupants for several seconds, fled off into the suburbs. Boris said to himself, "My God, what a country!" and decided then and there to move to Kathmandu. But first he needed an occupation. Since 1946 Boris had given up the direction of the "300" Club and, among other things, had attempted to set up a distillery in northern India. The distillery had failed, but the experience had convinced him that he might explore the prospects for alcohol brewing in Nepal, which up to that time had been carried on in an informal family basis, free of government tax. General Mahabir had become the Nepalese minister of industry, and he saw at once in Boris's proposed distillery a chance for the government to collect some new and badly needed revenues. Boris received a license to import alcohol and acquired the exclusive legal franchise for brewing it in the Kathmandu Valley. On the strength of this arrangement he brought his family to live in Kathmandu. (In 1948 Boris and Kira had been divorced, and Boris had married a beautiful Danish girl named Inger Pheiffer, a talented artist.)

At first, it looked as if the brewery would be a great success. But Boris had not realized that there were well over a thousand private distilleries in the valley and that many of these were owned by influential citizens, who were not in the least pleased either by the new competition or by the prospect of taxation. Pressure was brought to bear on the government and the matter came to a head late in 1954, when Boris's license to import alcohol was suddenly revoked. To compound matters, he was arrested for not having fulfilled the part of his contract which stipulated that he would pay the government a certain guaranteed minimum yearly tax. He protested that to earn the money to pay the tax he needed the alcohol that he could no longer import, but the protest was to no avail. He tried to bring suit, but the legal system in Nepal made it impossible for anyone to bring a suit against the government. Thus Boris went off to jail. He was apparently the first European to have been jailed in Nepal, at least in modern times, and hence it was not clear to anyone what should be done with him. By this time he had become a naturalized British citizen, and at the instigation of the British embassy he was taken out of the normal communal jail cell where he had first been put and incarcerated in the relative luxury of the tax office itself. Here he lived for six days, among the tax clerks, until he was transferred to a private cell, from which he was moved finally to the local hospital after he had become ill. After two and a half months he was released. King Mahendra, who had succeeded his father after the latter's death in March of 1955, agreed to release Boris on the condition that he would write a letter of apology. Boris refused, but a compromise was worked out whereby the king's secretary wrote the letter and Boris simply signed it.

Several months before this episode, Boris had begun to create the first international hotel in Nepal, the Royal, and had persuaded the government to issue tourist visas. For use as a hotel he had leased half of a former Rana palace. The other half was used by the Nepal Rastra (Central) Bank for its offices. All during the period in which Boris was in jail the new hotel was being put together, largely under the direction of his wife. Everything—knives and forks, plumbing fixtures, stoves and bake ovens—had to be imported or specially made. Boris was determined to serve first-rate European cuisine, a policy that meant that he had either to grow the vegetables or fruits himself (he brought the first strawberries into Nepal) or to import them by air from India or Singapore. Pigs were a case in point. The domestic pig could not legally be imported into Nepal because of the prevalent feeling that it was an unclean animal. But the Nepalese were very fond of wild boar. Thus, Boris imported a number of white Hampshire "wild boars" from England which he bred and raised. These animals appear to thrive in the valley, and Boris had a herd of some two hundred that he kept in a farm he had in the hills above Kathmandu. A certain number of them also used to wander around the hotel grounds, along with a large collection of dogs, birds, squirrels, and some Himalayan brown bears that were kept in a cage and fed by Boris's mother-in-law—a dynamic, outspoken, and delightful lady named Esther Scott. It was Mrs. Scott's claim that she was the éminence grise behind the hotel and that if it were not for her, Boris, whose spirit of Russian hospitality and generosity was legendary, would have given everything away. The pigs were a staple in the cuisine of the hotel, and Boris had visions of moving them to the south of Nepal, allowing them to multiply, and selling the extra meat to India. He imagined a fleet of refrigeration trucks moving south with the pork, coming back north along the India-Nepal highway and stocking what he hoped might become the first supermarket in Nepal. Like many such visions it never came to pass.

Two months after being let out of jail, Boris received a royal command from King Mahendra to cater his coronation, which was to take place on the second of May, 1956. There were to be several hundred invited guests, including newspapermen and photographers from all over the world. It was the first time that the coronation of a Nepalese king had been made an international event, and it became a symbol of Nepal's desire to join the world community. Boris had to fly everything in from abroad, including fifty-seven cooks and 150 trained servants from India, six thousand live chickens, one thousand guinea fowl, fresh fruit from India, whiskey, soda, glasses, and several tons of ice (there was no ice plant in the country). The coronation and the royal banquet, catered by Boris, were a great success, and Boris and the hotel became established fixtures in the valley. Until the 1960s, the Royal was the only hotel with cosmopolitan standards in Nepal, and Boris built up an extensive international clientele. For a time, his guests included several ambassadors and most of the personnel from the foreign-aid missions, who lived in the hotel until their residences in Kathmandu could be built. Nearly every mountaineering expedition that passed through the country stayed at the Royal at what Boris called his lowered "expedition rate." Besides feeding the expeditions, Boris used to bail out some of them from entanglements with governmental red tape. One of his prize possessions was a collection of rocks chipped out of the summits of several of the highest mountains in Nepal, including Everest, by climbers who had lived at the Royal.

The unconventional atmosphere at the Royal was not for everyone. The rooms were huge and somewhat cold at night during the winter. Some of them had stuffed tigers on the floor, souvenirs of Boris's days as a hunter. The plumbing was uncertain, the electricity a bit on the sporadic side, and the whole affair looked as if it needed rehabilitation. It closed in the 1970s.

Boris's next project was the construction of a restaurant—the Yak and Yeti—which, when completed in February of 1970, was one of the showplaces of the Kathmandu Valley. For his restaurant, Boris rented part of another Rana palace—there is no shortage of them in the valley—and in it created a mixed astrological and Newari decor that stunned the eye of even the most blasé. (When I visited the site shortly before opening day, about a ton of Newari carvings lay carefully stacked on the floor of the future kitchen, waiting to be mounted on walls and archways.) The Newar arts, like the wild animals in Nepal, are in danger of disappearing, since, in their urge to modernize, the Nepalese have developed something of a fetish for concrete. Concrete is a luxury in the valley. At present, mortar costs about ten dollars a sack. Although Nepal has a certain amount of limestone and a great deal of water power that will eventually be converted into economical electricity, neither is being fully exploited. (With the help of the West Germans the first cement factory in Nepal was constructed at the site of a limestone quarry near Kathmandu.) At the moment, most Nepalese who want to make a show of wealth and modernity build a concrete house, and the government has built a number of stark modern concrete buildings, such as the post office. There is a beautiful old grass parade ground and sports arena on the outskirts of Kathmandu which the government has ringed with a rather ugly concrete fence, apparently for decoration. In any event, and even in the absence of renovation, for travelers with a certain sense of whimsy the informality of the Hotel Royal and the personal charm of Boris more than compensated for the lack of modern conveniences.

On a Sunday afternoon when I stayed there in 1967, I went with Boris on a rather typical outing. A few days before, a large British Royal Air Force crew had come into town in a Beverly, a huge cargo plane soon to be replaced in the RAF, something like the American C-47. They were bringing in supplies from Singapore for some of the Gurkha military centers in the south of Nepal. As luck would have it, an air compressor in their plane failed, so they were grounded in Kathmandu for several days. The boys put up at the Royal, and Boris set about to look after their welfare. There were daily planning sessions that took place either in Boris's apartment in the hotel—which one reached by climbing a hazardous-looking tiny circular metal stairway from the second floor, and which contained an extensive collection of Tibetan art—or in the Yak and Yeti Bar of the Royal. The latter was one of the prime social institutions of the valley. It was wood-paneled and featured a splendid wood-burning fireplace in the middle of the room. In one of the planning sessions in the bar Boris decided to take the boys on a picnic, and he invited me along. "We will go to Sankhu in my Land Rover," he said, "and I will show you a wall that I bought"—an invitation that I readily accepted. Sankhu is one of the oldest towns in the valley, accessible only by jeep or Land Rover, since the road that leads to it is both unpaved and extremely rough. It is relatively rarely visited by tourists and is almost untouched by modernity.

At ten the following Sunday morning, we all assembled on the lawn in front of the Royal: about fifteen airmen, two Land Rovers, an Italian staying at the hotel whom Boris had also invited—the Italian had decided to hire his own transportation, which, as it turned out, was very fortunate—Mrs. Scott, and one of her dogs. Boris brought out some wicker baskets from the hotel containing a splendid picnic lunch, several dozen cans of chilled beer, and a couple of bottles of red wine. (Wine is practically unavailable in Nepal, and when it *is* available it is usually imported Chianti that costs at least ten dollars a bottle.) Mrs. Scott and I, the dog, and several airmen got into Boris's Land Rover, which turned out to be a rather ancient affair that he had driven overland from England. In fact, on the way to our picnic its transmission gave out, and we succeeded in getting to Sankhu only by being ferried by the other Land Rover. At a later stage, the Italian was sent back to Kathmandu in his car to fetch a jeep to pick us up. Sankhu turned out to be an extraordinarily beautiful Newar village, and if it were not for the sight of a few modern manufactured artifacts such as an occasional transistor radio or a wristwatch, one could have easily imagined oneself in sixteenth-century Nepal. We picnicked near a lovely pagoda temple many centuries old located on top of a hill, and after lunch Boris took us for a walk through Sankhu. He came to an ancient house with magnificently carved windows and wood paneling. Woodcarving was one of the great Newar skills. "I bought this wall," he remarked happily. "The owner was going to tear it down and put up something in cement. The carvings would have been burnt, probably, so I bought the whole wall."

Since 1955, when Boris persuaded the government to issue tourist visas, tourism has grown almost exponentially in Nepal and is now the number-one source of foreign exchange in the country. To give some idea of the growth, there were, according to government figures, 6,179 tourists in 1962. By 1981 the number had risen to 161,669. It is now about a quarter of a million. In 1961 tourism brought seventy-eight thousand dollars in revenue, and in 1981 fifty-two *million*. As a corollary to this, both the hotel and restaurant facilities have grown almost beyond recognition compared to what they were in the 1960s. Almost every major hotel chain has a luxury hotel in Kathmandu, and there are several indigenous ones that belong to the royal family. The hotels used to be under European management but, in the interests of expanding local employment, the Europeans have been replaced. At the high end of the luxury hotel spectrum is the Soaltee-Oberoi, which is hypermodern. It has four restaurants, one with nightly music, a casino that features blackjack and roulette, a swimming pool, air conditioning, and its own water filtration system. Drinking water is still a problem in Kathmandu. It comes in from pure sources in the hills and is, to a certain extent, treated chemically. But foreigners are advised not to drink it, although there is considerable difference of opinion as to what would happen if one did. Some people claim that the worst defect in the water is an occasional excess of mica, which causes diarrhea. Others say that it is possible to pick up amoebic and viral disorders of a much more serious kind. In any case, all of the hotels serve boiled water, and in Boris's establishment this used to arrive in various whiskey bottles that had seen prior service in the Royal's Yak and Yeti.

I went with Boris to the first anniversary celebration of the opening of the Soaltee, which was presided over by Prince Himalaya, King Mahendra's oldest brother and at that moment the acting ruler of Nepal. (King Mahendra was in Alaska shooting bear; the crown prince, Birendra, was at Harvard, where he was studying; and the king's other brother, Basundhara, also was temporarily out of the country.) It was a gala occasion that featured a floor show, consisting of some singers imported from India, an exotic dancer and an orchestra, and a free gift for everyone in the form of a ballpoint pen manufactured in China. The guests, dressed in tuxedos and ball gowns, represented Kathmandu society, the diplomatic missions, important government personalities, and the like, and the atmosphere was as remote from village life in Nepal as if the reception were being held in Paris or London. The Soaltee is located outside the city, and it so much resembles a Hilton or an Intercontinental in a Western city that someone staying there could, were it not for a few wall decorations and the Indian and Nepalese help, imagine that he was not in Nepal at all.

Most tourists spend a day or so in Kathmandu, looking at temples and the extraordinary street scene, and then pass on. Hence they are not aware of how really difficult it is to see anything of the country. A tourist visa is valid for at most thirty days and entitles the bearer to visit only the Kathmandu Valley, Pokhara, and a wilderness game preserve called Tiger Tops, in the Terai. Any other travel must be arranged specially with the Home Ministry. Even if permission can be obtained—and for many places not too close to the Tibetan border this is quite possible—the only way to get about is, usually, on foot. For example, it is essentially impossible for the average visitor to get to see Mount Everest; the mountain is not visible from the Valley of Kathmandu, and if one climbs some of the nearby foothills, the view of Everest is not very impressive. RNAC offers an hour's flight in the Fokker Friendship around the Everest area. From the plane one can get some rather spectacular, if slightly distant, views of the Himalayan chain including Everest. It is certainly worth taking, if one has no other way to see the mountains. But it is far from ideal since the chain is visible to only half the passengers on each leg of the flight while the other half strains across the aisle to get a glimpse of *something*. To see Everest well requires a trek to Solu-Khumbu some 190 miles to the northeast.

Some years ago the government set aside some one thousand square miles of the jungle in the south for a game preserve. Whole villages were moved out into other parts of the Terai. In the middle of the jungle a hotel was built called Tiger Tops, with the financial backing of two Texas oilmen. Its jungle setting near a large river is beautiful. To reach it one flies from Kathmandu to the Terai and then rides from the airfield to the hotel on the back of an elephant, a ride that takes about two hours. (It is also possible to get to the hotel by river rafting, something I did in 1979.) Riding in a seat on the back of an elephant, surrounded by elephant grass forty feet tall, is a remarkable experience, although a little wearing on the bones. The visitor to Tiger Tops is rewarded for his pains with solid food and drink served in a lovely thatched dining room. The accommodations, in thatched stilt houses, are simple but comfortable, and the visitor is taken on long Land Rover rides in the preserve with a chance of seeing some of the tigers, rhinoceroses, crocodiles, peacocks, pheasants, and barking deer that live unmolested in the jungle. At night, several buffalo are staked to posts alive, and tigers, if they are hungry, attack and kill the buffalo—a process that can, in principle, be viewed by the guests from safe hideouts in the jungle.

Not all tourists who come to Kathmandu, of course, can afford to stay at the Soaltee. In fact, there is a group of tourists who started coming to Kathmandu in the 1960s whose lack of obvious means of support was something of a headache to the Nepalese—the hippies. There was an international hippie circuit through Asia that had its ports of call in countries such as Afghanistan, Laos, and Nepal, where drugs were both legal and readily available in the open market. In Nepal, the hippies smoked processed ganja—hashish—that sold for about forty cents a pound. (Ganja grows more or less wild throughout the countryside.) Smoking pipes of hashish has long been a traditional aspect of Indian and Nepalese religious practice, and in Kathmandu one finds a number of pagoda temples in which people gather to smoke a common hashish pipe and listen to a guru chant, or sing together. I am not an expert on the extent to which drugs are presently used in Nepal, but from having been to a few of these musical temple ceremonies I have the impression that their religious use is largely confined to a minority of the older generation. Young Nepalese are tremendous cigarette smokers, and Nepal produces native tobacco and a vast assortment of different brands of cigarettes usually named after mountains or animals—Sagarmatha (Everest), Lion, Annapurna, and Nanga Parbat, to name a few. Many of these cigarettes are manufactured in a plant donated to the Nepalese by the Russians, at a cost of some six million dollars, some years ago. Like many of the industrial-aid projects in Nepal, it was designed to allow the Nepalese to manufacture something for which they would otherwise have to pay foreign currency. Cigarettes are sold individually or by the pack and are often used for tips and partial wages, especially in the countryside. In tiny villages far out in the hills one finds young children smoking constantly, and every little boutique sells a vast assortment of cigarettes. But one does not get the impression that there is much interest in drugs among the Nepalese. Among the young people who came to Nepal on the drug circuit, however (it is hard to say how many there were, although it was estimated that about two hundred gathered in Kathmandu for Christmas of 1966 and stayed until the government deported many of them), there did not seem to be much interest in anything else.

There are a few institutions in Kathmandu that cater to the hippie crowd; some of them used to allow hashish smoking on the premises, and some did not. Among the former, the most celebrated was the Tibetan Blue Restaurant (the restaurant was painted blue). It was owned and operated by Tibetans and served Tibetan food, as well as tea and hot lemon squash. Most of the clientele were bearded young Europeans or Americans, along with girls of varying dress and nationalities. The men often wore yellow monk's robes, more than likely purchased in some bazaar in Kathmandu. I made two visits to the Tibetan Blue. On the first one I was greeted at the door by a bearded American from Long Beach, California, who was wearing a yellow robe. At first I thought he must be the owner, but he cordially introduced me to two rather bemused-looking Tibetans for whom he seemed to be working as a kind of greeter. He offered me a turn at a pipe being passed around among the clientele. When I turned it down he said, "Man, if your cup is filled, there is nothing I can do for you," and disappeared into the kitchen. On my second visit, a month or so later, things seemed a lot quieter and the greeter had disappeared. I later found out that there had been a mass exodus of flower people to a site somewhere on the "Chinese Road" (so known because it was built by the Chinese), outside Kathmandu, where they were in the process of setting up an "LSD United Nations." It was rumored that for one Nepalese rupee a visitor to the "UN" could have his passport stamped "Hippieland." Apparently the Nepalese government was not especially amused by the whole affair; a number of citizens of Hippieland were asked to leave the country.

At the nonsmoking end of the spectrum was the Camp, a restaurant and hotel that was founded in February of 1967 by an Indian from Bombay named Ravi Chawla. Mr. Chawla, then a friendly and articulate man in his thirties, left a job with Burmah-Shell and packed his family off to Nepal to get away from what he called "the pressures of normal life." The accommodations at the hotel were rustic, clean, and very cheap. The Camp served American-style breakfasts of pancakes and eggs in its restaurant, as well as Tibetan food, and there was usually classical music playing from a hi-fi set. The atmosphere was more like a café in Greenwich Village than anything else, and the clientele looked and talked as if it might have been transported bodily from the Village. When Ravi was managing the Camp, his guests seemed to have a great affection for him, and they expressed it in poems and drawings that were inked into *The Camp Register,* a red Moroccan-bound book, and were often remarkable. I discovered one poetic offering that appeared to me to have considerable charm. In part it went:

This bloody town's a bloody cuss,
No bloody trains, no bloody bus
and only Ravi cares for us
     in bloody Kathmandu.

The bloody roads are bloody bad,
The bloody hash is bloody mad
It makes the saddest bloody glad
     in bloody Kathmandu.

And then:

To quench a thirst is bloody dear,
ten bloody bob for bloody beer,
And is it good?
No bloody fear,
     in bloody Kathmandu.

Ah, well!

For a Westerner coming from a complex technological society where one is, if anything, burdened by too much communication and transport, it is hard to imagine what it is like to live in a country where both communication and transport are difficult to impossible. Under such circumstances a "country" is hardly a national entity at all. Until 1951, when the Ranas were overthrown, Nepal was a geographical area divided by natural boundaries—rivers, valleys, high mountain passes—into units with practically no interconnection. There were (and are) at least thirty different tribal languages and dialects—twenty of them spoken by fewer than a thousand people each—and only a minuscule fraction of the population could read or write any language, still less the national language, Nepali. Nepalese currency was viable mainly in the Kathmandu Valley; in the north people used a simple barter system, and in the rest of the country Indian rupees were the only form of acceptable money. In many places paper money of any kind was not valid currency; the early mountaineering expeditions in the 1950s that first explored these regions had to take with them enormous treasure chests of metal coins. There had never been a national census—the first one was taken in 1952 through 1954. Only two cities, Kathmandu and Biratnagar, in the southeast near the Indian border, had electric power. There was no civil aviation. Until 1956 there were only 160 miles of all-weather and 230 miles of fair-weather roads in all Nepal. The wheel for transport, the electric light, tools, telephones, schools, doctors and hospitals, window glass, and airplanes were as remote to the average Nepalese villager as if they were located on the surface of the moon. Against this background, and despite the enormous tasks that lie ahead for the country, almost everyone who has studied Nepal in the last several decades comes away profoundly impressed by how much has already been done.

An incident occurred in 1967 that graphically summarized the kind of social progress that had been made in Nepal even twenty years ago. Late in October, a new telecommunications center in the very remote Bajhang District of northwest Nepal reported to Kathmandu that an outbreak of illness of some kind had taken place in Naura, a Hindu farming and herding village with a population of about fifteen hundred scattered over the east face of an eight-thousand-foot mountain. (The mere fact that such an event was and could be brought promptly to the attention of the medical authorities in Kathmandu was a very recent phenomenon and reflected the fact that most districts of the country had become linked to the capital by telecommunications. There is a dial telephone system in Kathmandu, which has been modernized and enlarged with the help of the United States AID, and the city of Biratnagar has internal telephone service. There is an international telephone and telegraph service from Kathmandu. The nearest hospital to Naura was in Doti, the district capital, three days' march away.* Of the fifty-one hospitals then in existence in Nepal, most were really medical dispensaries or clinics, and the ones in the countryside were and are not equipped to handle anything requiring complicated equipment or laboratory analysis. In fact, in 1967 there were some 220 doctors in all of Nepal, about 120 of them in the Kathmandu Valley; and there were four dental surgeons in the entire country. (There is at present no medical school in Nepal, but one may be established at Tribhuvan University in Kathmandu.) This worked out to be about one doctor for every fifty thousand Nepalese,** but even this figure does not give a real impression of the situation, since many Nepalese, especially the rural population, do not have sufficient education to make use of the health facilities that do exist and prefer to rely on the traditional practice of spirit healing and exorcism. (It was recently, and may indeed still be, the practice among certain rural people in Nepal to stroke a pregnant

* In the countryside the relevant unit of distance is the number of days' march. Of course, this unit is somewhat subjective, but the Nepalese can walk very fast and very far in a day. To give an example, we took fourteen days of stiff walking to travel the 190 miles from Kathmandu to Namche Bazar, near Everest, but the Sherpas can do it in seven.

** The present figure is about one doctor for every twenty-five thousand Nepalese.

woman's neck with a railway ticket—symbolizing the speed of transport—to ensure an easier delivery of the child.) In any event, because of the apparent seriousness of the outbreak in Naura, the Ministry of Health in Kathmandu was notified directly.

The only way to reach Naura quickly from Kathmandu is by helicopter. Since running the Russian and French helicopters that the army and the King owned would have been an enormous strain on the financial resources that the government had to spend on its health program, the Minister of Health asked the American AID mission for the use of its aircraft and pilots to fly personnel to Naura. During the first week in November, AID shuttled helicopters back and forth between Kathmandu and Naura carrying medical people, both Nepalese and those from the World Health Organization, which has a substantial program in the country. They discovered that quite a number of villagers were sick and that some had died. By the time the epidemic was over, there had been 27 human deaths and about 150 deaths of cattle. Preliminary examinations indicated anthrax, a disease that is passed from animals to humans. (They also discovered that the people of Naura had instituted, on their own initiative, a quarantine system. The village was ringed off by flags, and each house in the village where there were sick people had itself been ringed off with flags; to cross these flags, the villagers proclaimed, would be an affront to the gods. This quarantine certainly saved many lives.) The anthrax bacillus is very resistant, and since the herdsmen were disposing of the cattle by throwing them into the river, there was a great apparent danger of infesting the entire Karnali River system, which drains western Nepal. It would have been necessary for the government to burn Naura and perhaps the neighboring villages to eliminate the risk of reinfection.

Anthrax epidemics are extremely rare anywhere, and one of the important centers for studying anthrax is the Centers for Disease Control in Atlanta, Georgia. American AID, in cooperation with the American embassy, therefore arranged to have a team of specialists flown from Atlanta to Kathmandu and then to Naura a few days after the first report had come back to Kathmandu. By this time a laboratory analysis from the Ministry of Health in Kathmandu had given preliminary indications that the disease was not anthrax and that the people and the cattle were sick with quite different things—a diagnosis that the team from Atlanta helped to confirm. The cattle were dying from rinderpest, a disease that is specific to animals, and the people were sick with bubonic plague, a disease that is treatable with modern antibiotics. (There has been an extensive rinderpest eradication program in Nepal, which has been carried out largely in the Terai, with help from the Indian government, and which, since its inception in 1963, has been responsible for vaccinating about 950,000 animals. No vaccination program can be complete, however, especially in a country with remote farming areas, and after the outbreak in Naura the government accelerated the vaccination program in western Nepal.) Within a short time the plague outbreak in Naura was completely under control, and several of the people of the village who were sick when the medical teams first came to Naura responded to antibiotics and recovered. Forty years ago an epidemic like the one in Naura might never have been learned about in the rest of Nepal until it was too late, and would have gone on unchecked, with almost unimaginable losses.

Statistical data of any kind are hard to come by in Nepal, and medical statistics are no exception. The Ministry of Health, in cooperation with the Tom Dooley Foundation, did in the late 1960s the first comprehensive medical survey of the country. (One notable aspect of the Tom Dooley Foundation was that it was staffed in part by Pan American Airways airline hostesses, who were given a sort of sabbatical leave to work in Nepal.) Still, by talking to doctors and World Health Organization officials, it is possible to get some overall picture of the major health problems.

Since the beginning of the recorded history of Nepal, the

Terai has been notorious as the breeding ground of an extremely deadly malarial mosquito. The government of Nepal used to spend over half of its health budget on malaria control in the Terai. The terrain is so vast that there is no hope of eliminating the mosquitoes in their breeding grounds in the swamps and the rice paddies. Instead the government, in cooperation with the World Health Organization and the United States AID program, has concentrated in the villages. Malaria is spread by a man-mosquito-man chain. Thus, an epidemic can be averted if the mosquitoes can be prevented from passing the disease from person to person. This is done by spraying the interior of the houses in the Terai villages on a regular basis. At first, the campaign, which was begun in 1954, met considerable resistance from the villagers in the Terai, who did not understand the connection between the mosquitoes and the disease. As one AID official said to me, "How would you like someone to come into your house and spray the walls with DDT?" By now, the "DDT man" is a welcome visitor to the community, and much of the Terai, especially in the east, has been reclaimed from the mosquitoes. A specific, and often cited, example of malaria control in Nepal is that of the fifty-mile-long Rapti Valley—where the Tiger Tops Hotel is located—in the south-central part of the country just below the first Himalayan foothills. Before the United States AID and the World Health Organization, which began the malaria-control program in the valley in 1955, started their activities, the valley was essentially uninhabited and uninhabitable jungle. It is estimated that such population as did live in the valley suffered at least a ninety-percent incidence of malaria. By March of 1967 a study reported that the malaria rate had been reduced to four-tenths of one percent. In addition, with help from U.S. AID five thousand people had been resettled in the valley, which now has irrigation, medical facilities, and a school system; some fifteen thousand acres of land had been reclaimed from the jungle for farming; and with the aid of the World Food Program the Nepalese government started fish farms in the Rapti

Valley rivers. It is difficult to imagine a more striking example of what can be done, in an area of the world in which hunger is endemic, when modern technology is applied constructively. Because of the DDT resistance of the mosquitoes there has been some resurgence of malaria. The disease is now controlled by malathion, which is six times more expensive than DDT.

Nepal has its share of communicable diseases; tuberculosis, smallpox, diphtheria, and cholera are among the most prevalent. The country has made the most progress with smallpox, since it is the easiest to deal with. The Nepalese, with the World Health Organization, carried out a mass vaccination program that had its initial impact in urban areas like Kathmandu, where medical facilities are most easily available. It seemed too much to ask that a Nepalese farmer and his family walk several days to the nearest clinic to take vaccinations, especially when he may not understand their significance. In the countryside one often used to see people who have vaccination scars along with others whose faces have obviously been ravaged by smallpox. Nevertheless, Nepal was declared a smallpox-free country in April of 1975.

Tuberculosis is much more difficult to deal with, since both the diagnosis and the treatment are quite complex—the former requiring X-ray facilities, which are very rare in the country, and the latter a year or two of rest and drugs, which most Nepalese cannot afford. In the Kathmandu Valley it is thought that about one percent of the population suffers from tuberculosis. The high incidence certainly has to do, in part, with the fact that an entire Nepalese family and often more than one family will occupy one large room. Nepalese houses are small and, at least in Kathmandu, have two or three stories, with the bottom story often given over to some kind of shop. The houses are fitted tightly in together, and people often seem to be popping out of every seam. The population density in Kathmandu, even in 1970, was forty-eight thousand per square mile—a figure that is unbelievably high until one actually sees how little area an average family takes up.

(In the valley the density was 2,163 per square mile, and overall in Nepal it was 172 per square mile. In the United States, to give some sort of comparative measure, it was 50 per square mile. The Nepalese figures have increased substantially.) Even in the countryside, where there is plenty of space, families live in tightly packed rooms, with the result that an infectious disease like tuberculosis is easily transmitted from person to person. The people in the Kathmandu Valley suffer a good deal from respiratory coughs, which are thought to be caused by air pollution. The valley is a natural basin that traps the pollen from the crops, so people who are allergic to it tend to suffer. In addition there is the air pollution from automobiles and trucks. In the countryside there are similar sorts of allergic manifestations; one theory that seems to account for them is that the Nepalese develop an allergy to the grassy material out of which they make the thatch roofs for their houses.

One of the long-range goals of the health services in Nepal is to provide good drinking water for the villages. The villagers use water from nearby streams that are often polluted by man and animal. This, along with the primitive sanitation habits of the people, accounts for a great prevalence of amoebic and parasitic disorders among the Nepalese. Although Nepalese life expectancy is now thought to be fifty-one for women and fifty-four for men, this is a vast improvement over the estimate of twenty-six in the early 1960s. (This striking reversal of the life expectancies for men and for women—as compared, say, to those in the West—is not accidental. Girls are, in the main, treated less well than boys in a typical Nepalese rural family. Young boys are fed better and get better medical attention. They are also better educated. Eighteen percent of females are literate while fifty-two percent of males are literate. While these figures are distressing, some twenty years ago only fifteen percent of the population was literate. The education of women has been improving greatly and young girls are now encouraged by the government to attend school.) Almost one child in three still dies in its first year, often from acute dysentery. Throughout the countryside one sees posters in Nepali, with drawings for the majority of people, who cannot read, that stress the importance of washing before handling food. In health, as elsewhere, the key to progress is mass education and more food. In 1977, and things have not changed dramatically since, thirty-six percent of the population was subsisting on only 1,750 calories a day. The minimum adequate diet would require 2,256 calories a day.

Until the Ranas took over the country in 1846, education in Nepal was always associated with religious institutions. In the north these were Buddhist monasteries and in the south Hindu temples. Before 1768, when they were expelled, a few Christian missionaries founded schools. But in the century that the Ranas ruled, education became the exclusive privilege of the elite. The Ranas imported English teachers for their children, and before the Second World War some English high schools were founded in Kathmandu and the larger cities in the south. The Gurkha soldiers who came back from the British army after the standard fifteen-year period of service founded a few local elementary schools in the hills; even now in remote hill towns one often sees groups of children being taught, in an almost military rote drill, by an old ex-Gurkha soldier. After the war the Ranas were essentially forced by the example of the expanding drive for education in India and China to provide more schools. By 1951 there were 310 primary and middle schools, eleven high schools, two colleges, one normal school, and one special technical school.

It was at this time that one of the most remarkable figures in Nepalese education first appeared on the scene—Father Moran from Chicago. Father Moran, now eighty-three, founded a Jesuit school in Patna, in northern India, in the early 1930s. Several Nepalese, including members of the Rana family, attended his school, which was modeled after a typical English public school. He was therefore well known to the Ranas, and when they came under pressure in Nepal to do something about the educational system, they turned to him. This was in 1949. But Father Moran realized that a revolution was inevitable in Nepal, so he stalled off accepting the invitation for a year or so until there *was* a revolution. The new regime, the monarchy of King Tribhuvan, again asked him to come to Kathmandu and, soon after, he founded a private elementary school in Godavari, just outside the capital. There is now a high school there as well, and the elementary school has changed its name to St. Xavier's. The student body of St. Xavier's is made up almost entirely of Buddhists and Hindus. Although the school is run by the Jesuit order, there is no proselytizing (which is forbidden by the constitution of Nepal). There are about 250 boarders at St. Xavier's and an almost equal number of day scholars. While there is a tuition charge, many of the boys are there on scholarships, a fact that ensures a certain diversity of background. (There are no girls.) The classes are in English, and the level is such that a boy who does well at St. Xavier's can go to an English or American university and not be at a competitive disadvantage.

Father Moran is an enormously popular figure in Kathmandu. Many years ago King Mahendra conferred Nepalese citizenship on him, making him, to date, the only American to be so honored. He is an enthusiastic radio ham, and when I went to Godavari to have tea with him at the school, a former Rana palace, I was ushered into his radio room. He told me that he is a link in an international amateur communication system that extends all over Asia. He was waiting for his nightly signal from Singapore that would tell him if there were any messages to pass on to the next ham in the chain. (During the American Everest expedition of 1963, his station, 9N1MM, was one of the few links of the climbers to the outside world.) While we were drinking tea he was twiddling with various dials, and after a few minutes he got his call from Singapore, which said that there was nothing on the line, a bit of information that he passed on to the next member in the relay. Afterward he introduced me to a number of the boys, who spoke excellent English and seemed extremely bright. One of them was a young Sherpa from the hills whom Father Moran persuaded to sing a lovely Nepalese song. When I left, Father Moran, who had once been a premedical student, was on his way to make some sick rounds in the school. After seeing him in action for an hour or so, one gets the impression that he can do about anything he sets his mind to.

Father Moran is in the business of quality education, which, in an underdeveloped country—especially one such as Nepal where there is already an elite traditional class of educated people—is, in a sense, the easiest sort of education to provide, since only a relatively small number of students are involved. In principle, elementary education is compulsory in Nepal, but in practice there is an acute shortage of elementary schools and schoolteachers, especially in the countryside. It is probable that no more than twenty or thirty percent of the children now go to school, although the number is steadily growing. In 1981 a survey indicated that there were 10,340 primary schools, as opposed to 310 in 1951, and 918 high schools, as opposed to 22. There are also one hundred degree "colleges" in the country, most of them liberal arts colleges granting a BA degree. Even in the Kathmandu Valley, where the educational facilities are the best in the country, young children do not necessarily go to school. If one stands in the morning by one of the bridges that lead into Kathmandu over the rivers that bound the city, one sees streams of children driving animals to market or coming into town to work.

Apart from the shortage of facilities, one of the most acute problems in Nepal is that young people who might become teachers and who might contribute to the development of the villages often view education as a means to escape village life for the relative comfort and sophistication of the cities like Kathmandu. This attitude becomes more pronounced as students move up the educational ladder and is very extreme at the university level. There is only one university in the country, Tribhuvan University, which was founded, with the help of U.S. AID funds, in 1959. Several colleges affiliated with the university are located in towns outside Kathmandu, but the principal activities of the university, and especially its graduate schools, are in the valley. There are now some six thousand students at the university and since 1966 they have been attending classes in a new campus constructed a few miles south of the city. Shortly before the new campus opened I paid a visit to the then Vice Chancellor Upraity, whose office was in one of its attractive new buildings. Dr. Upraity received his undergraduate education in the English College in Kathmandu, took his doctorate at the University of Oregon, and then returned to Nepal, where he became involved with education. One of his principal concerns was the placement of university graduates. Many of them want to stay in Kathmandu, where, if they have been educated in the social sciences, the only career really open to them is with the national government, and such positions have been largely saturated—a situation that is a source of potential frustration among the students. It is aggravated by the fact that students (like everyone else) have been forbidden by law to engage in party politics. The present political system, centered on the local *panchayats*, does not seem to have captured the imagination of the students, and there has been a certain amount of agitation that has led to some student strikes and to the imprisonment of student leaders. King Mahendra and his son were both very skillful in incorporating opposition leaders into their governments, and it is said that some students feel that the best route into the government is to attract attention by agitation. King Birendra is encouraging a Go-to-the-Village campaign aimed at convincing students and others that they can best contribute to the development of Nepal by bringing their talents to bear on village problems. The paradox is that the more highly trained a man becomes, the less relevant are his skills to the condition of the villages. At its present stage of development, Nepal does not need highly trained engineers as much as it needs people who can and will construct simple wooden bridges; it does not need highly trained biologists as much as it needs people who can convince farmers to try new seeds; and it does not need doctors who have been trained to cope with Western medical problems, the diseases of technological civilizations where the life expectancy is much greater than what it is in Nepal, but it needs people who are willing to teach elementary sanitation in the villages in the hills. The present overproduction of intellectuals is not acute, since the number of Nepalese who are being trained at the university level is such a minuscule fraction of the population, but unless the development of the country can keep pace with the increasing educational opportunities, university graduates will be forced to go abroad to practice their professions.

One of the most effective outfits working with the Nepalese in an effort to improve their educational system has been the American Peace Corps. In 1963 an unnamed American author writing in an official publication made an attempt to assess the Nepalese impression of Americans. He noted: "A fairly large number of Nepalese have had some form of contact with Americans, mainly with tourists or those composing the official mission. The general stereotype which has arisen from this acquaintance depicts them as good-hearted, generous and friendly but basically simple people of somewhat limited perception." He went on to say, "According to all reports, volunteers of the United States Peace Corps have already had a measurable effect in improving the image of the United States."

In 1967, it was my impression that for the people in the countryside of Nepal, the Peace Corps volunteers *were* the image of the United States. Wherever one went in the back country of Nepal, if one said that one was an American it was almost immediately assumed that one must be in the Peace Corps. There were something like three hundred volunteers in Nepal. The volunteers go only where the Nepalese government asks them to go, and they work in fields chosen by the Nepalese. At present they are working in agriculture, rural construction—bridges and roads—education, and now computer-oriented occupations. The volunteers arrive in Nepal with a certain minimum skill in Nepali, and in a few months—they are generally there for a minimum of eighteen months—they become fluent and often learn one of the local languages as well. When they go into a village they usually work in collaboration with a Nepalese counterpart engaged in the same activity and share the experiences of primitive village life. I spoke to several volunteers who teach school. In one case there was a husband-and-wife team from the Bronx. He taught elementary school in the Kathmandu Valley, and she had organized the first school in Nepal for deaf children. Another young volunteer whom I met had had mathematical training and was attempting to write an elementary modern textbook in high-school mathematics, in Nepali, for use in the schools; he had, incidentally, chosen to live in a typical village house with no electricity or running water and with a straw mat to sleep on, although he was working near Kathmandu. In all instances, they stressed the fact that their major obstacle is the emphasis that has been placed in the past on rote. The Nepalese consider a man educated if he can recite by heart large parts of religious texts; no one ever taught children how to solve problems. The volunteers try to emphasize teaching children to deal with new and unfamiliar situations by reasoning them out. There was also a feeling among the volunteers that the Nepalese schools tend to teach English too soon. It is quite customary to start English in the third grade—a procedure that might be all right, except that many of the children do not yet speak their national language, Nepali, and so are forced to learn two languages at once.

In agriculture, the volunteers try to persuade the villagers to try new things—new seeds, new techniques for combating plant diseases, and the like. Young Americans are simply not used to a society in which progress is regarded as impossible, and perhaps the greatest contribution that the volunteers can therefore make is in sharing their optimism and opening up new options for the villagers. Simply giving practical demon-strations of how one goes about trying to solve problems is invaluable in a society in which people have been resigned to accepting the conditions of the past as inevitable. In general the Peace Corps volunteers fall in love with Nepal—with the beauty of the countryside and with the charm and kindness of the people,—and a substantial proportion of them stay on for a second tour of duty. Indeed, after leaving the Peace Corps many of them try to come back to Nepal to work with outfits like U.S. AID.

Most of the people I spoke to in our AID mission acknowl-edge that the first Americans to come to Nepal in 1952 to set up what was then the United States Technical Co-operation Mission seriously underestimated the difficulties of the job. At that time it was generally assumed that the people were aware of the possibilities of development—that they shared a "rising tide of expectations"—and that if they were shown what to do they would set off by themselves and do it. What the U.S. AID missions in fact found was that the people had, in general, no expectations at all and that there was, if any-thing, a profound resistance to change. This attitude meant that the only way to ensure the continuity of a project was for the advisers simply to commit themselves to running it indef-initely. In fact, many of the larger projects involving machines and mechanized factories, completely unfamiliar to the Nep-alese, simply stopped once they were turned over to the local people. For this reason, and because the battle to build and stabilize the Nepalese economy will be won or lost in rural Nepal, U.S. AID is now focusing most of its effort in rural development. The annual AID budget in Nepal now runs to about sixteen million dollars.

Nepal is one of the few countries in Asia which produces a surplus of food. This surplus is in the form of cereal grains—wheat, rice, millet—and in a normal year comes to about thirty-three thousand metric tons. It is sold to northern India, where there are chronic food shortages, especially in recent years in which there have been droughts and then floods. Food export is the country's largest source of income. If this were all there were to the agricultural situation, it would look quite bright. The problem is that the surplus is grown in the south, where the land is flat and agriculturally rich, but only about a third of the people live in the south. Two-thirds live in the hills in the north, where there is a food shortage that must be met by importing food from the south. In 1965 the deficit in the hills was estimated to be 230,000 metric tons, and what is shipped to India represents the excess cultivated in the Terai—the south—over what is needed to feed the rest of the population. This imbalance might be tolerated except that the birth rate in the hills is increasing faster than the rate of food production: in the hills the population is growing at a rate of about two and a half percent a year, while food production is increasing by about one percent a year. Moreover, as medical services improve and as the Nepalese enrich their diets (Nepalese typically now eat two meals a day, which are usually based on rice, millet, or potatoes—there is relatively little consumption of meat and vegetables), the population will grow even faster without a compensating increase in agricultural production. As it is, the country as a whole has only a bare surplus of food.

The situation is compounded by the transportation problem. Essentially everything that goes in and out of the hills is now carried on people's backs. This means that, because of the expense of transportation, prices are raised at either end. But the people in the hills have relatively few methods of earning cash; the most important is mercenary soldiering, which is gradually diminishing. Hence many hill people have already been forced to move south into the Terai—indeed, the Rapti Valley project is largely populated by resettled hill people—and others have emigrated to India or Bhutan where they work on roads. There is a good deal of seasonal migration back and forth across the southern borders for purposes of finding work. The government is confronted with a dilemma, since to reduce the cost of living in the hills it is essential to build roads there, but if the country builds roads it may simply help to perpetuate a situation that is fundamentally unsound economically. As one official puts it, "Is it a good idea to build a road that doesn't go anywhere?" Various plans are now under study, including the introduction of new hill crops such as tea, for example; apples are a relatively new crop which has been introduced into western Nepal. The climate in the lower Himalayan foothills is so diverse that almost anything will probably grow somewhere.

The most obvious things that the country has to do if it is to continue to have a food surplus are to increase food production and to decrease the birth rate. Family planning is just beginning in Nepal, and U.S. AID is cooperating in this program with the Ministry of Health. In Nepal, as in most underdeveloped countries, the problem is one of education coupled with a feeling among the people that because of the high death rates among children it is necessary to have large families in order to ensure the survival of some offspring into adulthood. (There do not seem to be any religious barriers among the Nepalese to family planning and they seem to accept the idea more readily than do Indian families.) While there is a good deal written about family planning in the press, and while it is included as part of the Go-to-the-Village program, one does not get the impression that it is being dealt with as yet on a scale large enough or with sufficient urgency to make much of a dent. On the other hand, the program to grow more food *is* having successes.

To increase food production requires both incentive and technology, and on both counts the Nepalese situation is extremely complex. Nepal has had one of the most intricate land-tenure systems in all of Asia. It is probably fair to summarize the matter by saying that in general about the only thing that is clear in connection with the ownership of land is that it is not owned by the tiller. Under the Ranas, land was given to all sorts of people and institutions on the condition that some fraction of the revenues be turned back to them. Hence large blocks of land were held by individual landlords who rented it out, often for rates consuming as much as eighty percent of the production. In addition, a tenant could be removed from the land more or less at the will of the landlord. Under such circumstances, it is hardly any wonder that the average farmer had little or no incentive to try to increase his production. Beginning in 1955, the government started a land-reform program that led to the proclamation of the Lands Act of 1957, which limited the landlord's rent to fifty percent of the produce and gave the tenant a good deal of protection and security. But it did not do anything about the accumulation of huge landholdings by individual landlords and their families. Hence, in 1964 a new Lands Act was passed that limited such holdings. Now, Nepalese units of measurement have been known to make strong men weep— the country is now engaged in a campaign to introduce the metric system to facilitate international trade—and this applies to the units of land area. Limitations on landholdings have been given in terms of the traditional Nepalese units, the *bigha* and the *ropani*. The maximum amount of land that any single owner can hold is twenty-five *bigha*s where a *bigha* is about 1.6 acres; thus, the maximum holding is just over 40 acres. But in the Kathmandu Valley, where land is very valuable, the landholder can hold only fifty *ropani*s. The *ropani* is equal to 608⁴/₉ square yards, while a *bigha* comes to 8,100 square yards. Excess land is to be purchased by the government and redistributed. A tenant who has cultivated an annual crop at least once cannot be evicted by the landholder on "arbitrary grounds," and the annual rent cannot exceed fifty percent of the produce and cannot be raised to fifty percent if it has been traditionally less on a given plot. It is generally agreed in Nepal that this is an excellent law, and the king has put behind it the full weight of his authority and his conviction about the need for land reform.

In practice, the law has been difficult to carry out. This is due in part to the fact that the Nepalese and, above all, the rural Nepalese, do not think quantitatively. Almost everyone who has traveled in rural Nepal has noticed how difficult it is to find out the distance to any place, even by asking people who live in the area. The farmers do not have the habit of measuring distances and areas, and the problem of learning who owns what certainly stems in part from the fact that plots of land have been only vaguely defined. Part of the problem also stems from deliberate attempts on the part of the land-owners to conceal ownership by dividing their holdings among in-laws and the like. A Nepalese "family" is often a very extensive unit that includes many "families" in the Western sense of the term. Hence one of the most important aspects of the land-reform program is to make surveys of the land to find out, in detail, who really owns it. Despite the difficulties, these surveys have been, or are being, carried out throughout Nepal, and a report in 1967 indicated that 537,120 farmers had been issued provisional land-tenancy certificates, that 90,064 *bigha*s of excess land had been taken over by the government, and that 15,408 *bigha*s had been redistributed to farmers. In addition, the government had taken steps to provide incentive for the farmers to increase production. In the Kathmandu Valley, for example, the traditional main crop has been rice. It is planted at the beginning of the summer monsoon and harvested in the fall. During the winter the fertile fields had been allowed, more or less, to lie idle. In recent years, with the help of AID, the farmers in the valley have been encouraged to plant wheat as a winter crop. To provide incentive the government has restricted the rent that the tenant pays to a percentage of the main crop only, so that a farmer who grows wheat as well as the main rice crop can keep the proceeds from the wheat for his family. New strains of winter wheat have been introduced into the valley, with the result that as of 1967 the Kathmandu Valley, long a food-deficit area, became, for the first time, a surplus-food area, producing 2,254 metric tons of surplus. To accommodate this, grain-storage facilities—*gowdowns*—were built in the valley (the Chinese have constructed *gowdowns* and warehouses both in the Kathmandu Valley and in the south as part of *their* aid program for Nepal) to counteract the adverse effects of seasons of drought. In the past, the Nepalese have been forced to import grain from abroad in bad seasons.

Along with the land-reform program, the government had instituted a compulsory savings program for farmers. It was designed to generate credit for farm investment and to free the Nepalese farmer from his traditional heavy indebtedness. For generations Nepalese farmers have been victimized when they have had to borrow money. In many cases the initial loan was to pay for a wedding ceremony or some other important social event, and because of escalating scales of interest the farmer was soon in debt for life. It has been, until recently, very rare for a farmer to borrow money for farm development—the purchase of fertilizers, seeds, and the like— since there was no way he could do this without being usurized. So long as he was earning so little for working on the land, the Nepalese farmer was not motivated to develop it. The compulsory savings program, which may be unique among developing countries, began in 1964 when the government simply decreed that, in the case of a rice paddy, the major Nepalese crop, a farmer would be required to set aside a certain fraction of his yield as savings. For rice the fraction, in Nepalese units, was one *maund* per *bigha*, where a *maund* is equivalent to about eighty-two pounds. This could be turned over to the savings association either in cash or in rice, which was then stored. In order to get the farmers to comply, the land-reform officer frequently showed up accompanied by an armed soldier and said to the farmer, "Where is your paddy?" The savings are completely distinct from a tax. The money belongs to the farmer, or is eventually available to him, and he earns interest on it. In only three years, well over thirteen million dollars was accumulated this way—a staggeringly large sum when one realizes that the entire assets of the Nepal Rastra Bank were, when the program started, about fifty million dollars. It is even more remarkable that this program was under the direction of a Nepalese, Mohan Man Sainju, who was then in his late twenties.

I had a chance to pay a visit to Mr. Sainju in 1967, when the program was beginning, in his office in the Singha Durbar, the labyrinthine palace which houses essentially all of the central government. An uninitiated visitor can get hopelessly lost in the place, and I was fortunate to have as a guide Dr. Raymond Fort, who was in charge of the Rural Development Division of the United States AID program in Nepal. Dr. Fort grew up on a farm in the Midwest and was very familiar with the problems of farming and farmers. He was also an old friend of Sainju. Sainju's office turned out to be a simple room with a cloth curtain for a door, and Sainju himself a delightfully informal man who looked even younger than his age. He had been educated in Nepal, and Fort remarked after our visit that this might have been a very good thing, since he had been able to come up with original solutions to Nepalese problems without preconceptions that he might have had if he had studied Western methods that did not necessarily apply to the local situation. Sainju told us that his department was working on formulating the best methods for returning the money to the farmers in the form of low-interest loans or credits. On the one hand, if this is done without close supervision the money may be used, as in the past, for weddings and other nondevelopmental expenditures; and, on the other hand, if the money is supervised federally it means increasing the burdens of the central government and retarding the development of local self-government. Like most Nepalese whom I met in the government, Sainju believed in strengthening the *panchayat* system, so that eventually each village can take the responsibility for its own development program and can raise its own local taxes to be used for the construction of local roads, schools, and medical centers. At the moment most of these things are done at the federal level, with a considerable loss of efficiency. Farmers were then beginning to take advantage of the development funds, which they used to buy new seeds and fertilizer, and Fort told me that in some areas production had increased by a factor of ten in three years. I asked Sainju what the main difficulties were that the program faced. He thought that education was the most se-

rious problem. As he put it, "In some households a farmer
wants to try new seeds, but his wife believes that if he plants
them then the gods will kill her oldest son."

There is a difference of opinion in Nepal as to how
successfully—and when, if ever—the country can be industrialized. Nepal has some mineral resources, including iron,
lead, and nickel. There is some mica, limestone, gold, oil, and
natural gas, but in many cases these deposits are located in
areas that are so remote that even if they were worked they
could not be economically exploited. The dream, shared by
many, that somewhere under the Himalayas enormous deposits of precious metals, perhaps even uranium, would be
found has so far not materialized. Apart from the soil, the
main resources of the country appear to be water power and
the forests. In 1967 about one-third of the country was estimated to be forest land. It is now much less. Sal, sisau, semal,
khair, karma, and ansa trees grow in the south. Salwood has
long been sold to India, where it is used for, among other
things, the construction of railway sleepers. Sisauwood is
used for making furniture, and semal, a soft wood, is used
for making matches. (In fact, the matches that one buys in
Nepal are so soft that they often break in two before one can
light them.) However, the forests in the country are in serious
danger of disappearing, since they have been exploited for
generations without thought of conservation. This despoiling
has contributed to a great deal of land erosion in the hills, and
the Nepalese are now making an effort to conserve and re-
claim the forests. (One of the consequences of the current
spat with India is that forest wood is being used to replace
cooking oil. In this respect I was appalled to find in a recent
edition of *Himal*, a journal devoted to the environment of the
Himalayas, an advertisement for a power saw that will cut
down a fully grown pine tree in five seconds!) In 1957 the
government established a Forest Nationalization Act, which
brought the forests under federal control, and a forest survey
was completed. There are forest reclamation projects in var-

ious parts of the country. On the other hand, Nepal has one of the greatest potential hydroelectric power sources in the world in the rivers that flow south from the Himalayas. In this respect, like so many others, Nepal resembles Switzerland, also a landlocked country with enormous power resources. Switzerland, of course, is highly industrialized and can sell its surplus power to rich neighbors who are, if anything, even more highly industrialized. Nepal's northern neighbor, Tibet, is less industrialized than Nepal itself, which makes India the only potential customer for surplus electric power. Indeed, India has already helped to build several hydroelectric plants in Nepal. An important side effect of these power projects will be the dams, which can be used to store water for irrigation. Nepal has very heavy rainfall during the summer months—the monsoon—but relatively little during the winter, and water storage will be an invaluable aid to the farmers.

Apart from the existence, or nonexistence, of natural resources, there are other uncertainties about the future industrialization of the country. Both India and China mass-produce consumer items such as shoes, cooking utensils, fountain pens, soap, and automobiles. (Most of the trucks that one sees in Nepal are Mercedes trucks that are made in the Indian Tata automobile works.) It is very unlikely that the Nepalese can produce these things at competitive prices for export in the near future. Therefore, there is now emphasis on building industries for import substitution—that is, manufacturing things for the Nepalese market that would otherwise have to be imported, and thus saving the valuable foreign currency that Nepal earns. There have already been some successes with this in matches, cigarettes, sugar, textiles, and soap, and the cement plant near Kathmandu. The largest uncertainty in the industrial development of the country is, perhaps, the question of whether an agrarian people can adjust to the requirements of working in factories. Some people say that the Nepalese are so devoted to the land that it is unlikely that they will ever make successful industrial workers. On the other hand, it is pointed out that young

Nepalese from the hills who join the British army as Gurkhas are very quick to learn how to handle and service complicated weapons and electronic equipment, and that there is no reason to suppose that, if given the proper training and motivation, they would be any less quick to pick up industrial skills as well.

There is no doubt that the key to Nepal's future is connected with, as much as anything, the country's foreign relations. Foreign aid has been decisive in the development of Nepal, and it is remarkable just how many countries have contributed. A survey done some years ago indicated that in the period from 1952 to 1967 the United States gave Nepal about one hundred million dollars in aid, while during the same period India gave over seventy-one million dollars, China over eighteen million, and Russia over twenty million. In addition, a large variety of other countries gave the Nepalese over nine million dollars. (India, China, and the United States, in that order, are now the largest donors.) Most of these countries have some sort of political ax to grind in the area—with at least one notable exception: the Swiss. It is difficult to imagine any possible political motivation for Swiss aid in Nepal, and yet the Swiss have one of the most effective, if small-scale, programs in the country.

The Swiss interest in Nepal goes back to the early 1950s, when, at the invitation of the government, the well-known Swiss geologist and explorer Tony Hagen began a series of geological studies of the country that lasted some seven years. Hagen, accompanied by a few Sherpas, walked thousands of miles in Nepal and probably came to know the country better than any Westerner—and perhaps any Nepali—before or since. Hagen wrote an excellent book, with superb photographs, on Nepal and concluded that rural Nepalese needed three things urgently: suspension bridges, hospitals and doctors, and schools. Perhaps because of Tony Hagen's work and writings and because of the Swiss alpine expeditions to Nepal, the Swiss have an especially fond relationship with this country whose geographical problems they find so similar to their own. They have built bridges in rural Nepal; and in Jiri, in the east, they have set up a sort of model village with a hospital clinic. Moreover, the Swiss introduced modern dairy farming to the country. In 1955, with financial support from New Zealand, another country that has had a close and disinterested relation with Nepal—probably because of Sir Edmund Hillary—the Swiss set up a cheese plant in Langtang, six days' walk from Kathmandu. Now there are several cheese factories in the country, and cheese and butter made from yak's milk (yak cheese is, by the way, delicious) have become an important export.

In 1950, when the Chinese moved into Tibet, a massive flow of refugees began pouring into Nepal, Bhutan, Sikkim, and India. There are now about eight thousand Tibetan refugees left in Nepal out of the original group of fifteen thousand, and the Swiss have made very important contributions to their resettlement. (A small number have even gone to Switzerland to live.) Outside Kathmandu, in Jawalakhel, there is a large refugee village under the general supervision of the Swiss aid program. Most of these Tibetans work at rug weaving. A Tibetan rug is a work of art. Made of thick, brightly colored wool, it is resplendent in traditional decorations of dragons and the like. There is a sort of rug factory in Jawalakhel run by Tibetans who chant in unison while they weave. In fact the Tibetan rugs made in Nepal are far superior to any being currently manufactured in Tibet.

Apart from the great powers, and the Swiss, many other countries have programs in Nepal. The British have set up radio broadcasting facilities and built roads, the West Germans have helped to establish a technical institute, the Australians have contributed to improving the water supply, the Japanese have been helping in hydroelectric power development, the Canadians furnished wheat to Nepal when there were food shortages, there are Nepalese studying in Poland, the French have opened up an embassy in Kathmandu and have been helping with the development of the Nepalese tourist industry, and the Yugoslavs and Bulgarians have entered into trade agreements with Nepal.

An interesting case is that of the Israelis. Contacts between Nepal and Israel go back to 1959, when the then Nepalese Prime Minister B. P. Koirala accepted an invitation to visit Israel. Shortly after his visit Koirala was swept from power by the King, and for a year or so contacts between Israel and Nepal were broken off. But in 1960 the king decided, despite Arab pressures, to open diplomatic relations with Israel, which he visited in the autumn of 1963. From 1962 to the present, Israel has financed the studies of many Nepalese students in that country and has been cooperating with the Nepalese in construction projects. Most recently the Israelis helped to train a Nepalese army paratroop brigade. One consequence of this for the Israelis is that Nepal has followed a generally moderate and friendly line in the United Nations, unlike India and Pakistan, who have sided with the Arabs. Social developments in Israel, especially the kibbutzim, appear to have captured the imagination of some of the young Nepalese. I met a young man in Kathmandu who told me that he was engaged in a program to start kibbutzim in rural Nepal. When I questioned him a bit more closely it turned out that what he really meant was that he was helping to set up cooperatively owned stores in the countryside that would compete with the privately owned stores and thus keep the prices down. But the word *kibbutz* had somehow stuck in his imagination and as far as he was concerned he was constructing kibbutzim.

In many ways Nepal's future depends on how it can maintain balance and independence with respect to its two giant and mutually hostile neighbors, China and India. Since the British left India, India's relationship with Nepal has gone through considerable evolution. The Nepalese have a long tradition of political independence, and Nepal's foreign policy with respect to India has been an attempt to establish its independence while, at the same time, having to face the political and economic reality of Indian power. (There is one curious manifestation of Nepalese independence—the time is ten minutes later in Nepal than in India since the sun gets to Kathmandu ten minutes earlier than it does to New Delhi. India has only one time—that of New Delhi. The Nepalese also regard Saturday as the day of rest while both the Indians and Pakistanis take Sunday.) Nepal's only outlet to the sea is through India, a fact that apparently inspired Nehru to state during the early 1950s, "We recognize Nepal as an independent country and wish her well. But even a child knows that one cannot go to Nepal without passing through India." This may have been true in 1950, but now a child can go by air to Kathmandu from Bangkok or Hong Kong (to be sure, with India's permission to overfly its territory), and if one is so disposed, one can come down from Tibet on the Chinese Road. As I have mentioned, for India, Nepal represents five hundred miles of strategic mountain frontier, since once the Himalayas have been crossed in Nepal, the country merges into northern India with no natural barriers. In 1955 King Mahendra invited the Chinese ambassador to India to visit him in Kathmandu. This marked a turning point in Nepal's relations with India and China and the beginning of Mahendra's attempt to balance off the influence of the two countries for the benefit of Nepal. In 1956 Nepal signed its first aid agreement with China, and in January of 1957 Chou En-lai paid a state visit to Kathmandu. In 1962 Nepal's relations with her neighbors took a dramatic turn when India and China went to war. It then became of crucial importance to India that its relations with Nepal be solid and cordial. There had previously been a good deal of friction between the two countries over tariff questions and, above all, over the fact that the Nepali Congress Party had mounted raids against the government of the king from northern India. But, with the Chinese at their doorstep, the Indians quickly moved to end all of the sources of tension with the Nepalese. (In particular they stopped the Congress raids.) King Mahendra, for his part, had already gone to Beijing and concluded the agreement with the Chinese that led to the construction of the road from Kathmandu to the Tibetan border.

At present, Nepal maintains a strict official neutrality as between the two countries. There were until the 1970s guerrilla incidents on Nepal's borders with Tibet, provoked by the so-called Khampas, refugees from the Kham province of Tibet, who were, in some cases, former members of the Dalai Lama's army. Much of this activity took place around the ancient Kingdom of Mustang, in the northwest part of the country—in fact, north of the Himalayas, on the Tibetan plateau. Mustang was, until recently, an independent, rarely visited principality loosely associated with Nepal, but it is now part of the kingdom. This Khampa activity was supported by the CIA and some Tibetans were actually trained in this country at Camp Hale, in Colorado. Under very heavy pressure from the Chinese, the Nepalese army put a stop to this guerrilla activity in 1974.

India's concern with China has given the Nepalese a certain room for diplomatic maneuvering, but it is still true that Nepal is extremely dependent on India economically. Since 1962, Indian currency has no longer been legal tender in Nepal, but the two countries are so closely tied economically that shortly after India devalued the rupee in 1966, a year or so later, and presumably as a direct consequence, Nepal followed. Whatever the government's attitude may be, it is quite clear to anyone who looks into the matter that the Nepalese "man in the street" has some, if not a good deal of, distrust of the Chinese. In the north this suspicion appears to be on religious grounds. The first thing that the Chinese did in Tibet was to destroy the monasteries that were at the heart of Buddhist religious life there. Those Nepalese who are Buddhist learned a sharp lesson from this, and do not want to see the same thing happen to them. Among the Hindus, in the south, the attitudes are more complex. Their religious orientation is toward India, and many Hindu Nepalese that I talked to seem to have attitudes about the Chinese that border on race prejudice. On several occasions people in Kathmandu told me that they did not like the Chinese, because they ate monkeys and snakes. There are Chinese in Kathmandu, where the Chinese embassy is, and they often appear in silent knots, dressed in blue Mao uniforms, in the local bazaars. At one time the Chinese were giving away Mao buttons, but the government of Nepal objected and then provided Mahendra buttons for the Nepalese people, who like to wear buttons and decorations so long as they are brightly colored. There are a few bookstores in Kathmandu that sell the latest works from Beijing. The Chinese in Kathmandu stay pretty much to themselves, and no one is really sure what their thoughts are about the future of Nepal. However, most people doubt that the Chinese are interested in taking over the country by force, for this would involve a large-scale war with India that the Chinese appear to want to avoid. In this respect there is a story, perhaps apocryphal, that made the rounds in Kathmandu. An American is supposed to have asked King Mahendra what he would do if the Chinese sent tanks down the road from Tibet. The king is said to have answered, "I would inform you."

The future of Nepal is very much tied to the strength and wisdom of the king and his relation to the people. The Nepalese people are honest, attractive, resourceful, and good-humored. Although it may sound romantic, it is true that they sing while they work. They sing in the fields and they sing when they carry loads up and down the countryside on their backs. They have lived for a long time in repression and ignorance, but, with modern communications and the ever-increasing presence of tourists from the West, they are becoming more and more aware of the potentialities of life. Some people who visit Nepal are somewhat appalled by what they regard as a loss of innocence—the replacement of the old village culture, with all its joys, sorrows, and beauties, by the transistor radio and the cement building. But one must understand that it is the Nepalese people who have chosen the road to development. They desperately want to enter the modern world, and they will do so, whatever anyone else may think about it. At the moment, the king is in full control of the country. He is genuinely loved by most of the people, who, even when they criticize the government, generally do so in a way that exempts the king. If the king is to continue to remain above criticism—and there are recent indications from Nepal that this may no longer be the case—then the villagers and townspeople must begin to realize their newly awakened hopes and visions of a better life. No individual, and no nation either, can live indefinitely on unfulfilled expectations.

3

Some Walk-Going

In many ways, Ila Tsering, who is now in his mid-fifties, is a typical Sherpa. Like most of his fellow tribesmen, he is, by geographic nationality, a Nepalese. Like all Sherpas, he is short (five feet three, the Nepalese average), dark and Mongolian-looking. (In Tibetan, *Sherpa* means "man from the east," but no one knows what "the east" refers to, exactly. Several centuries ago, it is thought, the Sherpa tribe migrated south into Nepal and northern India from Tibet. As for the Tibetans themselves, they look astonishingly like our American Indians.) Like most Sherpas, he wears his hair short. (Tibetans wear *their* hair extremely long, like a woman's, and tie it up in coils with bright ribbons.) Like most Sherpas, he is married to one woman (both polygamy and polyandry, though now forbidden by Nepalese law, are practiced by a few Sherpas, the most common arrangement being the marriage of a woman to two brothers) and has a fairly large family—

three boys and a girl. As is true of many Sherpa families, there is a history of tuberculosis in Ila's family—his wife had the disease until it was arrested by the arrival of modern medicine in his community. Like most Sherpas, Ila lives in the Solu-Khumbu region of Nepal. Solu and Khumbu are contiguous districts in the northeast, next to Mount Everest. Solu, the more southerly, is in the "lowlands"—its villages are at about nine thousand feet. In Khumbu, the villages are at eleven or twelve thousand feet, and the yak pastures, where the Sherpa herdsmen live in the summer, are as high as seventeen thousand feet, which is almost two thousand feet higher than Mont Blanc, the highest mountain in Europe. Ila and his family live in Namche Bazar, the district capital of Khumbu, which is at about twelve thousand feet. Like most Sherpas, Ila is multilingual. His mother tongue, Sherpa, is closely related to Tibetan but has no written form, so Tibetan serves as the written language. Ila speaks and writes Tibetan. He also speaks and writes Nepali. Most Sherpas now understand Nepali, and the younger generation, having had the advantage of formal schooling, read and write it as well. In addition, Ila speaks Hindustani, a mixture of Hindi and Urdu spoken in India. He understands English and speaks it with both a charming accent and a rather astonishing turn of phrase. (There does not seem to be any sound in Sherpa equivalent to the English "*f*" so *fruit* comes out "prut" and *breakfast* "birkpass.") Like all Sherpas, Ila is a Lamaistic Buddhist, his religious life being guided by the lamas who live and study in the monasteries in Solu-Khumbu. The spiritual leader of the Lamaistic Buddhists is the Dalai Lama, who lived in Lhasa before the Chinese occupation of Tibet. He is now in India, and for the Sherpas of Khumbu his spiritual representative is the abbot of the monastery at Thyangboche, a few miles from Namche Bazar. In addition, the Sherpas are animists—they believe in a complex set of spirits and deities who live in the streams, trees, and high mountains of Solu-Khumbu.

What distinguishes Ila from most Sherpas, who are

farmers, herdsmen, or traders, is his occupation, which he describes as "some walk-going." Before 1965, when the government temporarily banned all mountaineering expeditions because their number had become unmanageable, along with their irresponsibility (they would go where they had no permission to go, and, more important, several of them actually crossed the border into Tibet, inflaming the Chinese government), Ila's "walk-going" took him with English, Japanese, Indian, and American climbing teams. His function was what he calls "carrying go." There is carrying and there is carrying; Ila's version consisted of transporting food and other supplies to very high altitudes over difficult mountain terrain. Technically, Ila is a "tiger." The British, who discovered the extraordinary physical and human virtues of the Sherpas in the course of their first Everest expeditions, in the 1920s, gave the nickname "tiger" to those Sherpas who carried the highest or who showed special courage. It soon became a custom for the Himalayan Club of Darjeeling—the Indian hill station east of Nepal where many early assaults on the peaks were mounted—to make formal "tiger" awards to outstanding Sherpas. In the 1950s, a Himalayan Society was formed in Nepal and became a kind of Sherpa union. (It was temporarily dissolved in 1965 when the ban on climbing was imposed, and then revived in 1969 when the ban was lifted.) Every Sherpa registered with the society still has a sort of passport bearing his picture and his signature—a thumbprint if he can't write—along with a record of his work with various expeditions. The Himalayan Society also set the rates for "carrying," which are now somewhere between twenty-five rupees a day—about a dollar—for a porter to forty rupees a day for a *sirdar*—the head Sherpa. By Nepalese standards, this is very good pay. Ila has been with many expeditions throughout the Himalayas, but his most outstanding work was probably done with the American expedition to Mount Everest in 1963. On March 23 of that year, he was with a group that was caught in an avalanche on the lower slopes of Everest; an American climber, Jake Breitenbach, was killed, and a Sherpa, Ang Pema, was badly injured. Ila carried Ang Pema down to the base camp on his back. There the members of the expedition debated whether or not to continue, and decided to go on. The success of the expedition was due, at least in part, to the fact that the Sherpas were willing to carry on after the accident. On May 1, James Whittaker and a Sherpa, Nawang Gombu, of Darjeeling, made it to the top. On May 21, Ila and four other Sherpas carried supplies to an altitude of 27,250 feet on the west ridge of Everest—less than two thousand feet below the summit and higher than all but a handful of mountains in the world—in support of two successful American assaults, each by a different route. For his work on Everest (before the final push, Ila is reported to have said, "All smart Sherpas down sick. Only crazy Sherpas up here"), Ila was selected—along with four other Sherpas, two from Solu-Khumbu and two from Darjeeling—to visit the United States, with the aid of a grant from the State Department's Bureau of Educational and Cultural Affairs. On the way, Ila stopped in Switzerland long enough to climb the Matterhorn, which he found pretty tame. On July 8, President Kennedy presented the Hubbard Medal of the National Geographic Society to the American members of the expedition and to the Sherpas as well. Hanging in Ila's house in Namche Bazar is a delightful picture showing the president bending down to put the medal's ribbon around Ila's neck. Both men are grinning broadly.

After 1965, the expedition Sherpas of Solu-Khumbu fell on relatively hard times, because there was no expeditionary work for them. Their situation would have been incomparably worse if it were not for a retired British army officer, Lieutenant Colonel James Owen Merion Roberts, formerly of 2d King Edward VII's Own Gurkha Rifles. Roberts, who is now in his seventies, has been climbing in the Himalayas for more than fifty years, and served as the transportation officer for the 1963 American Everest expedition. (This was no sinecure, since the expedition required nine hundred porters to move

On the trail with Michele Jaccoux. (*Photo courtesy of Claude Jaccoux*)

The grounds of a monastery where we pitched our tents under the ever-watchful eyes of Buddha. (*Photo by Jeremy Bernstein*)

Michele Jaccoux and I discuss the wireless situation with young Sub-Inspector Rana. (*Photo courtesy of Claude Jaccoux*)

Ang Dorje with the yeti scalp. (*Photo by Jeremy Bernstein*)

Rocks and slabs filled with religious carvings, which add to one's *sonam* (the measure of credit which a Buddhist hopes to accumulate in his present life in order to escape the pain of rebirth). (*Photo by Jeremy Bernstein*)

Children of Nepal. (*Photo by Jeremy Bernstein*)

The cigarette is the consolation and perhaps the curse of the Nepalese. These children are twelve and thirteen years old. (*Photo by Jeremy Bernstein*)

A Nepalese farmer. (*Photo by Jeremy Bernstein*)

A merchant of Nepal. (*Photo by Jeremy Bernstein*)

A Tibetan porter with the face of a prince. (*Photo by Jeremy Bernstein*)

Our porters make their way down a small ladder joining terraced fields in typical scrub jungle farmland in rural Nepal. (*Photo by Jeremy Bernstein*)

The author crossing a typical Nepalese bridge. (*Photo courtesy of Claude Jaccoux*)

Jaccoux and I en route to Tiger Tops. (*Photo courtesy of Claude Jaccoux*)

Michele Jaccoux after several days on the trail. (*Photo by Jeremy Bernstein*)

Our party on Everest. (*Photo by Jeremy Bernstein*)

its equipment from Kathmandu to the base of Everest, a distance of more than two hundred miles through some of the most rugged terrain on earth.) There is probably no one in the world who knows the Himalayas better than Roberts; in addition, he served as military attaché to the British embassy in Kathmandu from 1958 to 1961, which has given him considerable familiarity with the intricacies of Nepalese governmental administration. He speaks both Nepali and Hindi, and is a brilliant mountain photographer. In 1965, Roberts, who lives in Kathmandu, founded an outfit called Mountain Travel. His idea was to organize and outfit small trekking expeditions into the back country of Nepal—which is completely inaccessible except on foot—for people who were willing to hike and camp but might not know how to get along in a strange, primitive country with an incomprehensible language. His first clients were three American ladies, aged fifty-six, sixty-two, and sixty-four, from the Midwest. They must have been in splendid shape, because, in the company of three Sherpas and nine porters, all supplied by Roberts, they made the trek from Kathmandu to Namche Bazar and back—a dogleg route of 190 miles each way as the crow flies—in a little over a month, and apparently enjoyed the trip thoroughly. (The distance as seen by a crow is not a very relevant measure of this trip, since so much of it is nearly vertical; some of the passes rise to nearly twelve thousand feet.) Today, Mountain Travel Nepal handles several hundred trekkers a year and employs the equivalent of three or four major expeditions' worth of Sherpas as guides and cooks, and at least 150 porters, who are recruited from the hill towns along the way. It also gives logistic support to many mountaineering expeditions. For a fee that comes to seventy dollars a day per person for the Everest trek—which, if one walks all the way from Kathmandu to the base of Everest, several days' march beyond Namche, lasts thirty-seven days, round trip—Mountain Travel supplies food, tents, and sleeping bags, along with sufficient personnel to carry the equipment and cook the food. All the trekker must supply is his personal gear and what Roberts used to call in one of his brochures "Feet in good, hard shape."

Ila Tsering was one of Colonel Roberts's *sirdars*, or expedition leaders. It was in this capacity that I came to know him. He was the *sirdar* for a thirty-five-day trek that I made in 1967 with my friends Claude and Michele Jaccoux (he is a French alpine guide, and she is a former member of the French national ski team and now a ski instructor) into the high mountain country of Solu-Khumbu in fulfillment of a childhood dream—to see Mount Everest. Its history and the almost legendary tales surrounding the attempts to climb it have always fascinated me. Mount Everest is a "British mountain," thanks to Edmund Hillary and Tenzing Norkay in 1953, although the British were nearly beaten by two Swiss expeditions in 1952 (and if the British had failed in 1953, an extremely strong French group had been granted permission by the Nepalese government to make an attempt in 1954). Until 1950, almost no foreigners had been allowed in; when that ban was lifted, the government started selling climbing rights to its mountains, which include eight of the ten highest in the world. The fee was arranged according to altitude. Up to 1965, when all climbing was temporarily banned, the eight highest—Everest (29,108), Kanchenjunga (28,208), Lhotse (27,923), Makalu (27,824), Dhaulagiri (26,810), Cho Oyu (26,750), Manaslu (26,760), and Annapurna (26,504)—cost 4,800 Nepalese rupees, then about $700 apiece. Any other mountains above 25,000 feet used to cost 3,200 rupees each, and mountains below 25,000 feet cost 1,600—then less than $250. (The last category have presented some ambiguities of interpretation, because northern Nepal abounds in "hills" and glacial passes that range between 18,000 and 20,000 feet but, in their context, hardly seem like real mountains at all. Although all of the "eight-thousanders"—the peaks over eight thousand meters, or about 26,250 feet—have been climbed, some of the mountains in Nepal have never been attempted, and several of them are not even named.)

In 1969 the Nepalese government lifted the climbing ban imposed in 1965. The Tourism Act of 1978 and the Mountaineering Expedition Regulation of 1979 set new terms and conditions for mountain climbing expeditions. Keeping in mind that in round figures the Nepalese rupee is now valued at about four cents, the regulations set a fee of fifteen thousand rupees for Everest and fourteen thousand rupees for any of the other eight-thousand-meter mountains. There is a sliding scale down to the so-called "trekkers' peaks." These are peaks, some of which are quite difficult, in the twenty-thousand-foot range that can be included as part of a trekking program. The fee for climbing these peaks is between two and three hundred dollars. In addition a mountaineering expedition is required to carry life insurance for the Sherpas and other personnel working for it. For work above six thousand meters a person must be insured for two hundred thousand rupees—about eight thousand dollars. Clause (f) of the regulations, the obligations, reads "To provide equal opportunity to climb the summit for those persons who have reached the last camp." This is surely a reference to the Sherpas, who carried supplies to such a camp and then might not be invited to join the summit teams. Most of the climbing reports one sees now from Nepal include Sherpa summit climbers.

In any event, it was the British who "discovered" Mount Everest. In 1852—according, at least, to the legend—a Bengali, Radhanath Sikhdar, who was working as a statistician for the British Survey of India, is said to have rushed into the office of Sir Andrew Waugh, the surveyor general, and announced, "Sir, I have discovered the highest mountain in the world!" Until that time, the mountain in question had been listed in the survey as Peak XV, with no altitude shown. It was not until 1865 that Sir Andrew formally named it for his predecessor, Sir George Everest. The first altitude given for the peak, in 1852, was 29,002 feet; on the basis of later measurements (in 1907 and 1921–22), this was raised to 29,145 feet; and it then shrunk back to 29,028 feet as the result of a survey made in 1955 under the auspices of the Indian government. Erosion, no doubt, reduces the height of the mountain, and there is reason to believe that the geological forces that raised the Himalayas from the sea in the first place are still at work, but these forces work rather slowly, and the discrepancies in Everest's altitude over the past century are certainly attributable to errors in measurement.* In 1987 there was much consternation caused by new satellite measurements of both Everest and K-2 in Pakistan which purported to show the latter was higher than the former. These measurements seem to have been wrong. The presently accepted altitude for Everest is 29,108 feet.

Of course, the Tibetans and Sherpas who lived near the base of Everest were aware of its existence long before the British arrived in India. Indeed, the Tibetan name for Everest is Chomolungma, which has been translated as "Goddess Mother of the World" or "Goddess Mother of the Snows." But big as it is, Everest is one of the most difficult mountains in the world to get a good view of. From the Kathmandu Valley it is not visible at all, although one can see it on a clear day from various hilly vantage points a short drive from the valley. Yet even then it does not seem like much; indeed, if one does not know just where to look one can easily miss it altogether. It is no wonder that the Nepalese thought several other peaks were higher. (In some books on Nepal written before 1850, Dhaulagiri, in western Nepal, was said to be the highest mountain in the world.) Because Nepal was completely closed to expeditions before 1950, the southern flank of the mountain, which lies in Nepal, remained unexplored until it was visited briefly in that year by a small British-American party.

* Dr. B. L. Gulatee, director of the 1955 survey, commented in the *Himalayan Journal*, a publication devoted to Himalayan exploration: "The new determination stands in a class by itself, and its close agreement with the older [1852] value does not signify that the latter was well determined. It is really due to the fact that like is not being compared with like. Judged by modern standards, the earlier deduction of the height of Mount Everest was vague in several respects, and was burdened with large errors on account of neglect or incomplete consideration of certain physical factors. It so happened that by chance the various individual errors, although large, have tended to cancel each other."

As for the northern approaches to the peak, Tibet too was closed to Westerners during the nineteenth century, but in 1904 Sir Francis Younghusband arrived with a contingent of British troops and opened up diplomatic and trade relations with the country. Still, it was not until 1921 that a British reconnaissance party made its way to the Rongbuk Valley, at the northern base of the mountain. In 1922 and 1924, British parties engaged in two absolutely extraordinary attempts to climb the mountain from the Tibetan side. A member of both parties was George Leigh-Mallory. (It was Mallory who, at a lecture in Philadelphia, replied "Because it is there" to a question about why he wanted to climb Everest.) Since first coming to Everest, in 1921, Mallory had become enslaved by the mountain. E. F. Norton, a climber with the 1924 party, wrote of him: "The conquest of the mountain became an obsession with him, and for weeks and months he devoted his whole time and energy to it, incessantly working at plans and details of organization; and when it came to business he expended on it every ounce of his unrivalled physical energy."

Reading the accounts of these pioneering attempts, one is constantly struck by the almost completely casual and innocent heroism of the participants. Almost all were public-school men (Mallory, indeed, taught at Charterhouse), and, when not otherwise occupied, could be found in small tents at various altitudes reading aloud to one another from *The Spirit of Man*, *Hamlet*, or *King Lear*. As Mallory wrote in his account of the 1922 expedition, "On another occasion, I had the good fortune to open my Shakespeare at the very place where Hamlet addresses the ghost. 'Angels and Ministers of Grace defend us,' I began, and the theme was so congenial that we stumbled on enthusiastically, reading the parts in turn through half the play." This reading of the Bard took place at twenty-one thousand feet, above the Rongbuk Glacier, and shortly thereafter Mallory and a companion, without oxygen, managed to climb to twenty-seven thousand feet— just two thousand feet short of the summit. A second team, using oxygen, got a little higher, but a third attempt on the peak ended in disaster when seven Sherpas were killed in an avalanche. This expedition marked the first use of oxygen (which the Sherpas called "English air") in climbing, and it also marked the first appearance of Sherpas in a mountaineering expedition. In 1924, the British were back en masse, with 350 porters and twelve climbers. Mallory was now thirty-seven, which seems to be a prime age for Himalayan climbing. (Young climbers usually lack the kind of temperament required to slog away day after day, often with little or no progress, on a Himalayan giant.) On June 4, E. F. Norton and T. H. Somervell reached over twenty-eight thousand feet, without oxygen. On June 7, Mallory started up with a young companion, Andrew Irvine. They were followed by N. E. Odell, the expedition geologist (who, incidentally, discovered marine fossils high on the mountain, showing its suboceanic origins). Odell had not come on the expedition primarily as a climber, but in the early stages he had shown himself to be so strong that he had been given the task of following Mallory and Irvine, one camp behind, to offer them whatever support they needed. On the seventh, Odell, who was in Camp V, at a little over twenty-five thousand feet, received a note from Mallory carried down from Camp VI by some Sherpas, which ended, "Perfect weather for the job!" The next morning, Odell started up after Mallory and Irvine, and his record of what he saw remains one of the most celebrated passages in all alpine literature:

At about 26,000 feet, I climbed a little crag, which could possibly have been circumvented but which I decided to tackle direct, more perhaps as a test of my condition than for any other reason. There was scarcely 100 feet of it, and as I reached the top there was a sudden clearing of the atmosphere above me, and I saw the whole summit ridge and final peak of Everest unveiled. I noticed far away, on a snow slope leading up to what seemed to me to be the last step but one from the base of the final pyramid, a tiny object moving and approaching the rock step. A second object followed, and then the first climbed to the top of the step. As I stood intently watching this dramatic appearance, the scene became enveloped in cloud once more. . . .

This was the last time that Mallory and Irvine were ever seen. Odell continued up alone—and in a driving blizzard— to over twenty-seven thousand feet in the vain hope of finding them. But there was no trace. Nine years later, on the next expedition to the mountain, Mallory's ice ax was recovered at a point not far above the place from which Odell had been watching. How did it get there? Did the men get to the top and fall on the descent, or were they lost in the snows before reaching the summit? No one will ever know.

In the 1930s, the British mounted four Everest expeditions from Tibet, the last one in 1938. All were stopped a thousand feet or so from the summit. In 1933, they sent two small planes over the summit of Everest, and for the first time the Nepalese approaches to the mountain were photographed. In 1934, a rather bizarre and somewhat pathetic English mystic named Maurice Wilson made a solo attempt on the mountain in order to publicize some of his theories, which included the notion that if a man were able to go without food for three weeks he would emerge in a state like that of a newborn child but with the benefit of all the experience of his past life. Wilson had never been on a mountain, but he somehow got the idea that if he could succeed in climbing Everest alone it would help to establish his theories. At first, he planned to crash a small plane as high as possible on the mountain and make the rest of the trip on foot. He got as far as Purnea, in India, where his plane was confiscated, and then walked the rest of the way—about two hundred miles—to Darjeeling. There he trained for months and arranged with some Sherpas to take him, disguised as a Tibetan, to the base of Everest. He, of course, had no permission to climb, but he made a favorable impression of the head lama of the monastery in Rongbuk, with whom he had many discussions. In May 1934 he started for the summit and died of exposure in his tent somewhere above twenty-one thousand feet. His body and diary were found by the British expedition of 1935.

Himalayan climbing was suspended during the Second World War, and it was not until 1950 that expeditions to Everest were resumed. (In 1947 there was another solo attempt by a Canadian, E. L. Denman, who also disguised himself as a Tibetan and who was accompanied by none other than Tenzing. They retreated safely from a point a little above where Maurice Wilson had died.) The political situation had completely altered. Tibet was now closed and Nepal open. In 1950 a small Anglo-American group made the first trek by Westerners into Namche Bazar, and in 1951 a very strong group led by the great Himalayan climber Eric Shipton and including Hillary set out from Dharan, in eastern Nepal, and explored the whole southern flank of Everest, mapping the general outlines of what became the climbing route up the south face. The next year, the Swiss got permission to try the mountain and again approached it via Namche Bazar. The party succeeded in forcing the great ice fall that leads from the Khumbu Glacier to the Western Cwm, a glacial valley that Mallory had seen from the north in 1921 and had given a Welsh name in honor of the fact that he had done his first climbing in Wales. In late May, Tenzing and Raymond Lambert, a famous Swiss guide from Geneva, reached a point on the south face that was a little more than a thousand feet below the summit. The Swiss were back in the fall of 1952, and once again Tenzing and Lambert were stopped at about the same point. Of course, on May 29, 1953, Hillary and Tenzing reached the top, following the Swiss route as far as it went, and in the snows of the summit Tenzing buried a little red-and-blue pencil, given him by his daughter Nima, as an offering to Chomolungma, the Goddess Mother. This was Tenzing's seventh Everest expedition.

Ever since the Swiss traversed Nepal from Kathmandu to Namche Bazar, all expeditions to Everest that have walked in from Kathmandu have used substantially the same route, and have set up their camps at more or less the same places. This was very convenient, since the Swiss published an extensive account of their trip across Nepal in a book called *Avant-Premières à l'Everest*, from which the prospective trekker could get an idea of what he was up against. Nowadays there are all sorts of trekking guides. In reading the book while my trip with Claude and Michele Jaccoux was still in the formative stages, I was immediately struck by the decisive role of the monsoon in determining when one can travel in Nepal. The monsoon comes to Nepal in early June and leaves, as a rule, by mid-September. It is caused by the fact that during the early summer the thin, dry air above the Tibetan plain becomes heated and rises, creating an enormous low-pressure system to the north of Nepal that draws up moist air from the Bay of Bengal. This moist air is wrung dry as it rises to cross the Himalayan barrier, with the result that to the north of the mountains the land is essentially a desert, while to the south it is something of a tropical paradise. During the monsoon, travel is all but impossible. The dirt trails, often exceedingly steep, become as slippery as ice, and the rivers are swollen with rain and with water from the melting snows of the Himalayas. The trek from Kathmandu to Namche— and all east-west travel in Nepal—involves crossing the innumerable rivers that flow south from Tibet. The bridges, if they exist at all, often consist of a few logs thrown across the stream. During the monsoon, the logs are carried away, and the bridge has to be rebuilt the following fall; it is quite rare to find a bridge that is high enough and strong enough to resist the monsoon waters. A third difficulty of travel during the monsoon is the insects, snakes, and, above all, leeches which abound in the tropical countryside during the summer. While a leech bite does not usually cause any serious trouble, there is nothing more revolting. The leeches of Nepal are, on the average, about an inch long. After a rain, they line the foliage along a muddy trail and sway back and forth until a man or an animal passes. Sometimes they drop down from leaves above the trail, but most often they climb into one's shoes, and lodge themselves between one's toes. It is useless, and even somewhat dangerous, to pull a leech off, since this causes a wound that tends to ulcerate. As a rule, leech bites do not hurt, so one is unaware of having been bitten until one discovers that one's clothes are covered with blood. Traveling over leech-infested terrain is no picnic.

All Everest expeditions have had to reckon with the monsoon. There are two possible strategies: to arrive at the base of the mountain in the late spring and climb until the monsoon strikes, or to arrive in the fall just after the monsoon and climb until the winter snows set in, during late November. In 1952 the Swiss tried both, and after reading their account of the trek to Everest in the early fall, before the monsoon had blown itself out—Lambert severely sprained his ankle when he slipped on a wet trail, and the leader of the expedition, Dr. Gabriel Chevalley, acquired a seriously infected ankle from a leech bite—I decided that, whatever else, we should avoid the bad weather. What with one thing and another, the earliest we could make the trek was in late September, a timing that worked out very well for Jaccoux, since it fell exactly between his climbing and his skiing seasons. Sometime in April I wrote to Roberts, and a few weeks later I got back a cheerful, businesslike reply on Mountain Travel stationery, which had printed across the bottom "Pack a suitcase and take off for Mount Everest"—rather as if it were a stroll in the park. Roberts indicated that a trek to Everest might well be organized for late September, when, with luck, the monsoon would have ended. Roberts was booked up months in advance, so monsoon or no, we accepted the dates he proposed and began making arrangements for the trip.

Among other things, Roberts sent his clients a detailed list of things to bring and medical precautions to take. Among the latter was a formidable set of suggested vaccinations, including typhoid, tetanus, cholera, typhus, smallpox, polio, and gamma globulin, to prevent hepatitis. During the spring, I involved myself in all but endless series of visits to my doctor for shots, and I assumed, naïvely, that the Jaccoux were likewise engaged. The French, although they invented vaccination, do not much believe in it, and when I arrived in Europe, in early June, the Jaccoux announced that they were going to take the bare legal minimum—cholera and smallpox—and *tant pis pour les autres.* Despite my fervent arguments about the terrible dangers they were exposing themselves to, they stuck to their intentions, and I must confess, got through the trek in splendid health. However, they did pay a visit to Dr. Guy de Haynin, the chief surgeon at the hospital at Mulhouse, who had been the expedition doctor for one of the French expeditions to Nepal and, the summer before, had been the doctor for a French expedition to the Peruvian Andes of which Jaccoux had been a member. In fact, Jaccoux served as de Haynin's medical assistant during the Peruvian expedition. Dr. de Haynin, in a gesture of great kindness, offered to supply us with a complete pharmacy, suitable for every medical situation that we might come up against, short of major surgery. Fortunately, as it turned out, most of the huge array of medicines that we took along came back unused.

Of much more relevance was the matter of clothing. From the Swiss account, it was clear that during the trek the climate was going to change from tropical to arctic. We planned to wind up our trek somewhere near the base camp of the British 1953 Everest expedition, which is at 17,800 feet, and from all accounts we could expect extreme cold, high winds, and snow. On the other hand, during the first week or so of the trek we would be passing through tropical jungles, and our main problem would be avoiding heat prostration. Shorts, bathing suits, and parasols would solve the heat and sun problem, but the cold was something else. The Jaccoux teach skiing and, as Michele said when we were discussing the matter, *"Nous, on connaît le froid."* Following their advice and a clothing list supplied by Roberts, I ended up taking along—working from the inside out—long thermal underwear, two wool shirts and a pair of heavy climbing pants, two heavy sweaters, two windproof light nylon jackets, a heavy down jacket, two wool hats, a pair of wool gloves, a pair of leather gloves, a pair of enormous mittens, hiking shoes and climbing shoes, several pairs of extra-heavy wool socks, and a track suit, which Jaccoux had suggested would make a good pair of pajamas. (On one memorable evening when we were camped in our tents in the snow at sixteen thousand feet, I wore almost all of it, and Michele claimed that she had on seven layers.) In addition, we took three cameras and enough film for several thousand pictures, a portable electric razor, a sewing kit for Michele, a portable radio (which broke down almost immediately), Malraux's *Anti-memoires* for Jaccoux, two months' supply of Gauloise cigarettes and an equivalent quantity of pipe tobacco, two decks of cards, two small ice axes and a coil of light nylon climbing rope, and several boxes of laundry soap. I had also purchased twelve aerosol cans of the best Swiss insecticide, and twelve cans of insect repellent, as well as several thousand chlorine tablets for purifying the drinking water. As a last-minute inspiration, we stocked up with vitamin-C tablets, on the ground that there might not be much available in the way of fresh fruit. Actually, we had fruit of one kind or another almost every day.

As it happened, I spent most of that summer near Geneva, which allowed me to undertake an extensive training program of hiking in the Alps. About a month before we were supposed to leave, I slipped on a wet rock during one of these hikes and sprained my ankle, which nearly finished the expedition right then and there. Fortunately, by the time we left, the ankle, although weak, was usable. Jaccoux, on the other hand, was in superb condition after a summer of guiding, and Michele, despite a decidedly svelte appearance, had the natural stamina of a musk ox. By early September we had everything in one place, including our visas. Nepal is one of the few countries in the world where one's entry visa does not allow one to travel in the country. Our visas, valid for fourteen days, gave us permission to visit only Kathmandu, Pokhara, and Tiger Tops. For our tour, Roberts had had to apply for a "trekking permit" for each of us—a sort of passport, with photograph, which spelled out precisely where we could go. The fact that one is required to have such a document, and the fact that one is not allowed to vary at all from the assigned route, are reflections of the Nepalese government's concern about letting foreigners get too close to its northern border. Under almost no circumstance is a foreigner allowed to get closer than twenty-five miles from Tibet. Even if one charters a plane to see the Himalayas, the government insists that a representative from the Foreign Ministry be aboard to make sure that the plane does not stray too close. The Nepalese walk a delicate tightrope between China and India, and they are determined not to have their balance disturbed by incidents on the borders. So we filled out long forms for our trekking permits and enclosed several pictures, and in the middle of September Roberts informed us that everything was in order.

By the end of September, Claude and Michele and I were flying over the flooded rice paddies of northern India, across the Himalayan foothills, past the great snow-covered peaks of western Nepal, and down into the Valley of Kathmandu— surely one of the most spectacular flights in the world. Roberts had sent a Land Rover to meet us at the airport, and later in the day, when we had settled in, he dropped by the hotel to say hello and introduce us to Ila Tsering. Roberts, a courtly, soft-spoken man with a slight limp that apparently does not impede his walking and climbing, has the air of someone who has spent a great deal of his life out of doors. I asked him whether he thought the monsoon was over, and he said that it hadn't rained in two days, which was a good sign. He told us that the leeches had been particularly bad during this monsoon but added, "I shouldn't think you will have much trouble if the rain holds off." While this conversation was going on, Ila stood silent, studying us. I suppose he was wondering what sort of people he was about to spend the next five weeks with. After Roberts left, Ila came to our rooms to see how our equipment was arranged. We had been instructed to have everything packed in plastic bags, which, in turn, were to be put into wicker baskets carried by the porters. Each of us had been allowed about thirty pounds of gear, plus whatever we wanted to carry ourselves. When Ila saw the climbing rope and ice axes, he remarked, "Climbing something?" with a cheerful laugh that seemed to indicate that he didn't take the prospect very seriously.

Early on the morning of September 30, we piled our gear into one of Roberts's Land Rovers and left Kathmandu on the first lap of the route to Everest. For the first thirty miles, we were able to take advantage of the Chinese Road, which runs from a point near Kathmandu to the Tibetan border at Kodari. Foreigners were then allowed to travel only the first sixty miles of it, but for our purposes only the first thirty-odd miles—to a point called Dolalghat, which is at the junction of the Indrawatti and Sun Kosi rivers—took us in the direction we wanted to go. At Dolalghat the rivers are crossed by the Chinese Bridge, a magnificent structure "just wide enough," as someone had said, "for two tanks and a motorcycle!" The Land Rover let us out in front of an open shed on the near side of the bridge. Clustered around the shed was a large assortment of people of various races—Tibetans, Sherpas, Tamangs, and Newars. It took several minutes before it dawned on me that most of them were connected with our trek. When I finally got them sorted out, our roll included three Sherpas, in addition to Ila; six Tibetans, who, it later turned out, were "high-altitude porters," with considerable experience on expeditions and absolutely unbelievable resistance to the cold (among them a mother and daughter, who, like most Tibetan and Sherpa women, were capable of carrying almost as much as the men, and who had walked to Kathmandu from Solu-Khumbu and done a good deal of shopping, the results of which they were taking back home); and a group of eight or ten (it varied from day to day) Tamang porters, members of a tribal group that lives in the high hills near Kathmandu and speaks a Tibeto-Burman language which is distinct from either Sherpa or Tibetan. The Newars apparently owned the shed, which served as a kind of open-air refreshment stand. We tried to keep out of the way while Ila began the task of putting various things of ours into various wicker baskets. There was a total chaos of people and animals. (It turned out that we were taking along some live chickens.) For a while we stood in the sun, but it beat down with such a leaden, tropical intensity that we soon moved into the limited shade afforded by the shed. Jaccoux had had the inspiration of buying three Indian parasols in the market the day before, and in addition, we had brought along two sun helmets (Michele preferred bandannas), all of which were indispensable. After half an hour or so our caravan was organized, and we crossed the bridge and started up a nearby trail that turned east, away from the road.

The tone the trek was to take for the next two weeks was set right at the beginning—up and down. We began at once what Roberts referred to in his notes for Everest trekkers as "a long and rather tiring climb to over 6,000 feet." To be sure, in comparison with any of the training walks I had taken in the Alps, this should have been a bagatelle, and still more so for Jaccoux. But the trail was steep and the heat overbearing. Perspiration streamed down our faces, and at one point, as we passed a little village, Michele bought a length of cotton cloth, out of which she made a sari to take the place of the jeans she had been wearing. The trail was jammed with people. Almost all commercial transport in rural Nepal is done on human backs, and we saw men, women, and children carrying sacks of grain, reams of paper, and cloth, long bundles of bamboo poles, salt, and animals too small to be herded. The beginning of our trek coincided with the ten-day Dassain festival, which celebrates the victory of the goddess Durga over the buffalo-headed demon Mahissasoor. Animals are brought from the countryside to Kathmandu for sacrifice, and many of the animals we saw—chickens, goats, and buffalo— were on their way for that purpose. At one point, I met a man who spoke excellent English and said he was a doctor out on a call in one of the villages—a rare sight in the countryside. The doctor asked where we were going, and when I told him that we were on our way to Namche Bazar and the base of Everest, he looked at me as if I were slightly daft and suggested renting a helicopter.

After walking a couple of hours, we came upon a large pipal tree under which the residents of a nearby village had constructed stone blocks just high enough so that anyone carrying a load could set it down by backing into the block and leaving the basket, or whatever, on the top. It was a delightfully shady spot, and we joined a dozen or so Nepalese who were resting in the shadows. By this time, although we had walked only a few miles, the heat had become so intense that every step in the sun was a major effort, and we were grateful when Ila announced that we would make an early halt and camp close to a spring by some nearby rice fields. We crossed the fields, which were wet and green from the rain of the recent monsoon, and got ready for our first night on the trail. This involved a routine that was maintained for the next five weeks. First, the tents were taken out. We had two light-green ones—one for the Jaccoux and one for me. They were carried by a Tibetan with an extraordinary face, rich with humor and deeply lined. Michele nicknamed him *l'Indien* because of his remarkable resemblance to an American Indian chief. (The Indian had a marvelous sense of balance, which he demonstrated later by carrying me on his back, like a child, across some thin planks that spanned a monsoon-swollen river. I had started out on the planks but didn't like their look, and had climbed back to solid ground. Before I knew what was happening, the Indian had hoisted me on his back and was trotting across the narrow, swaying boards with the agility of an acrobat, setting me down gently in the grass on the other side.) At our nightly camps, there would be a general flurry of activity, usually accompanied by singing, while the tents were rolled out and set up. Another porter—also a Tibetan, whom Michele called *le Chanteur*—always led the singing, which consisted of some eerie, haunting, and terribly sad-sounding songs of Tibet. Meanwhile, two of the Sherpas, a cook and an assistant cook—a Roberts trek had a certain chic—had started a fire to boil water for tea. At first we had some misgivings about the water, and Michele had been allotted the job of discreetly keeping an eye on the cooking, to make sure that everything was washed and boiled. However, after a few meals it became clear that the Sherpas were absolutely scrupulous about all hygienic matters connected with us, although they themselves drank water of every description without treating it and without giving it a second thought. Apparently they had learned that a trekker is a delicate creature who must be treated with extreme care if he or she is to be kept moving.

As soon as the water came to a boil, tea was served—really a light meal consisting of biscuits, sardines, cheese, peanut butter and jam, and sometimes Sherpa bread, a rich concoction made of millet and nuts. We were then free to do what we liked until dinner, which was served between five thirty and six. During the interval, we washed, mended clothes and read, and sometimes Jaccoux conducted a little clinic for any of the porters or Sherpas who were ailing—mainly from sore throats and from infected blisters acquired from walking barefoot, both of which responded very rapidly to antibiotics. We also had a chance to study the scenery. What we saw the first afternoon was typical of the Himalayan foothills in early fall. Everywhere we looked, there were rich fields of green set in terraces that climbed the hills. The earth was carpeted with flowers in explosive tropical colors. We could make out neat-looking villages of stone houses, often painted white and pink, some with wooden roofs and some with thatch and some with slate. The Nepalese in the countryside have a keen sense of color and are fond of brightly decorative flower gardens. Since our campsite afforded a view to the north, we could see the great Himalayan range—a sort of distant white wall, with the summits so high that we often confused them with clouds. Jaccoux wrote in his diary the first night, *"Sentiment de paradis."*

Dinner was always our gala meal. If it was warm enough, as it was on the first nights of our trek, we would eat outside, instead of in our tents, in the light of a candle or a kerosene lamp. (In the tropics the sun appears to set all at once, and by five thirty or six it was night.) The first course was inevitably soup—usually powdered, but sometimes fresh chicken soup made from the remains of one of the birds the Sherpas had cooked. As we wandered through the villages, Ila would call out in Nepali to any of the local women who might have some fresh food to sell, *"Hey didi! Macha? Kukra? Phool? Phal?"* ("Hello, lady! Fish? Chicken? Eggs? Fruit?"), and sometimes he would be successful. If not, we ate rice and peas mixed with onions, and sometimes canned sausages and spaghetti. Later, when we got into the Sherpa country, we were treated to some of the Sherpa specialties like *mo-mo*—a delicious spiced dough wrapped around chopped mutton or goat and then fried crisp. Dessert was fruit—fresh tropical bananas, mangos, or mandarins, if they were available, or, if not, canned fruit from India. It was a thoroughly nourishing and adequate diet, but as the weeks wore on we began getting odd cravings for different tastes—Jaccoux had visions of *boudin* (baked blood pudding with apples), Michele of red wine, and I of ice cream. (We never managed to consume enough sugar to restore the energy that we expended walking ten or so miles a day—up and down—and when we returned to *chez* Boris in Kathmandu, thin as rakes, we fell like vultures on every rich dessert we could lay our hands on.) By the end of the dinner, the Sherpas had put candles in our tents, and I was generally so tired that it was no trouble to fall asleep at seven or seven thirty, while the Jaccoux read or played endless games of cards.

At our first camp, Ila suggested an early start the next day to escape the sun, so we agreed to get up at six thirty and to drink a light tea in order to skip breakfast and get under way as quickly as possible. As the days went on, our rising time grew earlier and earlier; in our eagerness to avoid the heat we were usually on the trail well before six. Our second day was eventful in that, on the one hand, Jaccoux was bitten by a leech and, on the other, a new and remarkable Sherpa personality was revealed to us. The leech bite was completely unexpected. We had been bathing in a warm, azure jungle stream and had left our shoes on the bank. When Jaccoux started to put his shoes back on, he noticed that blood was flowing from between his toes. He removed a grisly-looking black leech by touching it with a cigarette ember—the classic method—applied alcohol, and put his shoes on. Neither Michele nor I was bitten, but it was a signal to watch out. As for the Sherpa, his name was Ang Dorje, and he was Ila's assistant. He had the broad, sad, wise face of a circus clown, and as I got to know him better I realized that he was one of the kindest people I had ever met. On the first day, my weakened ankle had been giving me a good deal of trouble, and I had used my parasol as a kind of crutch, which had not done much good. The following morning, when Ang Dorje appeared at my tent with tea, he was carrying a long stick that he had carved more or less in the form of a ski pole. "Horse," he said, giving it to me. From that day on, Ang Dorje and I and the "horse" were inseparable. Nothing was ever said, but whenever I was limping along the trail behind the rest of the group, I would notice Ang Dorje sitting on a rock a little way ahead of me and staring off into space, as if taking a rest. His resting places would always be at a point where the trail forked or where it was rough or slippery, and as I reached them he would materialize at my side discreetly, as if he just happened to be there by accident. It was never very clear to me how much English he understood. We carried on long conversations in which he taught me Sherpa words in exchange for their English equivalents, and I was confident that he followed everything I said. However, one very cold night we were camped in a small windy wooden cabin not far from Everest. Sherpas do not have chimneys in their houses; they leave the doors open to let out the smoke. This cabin did have a chimney, but the Sherpa domestic habits prevailed. I gave Ang Dorje a long and feeling discourse on how comfortable it would be in our cabin if the door were kept closed and the heat kept in, and he nodded sagely. Then he left the cabin, only to return a few minutes later, leaving the door open, and ask, as he pointed to it, "What English word this?" Curiously, if Ang Dorje had been a bit younger he would not have had to ask, for today the Nepalese educational system starts instruction in English at a very early age—as I later discovered to my advantage. One day I was moving along the trail alone; the Jaccoux had raced off ahead, Ang Dorje had gone off for something, and the porters were far behind. Without paying much attention to where I was going, I found myself in a scrub jungle where the trail, as far as I could make out, completely disappeared. After wandering around aimlessly for half an hour or so, I began to get really worried that I was lost. To add to the general tone of things, the sun was setting, and I had just been bitten by a leech. At this point, a small Nepalese boy appeared from nowhere. He was carrying a large kukri and looked to be about ten. I began to gesticulate in the general direction of Tibet and to babble, "Sherpas, sahibs? Sherpas, sahibs?" in some desperation. He looked at me calmly and, in splendidly articulated English, said, "Where are you going?" Considerably abashed, I allowed myself to be led off in the direction of our party.

The days rolled on in a succession of jungle valleys, mountains, ridges, and rivers, and as we approached the high mountains the valleys grew steeper, the ridges higher, and rivers swifter and colder. Each morning, Ang Dorje would arrive at my tent with tea and an outline of the day's activities—"Some down-go river, river, birkpass, up-go steep road." (Breakfast was the other substantial meal of the day, with eggs, pancakes, toast, and coffee, and it was meant to do us from ten in the morning until teatime.) When we camped in towns, the children would come and surround our tent and stare at us and, at times, a man or a woman would come to us and ask for medicine for a child (if there is one English word that the Nepalese in the countryside know, it is *medicine*), and

Jaccoux would try to find something in our pharmacy that would do some good. Once he told a mother whose baby was suffering with infected sores to wash the child with soap. She said that she did not have the money to buy soap, which cost a rupee and probably represented a day's wages. We gave her several bars of our soap.

The Swiss route that Roberts suggested was, in general, so arranged that all the camps are on high ground, which is dry and hence relatively free of jungle fauna. Sometimes, though, we found it convenient to do a stage and a half, especially if the following day featured an especially severe climb. (We would make the descent in the late afternoon so as to be able to climb in the very early cool morning.) Hence one night we camped in a tropical jungle near a stream. That night Ila displayed his talents as a barber. Michele had been talking with Ila about his activities during the monsoon season and had learned about the barbering. Jaccoux is celebrated in Chamonix for his long, elegant blond plumage, and it was out of the question that he would submit to have any of it removed by a barber of unverified skills. On the other hand, I had forgotten to get a haircut before leaving France and my hair was beginning to curl down over my neck—an annoyance in the heat. So I became a willing victim. I was seated on a rubber poncho, and Ila went to work with a pair of scissors under the watchful gaze of our entire expeditionary force. Amid murmurs of general approval Ila proceeded to remove most of my mop, leaving a sort of crew cut. When it was over, Michele commented, *"Ça te va,"* and that was that.

We decided to celebrate the event with a small toast with our expeditionary cognac, purchased in the New Delhi airport. One of the two bottles was brought out and we settled back to contemplate the tropical night. Suddenly something came hurtling out of the jungle, ran past our tents, and jumped out at me. I leaped up in the air and emitted a bloodcurdling yelp, which brought Sherpas running from all directions. Ila, who had seen our visitor disappear into the jungle, said, "Eats snakes," from which I concluded it must have been a mongoose. It dawned on me that if it was a mongoose, it might well have been in search of its dinner. Jaccoux, armed with a long stick, led a thorough search of the tents but failed to turn up anything.

The next morning, as we walked through the jungle, we saw huge silver-gray gibbonlike monkeys swinging from tree to tree. Michele and I were bitten by a leech, and after my bite we made a major scientific discovery. The leech had been removed by applying a cigarette to it—the Sherpas favor salt—and was lying in the grass still moving. It occurred to me that we might try an experiment on it. We had, more or less intact, our twelve cans of insect repellent, which had turned out, if anything, to attract the Himalayan flies, and which I had suggested we chuck into the nearest ravine since the cans were taking up space. Before doing this, we decided to spray the leech with the insect repellent to see what would happen. Instantly it curled up into a ball and died. We now had a first-rate antileech weapon, and during the next several days, until we reached the high mountain country, one of us always walked with the aerosol can of insect repellent at the ready.

After a week, we reached the important Hindu village of Those, which has a large school and an ancient ironworks, one of the few then functioning in Nepal. The village is located just on the frontier of Sherpa country; in fact, after leaving it we crossed an abrupt nine-thousand-foot pass, and, as if by magic, the character of the countryside, the people, and the architecture was transformed. Since the Chinese invasion of Tibet there has been a sharp change in the attitude of the Sherpas toward Nepal. Until the invasion, they did not really regard themselves as Nepalese. ("Nepalese," to them, referred to the inhabitants of the Kathmandu Valley.) However, when the Chinese smashed the monasteries in Tibet and broke down the whole traditional structure of Tibetan society, the Sherpas began to turn toward their own government. In most Sherpa homes one sees, side by side, portraits of the Dalai Lama and the king of Nepal. The older generation of

Sherpas have a deep-seated fear of the Chinese after what happened in Tibet; indeed, when I once visited an old lama in a small monastery south of Namche, he insisted on lifting up my sunglasses and looking at my eyes to be sure that I was not Chinese, before he would talk to me.

The Himalayan ridges have divided Nepal into small sections, and the ruggedness of the terrain keeps the different populations almost intact. We were now in Buddhist territory. The people had a definite Mongolian look, and the countryside was dotted with *chorten*—monuments in the shape of the contemplating Buddha. There were also numerous *mani* mounds (*mani* means "prayer" in Tibetan), usually erected in the middle of the trail and covered with carved stones on which the sacred formula *"Om mani padme hum"* was etched again and again. Sherpas passing a *mani* always leave it on their right, so that if they come back by the same trail they will have made a full circle around it, in deference to the full circle of the wheel of life. On each ridge, now sprinkled with snow, there would be a cluster of prayer flags printed with religious messages. The houses had wooden shutters that could be closed against the winter winds. (Glass was then almost unknown in the Nepalese countryside.) We had definitely left the tropical jungles and the rice fields of the Himalayan foothills, and the cold nights told us that we were approaching the high mountains. We crossed a pass nearly twelve thousand feet high and felt the first effects of the thin air, which made us a little dizzy and short of breath. Coming down through some lovely pine forests, we reached the village of Junbesi—one of the largest and most attractive villages in the district of Solu. We had now been walking ten days, and although we had seen a number of high mountains, Everest had remained hidden behind the nearby hills. Ila promised us that if the sky was clear we might catch a glimpse of the mountain from a high ridge beyond Junbesi. The next morning, we churned up the ridge and from it got a stunning view of the Himalayan wall near Everest, but the Goddess Mother herself lay hidden in clouds. Ang Dorje flapped his arms and blew in a gallant attempt to disperse them, but after a half hour or so we gave up and continued along the trail to a campsite above the Dudh Kosi, the river that drains the whole south side of the Everest range.

We intended to follow the Dudh Kosi Valley up into the mountains, but first we had to cross the river and go through some low, damp fields. It had rained the night before—a last trace of the monsoon—and the trail was muddy, slippery, and alive with leeches. I have never seen anything like it. Leeches were everywhere—on our shoes, our legs, our arms. I was bitten four times in ten minutes, and the legs of a porter in front of me were streaming with blood. We kept spraying ourselves with insect repellent, but every time we stopped to do this, more leeches attacked us. Finally Ila said, "Now quickly go!" and, all but running, we raced to higher ground. When we stopped, we were all thoroughly shaken. It was at this point that we began to wonder if it would be possible to come back by air. As it happened, every morning at about eight or so, when the sun began to beat down and we were starting up a hill, we had been hearing the sound of a small plane passing overhead. "Swiss people," Ila had said. "Lukla going." Lukla (at 9,200 feet) is a small village above the Dudh Kosi Valley; a few years prior, Edmund Hillary had carved a small grass airstrip out of a field on a hillside there. There were no regular flights to Lukla, but from time to time Mountain Travel, Roberts's outfit, was able to charter one or another of the STOL planes that are usually based in Kathmandu. It had been our original idea to walk to Namche and then fly out from Lukla, but this plan had been abandoned when it appeared that it would be difficult, if not impossible, to arrange a charter. Given the leeches, however, we thought we might take another crack at it. (As it turned out, the monsoon was over for good in a few days, and people who took our route a week or so later told us that it was completely dry, with not a leech in sight.)

Our hopes were raised a few hours later. I found the Jaccoux talking, in French, to a Sherpa on the trail. The Sherpa explained that he had learned French in Montpellier, where he had gone to study viticulture with the intention of growing grapes and making wine in the Kathmandu Valley. He had flown into Lukla in the morning to spend the Dassain holiday with his parents, who lived in the region, and his plane, he said, had returned to Kathmandu empty. A bit later, as we pushed along a wooden trail leading up the Dudh Kosi, we met a British Gurkha officer who had been in Namche on a holiday to see Everest, and he told us that behind him on the trail was a party of four—an Australian forester working in Nepal in the forest conservation program, and three British ladies whom he was escorting. They had booked a plane out of Lukla in a day or so, the Gurkha told us, and could speak to the pilot to see if something might be arranged for us. After a few hours, we ran into the Australian and the three ladies, all looking fit and sunburned, and the forester said that he would be glad to talk to the pilot, and that we could expect to get a radio message at Dr. McKinnon's in a day or so. From reading Roberts's notes, I knew that there was a New Zealand doctor named John McKinnon who ran a small hospital— also set up by Hillary—in the Sherpa village of Khumjung, in the hills beyond Namche. The notes also mentioned a radio at the hospital, and our whole aviation scheme seemed to be falling into line. Little did we know.

That night we camped by a pair of excellent wooden bridges built in 1964—again by Hillary—across the Dudh Kosi and its adjoining tributary, the Bhote Kosi. The bridges have made an enormous contribution to the life of the Sherpas, since Namche is the trading center for the whole area and can now be reached from the lowlands by a relatively convenient trail; previously, crossing the rivers had been a major, risky operation. Our camp was on the Dudh Kosi itself, and from it no mountains could be seen at all, since they were blocked by the huge cliffs etched out by the river. However, the next day, given clear skies, we were promised a full and dramatic view of Everest and its satellites. By now, the winter weather pattern was beginning to settle in, which

meant bright clear skies in the morning, followed by a clouding over in the afternoon and sometimes snow in the evening.
To be as sure as possible of getting a good view, we left at the
crack of dawn the next day. We were now over ten thousand
feet—the lowest altitude we would be at for the next three
weeks, but still sufficiently high so that we could not move
too fast on the stiff uphill trudge toward Namche. As we
climbed slowly, mountains began revealing themselves in all
directions, and soon we were surrounded by great snow-
covered peaks. Every now and again we would stop while
Jaccoux took out his map and compass and tried to identify
some of the mountains, to make sure we were not overlooking
Everest. Up ahead, we saw a level place in the steep trail and
an array of prayer flags near a *mani*—a sure sign that there
was a special view of the snows. When we reached the *mani*,
we looked to the north, up the valley, and fell into a stunned
silence. First, like the brim of a glistening crown, we saw the
massive ice wall of the Nuptse, perhaps ten miles away. Soar-
ing above it was a black majestic pyramid, seamed with snow;
from its top a plume of white floated off into space. It was
Everest, and it looked like the Queen of the World. We stood
fixed to the spot for nearly an hour, with all the Sherpas and
Tibetans seated around us. Finally Ang Dorje said, "Beautiful. Now Namche go," and we started up the trail, which
swung off to the left, hiding the mountains.

Ila had gone on ahead the night before to spend the evening with his family in Namche, and before we reached the
village we were met by a lively-looking young boy who Ang
Dorje said was Ila's son. Soon after, Namche appeared from
around a bend. It is set in a horseshoe-shaped arena and
clings to the side of an enormous gorge that drops down into
the Bhote Kosi. There are about eighty stone houses in the
village, and also a police checkpoint. Our trail led right into
the police station, where Ila was waiting, along with a couple
of sleepy-looking Nepalese constables dressed in khaki. We
had to hand over our trekking permits, and there was a
lengthy pause while they were passed around, commented

on, and noted in various books. Next, we were taken to visit the district governor of Khumbu, a distinguished-looking former Nepalese army officer named Colonel Bista. The colonel greeted us in his pajamas and bathrobe and invited us to have morning tea with him while we explained where we had come from and where we planned to go. "If there is something I can do for you, let me know," he added—an offer that we were soon grateful for. In the meanwhile, Ila had set up our tents on a hillside a little above the town, and as it was clouding over and beginning to snow, we retired inside them.

During the afternoon, an almost endless series of Tibetans stopped by to sell us scrolls, rings, beads, bracelets, silver cups, and prayer wheels. We had just seen off the last vendor and had broken out what was left of the now remaining bottle of cognac, when a figure appeared outside our tent in the now driving snow. I peered out and saw a rather elegant-looking young man wearing white pajamalike pants, a somewhat oversize army overcoat, and brightly colored wool gloves. Before I had a chance to say anything, he invited himself into the tent and introduced himself as Sub-Inspector Rana, of the Nepalese police. The name rang a bell. A few days before, we had met on the trail a young Swiss who had come to Namche without a trekking permit and had spent the better part of two weeks trying to arrange for one by telegraph. During this period, he passed a good deal of time discussing life and literature with Sub-Inspector Rana, whom he had come to regard as something of a cultural oasis and bon vivant. "Rana has a garden in which he grows six kinds of vegetables," the Swiss had told us.

We offered Rana a seat on one of the sleeping bags and a beaker of cognac.

"*Merzi, madame,*" he said to Michele, whose nationality he had apparently learned from studying our entry in the official book. "Do you pronounce it '*merzi*'?" he asked, and Michele spent five minutes repeating *merci* over and over, until Rana's pronunciation was about right.

"You are an American," he said to me, and added, "I admire your John Steinbeck and your Agatha Christie," helping himself to another bit of brandy. In this general vein, the conversation flowed along until dinnertime, when we invited Rana to share our meal—which consisted mainly of rice, peas, and onions. "I admire your onions, madame," he informed Michele, who was staring gloomily at the now empty cognac bottle. We had told Rana that we planned to go to see Dr. McKinnon the next day, and he offered to join us, provided that the police station was in "perfect order" in the morning.

The next morning there was no Rana, so, assuming that the police station had not been in the best order, we left for Khumjung and the McKinnons. Khumjung is a typical high Sherpa village. It is at 12,300 feet and consists of a large number of sturdy-looking stone houses set among yak pens and potato fields. The walk from Namche to Khumjung is surely one of the most beautiful in the world. On it one sees another group of the satellites of Everest, especially Ama Dablam. While Everest impresses one with its size, Ama Dablam, which is only 22,350 feet, impresses one with its elegance. It is a perfectly shaped mountain—a sort of ice Matterhorn—with steep faces of delicately fluted ice. (It was first climbed in 1961 by a mixed New Zealand–American group. The sole American in the party, Barry Bishop, who later climbed Everest, was in Nepal when we were there, and he said that Ama Dablam was technically more difficult than Everest by several orders of magnitude, although much lower.)

Leaving the fields and the yak pens, we followed a series of neat paths up to a modern building—the Khumjung hospital. The McKinnons, then both in their twenties, turned out to be an extremely cordial and attractive couple. He said that he had first come to Nepal with Hillary in 1964 when he was still a student, to climb and to help build the bridges. He fell in love with the country, and two years later, when Hillary succeeded in building a hospital with funds raised through his speaking tours in New Zealand and with private contributions, McKinnon volunteered to be its first doctor, a post he held until 1968 when he returned to New Zealand. It would be difficult to imagine a better choice. He and his wife Diane, who taught English in one of the Hillary schools (since 1961, Hillary, with the aid of the local villagers, had built six schools in the Solu-Khumbu area), succeeded in immersing themselves in the life of the community. (Some time later, Mrs. McKinnon took us to visit one of the Sherpa schools. It was a two-room affair in a modern Quonset-hut-like structure. The "headmaster" was a multilingual Sherpa from Darjeeling. Although it was November, the school was about to close for a long winter recess, since many of the pupils were to leave for the lowlands with their parents, who had homes in the lower valleys where the winters are less severe. The major school term is in the spring and summer. The children, perhaps a hundred of them of various ages, were engaged in their English lessons and were reciting in loud choruses. I noticed several English mottoes on the walls, including GOD BLESS OUR KING and FORTUNE HAS WINGS, and wondered if any of the children realized how much "wings" in the form of the airplane had to do with their futures. The increasingly active link that the Sherpas have with the rest of Nepal is coming to depend more and more on the fact that Solu-Khumbu can now be reached fairly conveniently by air. I wondered at the time if Namche Bazar or Khumjung would one day be transformed into the Chamonix or Zermatt of Asia, with a profusion of hotels all guaranteeing fine views of Everest. It was both a heartening and a somewhat dreary prospect.)

Being a doctor in Solu-Khumbu was not a passive matter, since the Sherpas had had relatively little experience with modern medicine and until recently were inclined to put their faith in spirit mediums and magic potions. McKinnon had to prove that modern medicine is more effective than looking into the silver mirror of a spirit medium, and to do so he had to put in many miles of walking over very steep terrain to visit his patients, since Sherpas who feel that they are really sick prefer to stay in their own houses and die. Treatment is free. The most persistent problems were tuberculosis and goiter. Goiter, which was brought on by a lack of iodine in the diet, was common throughout the Himalayas, because such iodine as there is in the soil is removed by erosion and not replaced by the rains, which are iodine-free, the mountains being so far from the sea. There was a move to make the import of iodized salt obligatory (Nepal has no salt of its own), but at that time whole villages in Solu-Khumbu were afflicted with the disease and, what was worse, there was a high incidence of cretinism among the children. Until the diet could be changed, McKinnon attempted to treat his people with iodine tablets and iodized oil. There was a problem of knowing just how big a dose to administer, and he had conducted a series of experiments to find out. I nearly gave him a fit when I innocently announced that we had been dispensing iodine on our walk. What I meant was that we had been treating cuts with liquid iodine, but he assumed that we had been handing out tablets.

Tuberculosis is a much more serious matter. It is hard to detect in the early stages, unless a Sherpa is willing to come to Khumjung for an X ray or, at least, a skin test. Moreover, the treatment, while very effective, is lengthy. No Sherpa can afford to spend a year or so in a hospital. McKinnon worked out a program that allowed Sherpas with tuberculosis to live in a wing of the hospital for three months—with their families, if necessary—and then return to their villages. In each village he trained two people to act as nurses. They were able to give the necessary shots twice a week, and they knew enough about the symptoms to recognize if someone appeared to need help. In Namche I met one of McKinnon's "nurses," who turned out to be a very intelligent fifteen-year-old boy. He was, among other things, responsible for treating Ila's wife. In addition, McKinnon gave all the children in the area skin tests and smallpox vaccinations. Even as late as 1963, when the American Everest expedition came through Solu-Khumbu, whole villages were being ravaged by smallpox epidemics. It was about that time that Hillary started his vaccination program, which saved many lives and which was carried on by McKinnon.

During the monsoon, the McKinnons hardly ever saw any Europeans, and such rare mail as they got was carried to the hospital by porters. In the winter, many of the Sherpas head south. They are quite nomadic, and it is common for a family to have as many as three houses—one in the high mountain country, one in a village like Khumjung, and a third down below, where it is relatively warm in the winter. McKinnon said that he did not miss either his mail or his visitors, since he and his wife shared the social life of the Sherpas—the weddings, the naming ceremonies (a baby is named by its grandparents in a lively ceremony in which a good deal of *chang,* the local beer made of corn or rice, is drunk), and the funerals. (Sherpas cremate their dead, as do the Hindus of southern Nepal. The Hindus preserve part of a bone from the cremation and bury it in one of the sacred rivers beside which cremations take place.) He was also engaged in a potato experiment. The potato is the cornerstone of the Sherpa diet, although, oddly enough, it seems to be a relatively new arrival in Solu-Khumbu. Christoph von Furer-Haimendorf, a noted anthropologist who has made an extensive study of the Sherpas, noted, in his book *The Sherpas of Nepal,* that "it is certain that the potato was not known in the Himalayas until comparatively recently and the two most likely sources of its spread into Eastern Nepal are the gardens of European settlers in Darjeeling and the garden of the British residency in Kathmandu." This would make the potato about a hundred years old in Solu-Khumbu, and Furer-Haimendorf connects this dating to the time when the monasteries were built in Solu-Khumbu. There have been monasteries in Tibet for centuries, but the monasteries in Solu-Khumbu are quite new. The thought is that they were built and monks were allowed to withdraw from the population after the introduction of the potato gave the Sherpas enough food so that not everyone was required to scratch crops from the rather meager soil. The Sherpa "method" of growing potatoes was to throw the plants into the ground and to hope for the best. McKinnon took a plot of land belonging to the hospital and cultivated half of it Sherpa style and half of it using careful agricultural methods. What he found, perhaps not surprisingly, was that on the careful half he grew twice as many potatoes as on the Sherpa half and that the potatoes were larger and freer of blight. He hoped the lesson was beginning to sink in.

Among the letters that McKinnon had received in the last delivery from Lukla before our arrival was one from Mountain Travel saying that space was available for a flight to Kathmandu on the second of November—in about two and a half weeks—for three people. However, we learned to our dismay that McKinnon had no radio—one had been ordered but had not arrived—so we had no way of communicating with Kathmandu. McKinnon said that our only chance was to persuade the authorities in Namche to send a wire to Mountain Travel on the police wireless, and to pray that it got there. Leaving Khumjung, we walked back to Namche to look for Sub-Inspector Rana in the hope that we could convince him to send the wire. We stopped by the police station, which was manned by a lone constable who, from time to time, jumped from his desk to chase an errant goat out of Rana's vegetable garden.

In due time, Rana was found. *"Bon soir, madame,"* he said to Michele, bowing, kissing her hand, and apologizing for not appearing in the morning. We explained our plight, and after thinking the matter over he said, "I would, of course, like to help you. But it would be very courteous if first you were to talk to Colonel Bista. If he signs the telegram, then I would be honored to send it by our very wireless."

Colonel Bista was engaged in the nightly volleyball game that took place between the police and the soldiers in Namche, and we had to wait a half hour or so before we could see him. I had, in the meanwhile, written out a telegram, which the colonel, when he was free, read very carefully, offering a few suggestions for its amplification, and then signed, remarking that it was the Dassain holiday in Kathmandu and he was not sure how soon it would be delivered. In any case, we had done what we could, and the next day we were off to the base of Everest with the understanding that if an answer ever came through it would be sent up by runner.

The following morning, our Tibetan porters showed up early. They were dressed in heavy clothes, and instead of the Chinese-made basketball shoes that they had been wearing since leaving Kathmandu, they now wore wonderfully color-ful heavy cloth boots with thick soles. Ila appeared with some expedition gear, including a down-filled sleeping bag, that he had used with the Indian expedition at an altitude of twenty-six thousand feet on Everest. "Next days, some cold," he announced. The evenings had already been "some cold," and we were putting on more and more clothes to keep from freezing. However, the day of our departure was bright and warm, and we set out for the Thyangboche monastery, the home of the reincarnated lama who is the religious leader of the Sherpas of Solu-Khumbu. It was a beautiful walk, with Everest and all of her satellites in full view, and in a few hours we struggled up a steep hill, 12,600 feet high, where the monastery was, and into a nearby cabin built by an Indian expedition for Everest trekkers. It was drafty, but Hillary—leave it to Hillary—built a splendid wood-burning stove in the living room which kept everything warm as long as one continued to feed it and kept the doors shut. The walls were covered with signatures of members of former Everest expe-ditions and trekkers who have spent the night there. For us, it was the first time in more than two weeks that we had slept in a building, and we were happy over the change. Ila had promised us a visit to the head lama before we headed off into the mountains, and for that purpose he had bought three white ceremonial scarves, which we were meant to present to the lama; in return, he would give each of us one of his own scarves.

The head lama of Thyangboche was chosen for his role while still a small child. He comes from a Sherpa family in

Namche, and when he was very young he began to talk about his "home" in Thyangboche, where he had never been. The monks at Thyangboche, hearing of this, got some of the clothes of their head lama, who had just died, and mixed them with objects not belonging to the lama. The child, who was then four, picked out the clothes of the old monk and said that they belonged to him. He was immediately heralded as the reincarnation of the old lama and brought to Thyangboche to study. When he was sixteen, he was sent to Tibet for more study, and in 1956 he came back to Thyangboche as its abbot. He was then in his early thirties. I was immensely impressed by him. He spoke no English, but his brother did, and he acted as our interpreter when Ila's English failed. The abbot's apartment was simple, but he had many modern devices—a radio, a camera, a watch—that had been given to him over the years by people on expeditions. Apart from study, religious ceremonies, and running the affairs of the monastery—the monks depend partly on donations and partly on a certain amount of commerce that they carry on in the community and in Tibet—the abbot's main interest was in flowers. He had a small hothouse, which he and his brother built to protect his flowers during the winter. Friends send him seeds from all over the world, and he has a book filled with all the seed envelopes, along with the names of the donors. The abbot accepted our scarves and took three of his own and touched them to his forehead as a blessing. While this was happening, Ila stood beaming. It was obviously a ceremony that meant a great deal to him, and he later told me that he would not go into the high mountains without the blessing of the abbot.

One of the things that I discussed with the abbot was the yeti—the legendary abominable snowman. It is safe to say that no reliable Western observer has ever seen one, although some curious bearlike tracks have been photographed on the remote glaciers near Everest. On the other hand, the yeti does play a persistent role in the mythology of the region. Sometimes it is given semihuman characteristics, sometimes it is said to carry people off, but most often it is said to look like a bear, or perhaps some sort of simian. The abbot has never seen one, either, but he said that when the snows are very heavy around the monastery some of the other abbots claim to have seen such a creature. (Among the Sherpas it is usually a distant cousin or an uncle, now passed on, who saw one once.) He told us that in one of the monasteries down the valley there were a scalp and a hand (a bone from a hand) that were claimed by the local authorities there to be from a yeti. At this point the abbot smiled and pointed to a chair which was obviously covered by a goatskin and said, through his brother, "It is the same kind of yeti as this." Later we visited the monastery itself, and for a small donation the ancient abbot there produced the objects in question. Ang Dorje, who, I gathered, did not have a very high opinion of the yeti question in general, donned what is presumably a goat scalp, and we took his picture with great solemnity. Most of the other Sherpas seemed to take the whole thing as a joke, so we did not learn anything more about the yeti than we knew before we went to Nepal.

We left Thyangboche and headed north. The villages became cruder and cruder, and the terrain more barren. The tree line in the Himalayas is very high, and we were now at nearly fourteen thousand feet—the altitude of a good-size Swiss Alp—and it was still grazing land for yaks. Wood was scarce, so we used dried yak dung for fuel. It makes an excellent smokeless, odorless fire. On the trail we passed yak caravans being driven down for the winter. The yak is a great, shaggy beast, but incredibly timid; it will all but climb a vertical bank to get out of one's way on the trail. (I did once encounter an aggressive yak. Not far from Thyangboche, I was walking along peacefully when I heard several people ahead croaking *"Ee-yuk, Eee-yuk"*—a series of sounds that the Sherpas make if there are yaks around. Above the general din I heard Michele yelling, *"Attention,* Jeremy—*un yak fou!"* I looked up and found myself staring into the eyes of a rather malicious-looking brown yak that was attached by a string to a Sherpa who was trying to restrain it. It lowered its horns, and I went up a rock embankment in very great haste, and stayed there until the animal was led away.) The Sherpas have great affection for yaks. (One night, we heard some piercing cries not far from our camp, and I at once thought of a leopard, since I had read in a book on the British Everest expedition that its camp had been visited by one after dark. Moreover, Jaccoux claimed that he could make out a pair of glittering eyes off in the scrub. But when I asked a Sherpa what kind of animal it was, he replied, "Doesn't eat yaks," which seemed to settle the matter. It was probably a small wildcat of some kind.) Being Buddhist, the Sherpas will not, in general, kill any animal, but if a yak should happen to drop dead, or if someone else should kill it, they are delighted to eat the meat. Sherpas are profoundly religious, but not dogmatic. As Buddhists, their greatest concern is to add to their *sonam*. There are many ways that one can increase one's *sonam*. For example, a rich man can increase it by having a temple built for the community. There are some very wealthy Sherpas in Solu-Khumbu. Namche Bazar was the great trading station on the way to Tibet, and before 1950 enormous yak trains passed through the town en route to the Nanpga La, a nineteen-thousand-foot pass leading to Tibet. From Tibet, Sherpas got salt, copperware (all the cooking utensils in Solu-Khumbu were of copper—and very beautiful, too—although now they have been supplanted by tin and aluminum objects, usually of Chinese manufacture), and animals, for which they traded rice, carried up from the lowlands, and dyes, among other things. Even now there is some trading into Tibet, and it is a very profitable business. We were told of one trader who came back from Tibet with a profit of eighty thousand Nepalese rupees—now about $3,200—from the sale of one yak train's worth of goods. He was building a small temple in Namche, and while we were there we watched the famous Sherpa artist Kapa Kalden in the process of decorating the interior and the huge prayer wheel. One can also lose *sonam*. In his book on the Sherpas, Furer-Haimendorf gives a list of some of the sins that can lead to loss of *sonam*. It is an extraordinary list, and it gives an idea of why people who have come to know the Sherpas are so fond of them. Among the items are the following:

1. To threaten children or make them cry is sin, whatever the reason.
2. To fell trees is sin, though on occasion it is inevitable; even to pluck flowers is sin, and it is sinful to set fire to the forest.
3. To marry a girl who is unwilling is sin both for the husband and for her parents, who arranged for the marriage.
4. To talk ill of someone behind his back is sin, particularly if what one tells about him is not true.

We camped in some deserted yak pens in Pheriche, a summer village, now abandoned, since the yaks had gone below for the winter. The nights were now desperately cold. As long as the sun was up, it was quite comfortable, but as soon as the shadows began to creep over the ground the temperature plummeted to near zero, and we made a dash for the tents, to put on every ounce of warm clothes we had brought along. It was much too cold to bathe, and Jaccoux said that it would be inadvisable even to wash, since the dry air was so dehydrating that we risked being severely burned and chapped by the sun. By now, we were all beginning to feel the effects of the altitude—headaches and dizziness. The streams that led down from the Khumbu Glacier—the glacier that comes down from the sides of Everest—were frozen, and we crossed them gingerly. Our next, and highest, camp was at sixteen thousand feet—higher than the summit of Mont Blanc—and the three of us were beginning to feel truly worn down by the altitude and the cold. We were merely a mile or two from the Tibetan border. This is the only place in Nepal where the government allowed one to get that close to the border, since the way is blocked by the Everest range and it would take a full-scale alpine expedition to cross it; trekkers have all they can do to haul themselves up to the high yak pastures. However, we could see some of the peaks in Tibet, and also the Lho La and the Shangri La. *La* is the Tibetan word for "pass," and Shangri La is an impressive but bleak-looking pass that leads into Tibet.

We now began to find out for ourselves why the Sherpas and the Tibetans do so well on the high climbing expeditions. While we were literally trembling with cold and fatigue, Ang Dorje was wandering around happily in a light shirt and wearing tennis shoes with no socks. I asked Ila if the altitude ever bothered him, and he said, "Twenty-six thousand feet, some headache getting." At sixteen thousand feet my head felt like a melon. The next day, we climbed the Kala Pattar. By any standard, it is a *montagne à vache*—a gentle, grassy slope with a few rocks on top. But the summit is at 18,200 feet— 2,300 feet higher than any mountain in Europe—and I found it very tough going. I seemed to be held back by a sort of invisible wall, and every time I moved I felt as if I were hauling a ton of bricks. From the summit we got an incredible view of Everest and the Khumbu Glacier. Everest was perhaps a mile away, but the summit was still two miles above us. I asked Jaccoux, who had been to 22,200 feet in Peru, how people could climb at such heights. (I was having all I could do to walk.) He said that of course they trained for weeks before the summit climb. In addition, there was a morale factor that comes from being part of a large, dedicated group; also when one actually comes to grips with the difficulties of the mountain, one tends to forget one's aches and pains. It was now beginning to snow, and we hurried down. In passing, we had a chance to look at the memorial tablet that the American expedition had erected to Jake Breitenbach, the climber who was killed on the Khumbu ice fall in 1963. (In 1970 his remains were discovered on the Khumbu Glacier.) When we got back to our tents, it was snowing heavily. I was so tired that when Jaccoux handed me a headache pill I just stood there holding it, not knowing what to do with it. I somehow got back in my tent and lay gasping on my sleeping bag. After a few minutes, the head of Ang Dorje appeared in the tent. "Soup ready," he announced, and in came a tray of warm tomato soup and crackers. He stood there while I ate it, to make sure that I was all right, and then left.

We had had some vague plans to do more climbing and hiking, but the snow was coming down in thick gusts, and we were really exhausted by the altitude. So the next morning we began the trip back. On the first day, we passed a huge lake, ice blue, that nestled against the mountains. "In summer, many yaks," Ang Dorje told us. When we got a little farther down, we were met by a runner from McKinnon bearing a letter from Mountain Travel that had just arrived. The office had received both our telegram and a personal message from the Australian forester, and we could take the plane on the second of November.

We had several days to fill before that date, some of which we passed in the monastery grounds in Thyangboche, some with the McKinnons, and some in Namche. In Namche, Sub-Inspector Rana told us that while we were gone a yak had got into his garden with the six kinds of vegetables and had eaten every last one of them. Ang Dorje and Ila and a small group of our Tibetan porters had to hurry back to Kathmandu to meet some new trekkers, whom they were taking to western Nepal, near Annapurna. To make sure that we didn't get into any trouble and were fed periodically, Mountain Travel had assigned two young Sherpas to look after us until the plane came. They were eighteen, and at first I was worried about how two young boys would fare as cooks and guides. There was no need for concern. Both of them had been on expeditions since they were fourteen, both had gone to the Hillary schools, and they spoke excellent English. They were dressed in Western-style blue jeans, and when we left Namche for Lukla one of them was carrying a transistor radio on which he listened to music from Radio Nepal and India.

For the next three days, we camped next to the tiny airfield. The boys turned out to be fine cooks, and we feasted on pancakes and chapattis—Sherpa unleavened bread. Each morning at about sunrise, the Swiss plane came in to leave off people. It was not yet our turn to go, and the pilot informed us rather tersely that we would have to wait until it was. One morning the passengers turned out to be the German ambassador to Nepal and the United Nations High Commissioner for Refugees; they had come up to look at some Tibetan refugee villages. Another morning, a U.S. AID helicopter came floating in with a passenger who said that he had been sent by the Smithsonian Institution to collect Tibetan manuscripts. At eight forty every morning we got the English-language news broadcast from Kathmandu. Otherwise we sat around, somewhat bored, waiting for our plane. Finally, on November 2, as scheduled, it came in over the mountains. We had been joined by two trekkers also waiting to be flown out, and the five of us piled into the plane with our gear. There was the inevitable Nepalese observer from the Foreign Office wedged into one of the back seats among the rucksacks. The plane took off, and for the next hour we saw unfolding beneath us the whole route that we had taken over the previous month. There were the tiny trails that we had climbed up and down, over steep ridges and through the terraced fields and jungles. Here and there we could spot a familiar village clinging to a mountainside, and to the north we could see the great white mountains, with the clouds hovering near their summits. As I looked at them, I thought of a Nepalese legend that tells how they came to Nepal. In the beginning, the mountains, which were the oldest children of the god Prajapati, all had wings, and they flew about the world as they liked. However, Indra, the god of rain, wished to bring the waters to the people of Nepal. So he cut the wings from the mountains, which then fell to earth and could no longer fly. The wings became clouds, and still cling to the mountains. So wherever there are mountains there are clouds, and water from their rain nourishes the earth beneath.

4

Afterthoughts

Forsco Maraini, the noted Italian travel writer, in his book about Asian travel, *Where Four Worlds Meet*, introduces the notion of voyages of the first and second "type." In a voyage of the first type the traveler never really crosses a cultural frontier no matter how far he may actually have traveled. He may encounter new languages or religions or the people may appear very different, but in a subtle way these differences only emphasize the common elements that the voyager shares with the peoples he is visiting. As Maraini puts it, there is "some fundamental essence common to both your country and theirs. You are still within the orbit of those peoples who developed and matured together, to a greater or lesser degree, through thousands of years of history. . . . They will all tell their pupils *something* about Christ and Aristotle, Moses and Homer, Shakespeare, Dante, and Goethe, Descartes, Galileo, Beethoven, Cervantes and the rest, right down to Tolstoy and

Van Gogh. But bring up such names as Jalal-ud-din Rumi or Valkami, Nagarjuna or Milarepa, Lao-tzu or Chu Hsi, Genghis Khan or Hideyoshi, and you realize that you are treading on ground which (at least as things are at present) is basically alien, exotic, to be cultivated only by specialists: something concerning other 'fields of intelligibility' than one's own. You have crossed the ideological barrier"—and thus have made a voyage of the second type.

Even in a country as "exotic," from our point of view as Nepal, it is possible for a traveler to so limit his contacts that the "cultural frontier" is perceived dimly if at all—from, for example, the window of a rapidly moving automobile. As the country "develops"—moves more and more toward acquiring the technological standards of the West—it becomes easier for a visitor to ignore ideological barriers completely. This is, in a way, a pity, since one of the most fascinating things about Nepal is just this cultural frontier. In Nepal one may discover how a people—or, really, many separate peoples—evolving in all but total isolation from the West came to deal with the great realities that affect human beings: death, love, birth, law and the meaning of life itself. As we in the West face these realities, we bring with us a vast tradition of what we like to think of as rational inquiry. We have come to believe that there are "scientific" explanations of most things, and for most of us this is a source of comfort, since what we can explain in terms of scientific principles we can also, to some extent, manipulate. It is reassuring to know that microbes cause disease, for microbes can be destroyed. It is reassuring to know that lightning is an electrical discharge, for physics then teaches us how to act so as to minimize the risk of being felled by a lightning bolt. In truth, of course, most of us understand as much about the underlying scientific explanations of these natural phenomena as we do about the magical incantations of the spirit mediums of Nepal. But we are usually willing to accept this partial understanding, since the incantations of our scientists, even our computers, lead to effective and practical solutions to many of our problems.

For a Westerner to get a feeling for the cultural life of Nepal, and especially of rural Nepal, he must try to imagine living in an extremely vivid natural environment, frequently hostile, surrounded by mountains, jungles, wild animals, often plagues, without doctors to cure the sick, without electric lights to illuminate the night, and above all, without our scientific tradition that informs us that what we see around us can be explained by natural laws and principles.* In such an environment every object of nature becomes charged with mystical powers. The Himalayan snows floating above the Nepalese countryside in serene, remote grandeur become the abodes of gods. The smooth stones of the rivers become charged with magical powers, and even the animals become representatives of unseen but powerful forces.

In 1954 Giuseppe Tucci, an Italian scholar and Orientalist, who had made eight journeys into Tibet and six in Nepal, took an extensive trip by foot in central Nepal. He was in search of the origins of the Malla kings, the dynasty that ruled the country, or at least parts of the country, from the thirteenth to the eighteenth century. (He found traces of the Mallas in some of the remote central hill towns and concluded that there was evidence that linked them to prior Indian nobility.) On his way back south toward the Indian frontier, Tucci came upon one of his Nepalese guides in a striking attitude of prayer alongside the trail. Tucci writes:

* The closest thing to a scientific tradition in Nepal was, until recently, the practice of astrology. There is no doubt that astrology plays a very important role in the life of the Nepalese. For example, the date of the wedding of King Birendra, to a Rana—February 27, 1970—was decided in collaboration with the court astrologers. Not long ago I was told of an incident involving a Nepalese village child that shows just how deep the faith in astrology runs in the countryside. When the child was born it had a bad horoscope, and, unhappily, six months later, the child's father died. The mother, because of its horoscope, blamed the death on the child and left it to starve. It was found in this condition by a U.S. AID worker and eventually was adopted, with a special dispensation from the king, by a U.S. AID official. The child, a young boy whom I met in Kathmandu, appears to be thriving, although his new father says that, according to the horoscope, his eighth year should be a difficult one. In his twenties, however, he is expected, if all goes well, to take a long and profitable voyage of some three years to a distant place.

I saw the man who led the march and who was acting as our guide standing with his hands raised in prayer. At his feet was a cobra with distended hood watching him threateningly. But he did not move and would have preferred to be bitten rather than kill it. The snake is a naga, a mysterious creature linked with the obscure forces of the underworld, which guards the treasures hidden in the womb of the earth and the springs which give it life, it is the symbol of Shiva, the sign of time that always renews itself. Between killing and being killed many would still choose the second alternative.

As should be clear from the earlier parts of this book, an increasingly large number of Nepalese would find this kind of primitive religious expression as strange as we do. In an interview given to New York Times reporter Joseph Lelyveld some years ago, King Mahendra was asked if he himself believed that he was the reincarnation of the god Vishnu, a traditional Nepalese belief. Mahendra replied, "Personally speaking, I don't believe in all those things. First of all I am a human being. And whatever I am, I must serve my country." However, the traces of the ancient religious attitudes are in Nepal, and the farther one travels into the remote country-side, the more they merge with present practice and belief.

The ambiguities in the religious attitudes of the Nepalese are nowhere more evident than in their art. There does not seem to be a tradition of secular art in Nepal, unless one wishes to count the Newar building decorations or the few rather stilted portraits of the early kings. Art in Nepal is an essentially religious activity. It has been remarked that Himalayan art differs from Indian or Chinese or even traditional Tibetan art, with which it has pronounced similarities, by a kind of savage dynamism. The Nepalese Buddhas are not always serene, and their expressions frequently appear to exhibit cruelly ironic smiles. Gods and their consorts merge with each other in a frenzy of sexual energy. (One of the more striking aspects of the temples of Kathmandu are the erotic carvings that often decorate friezes around the pillars supporting the pagoda roofs. These carvings, oddly stylized as if illustrating a text, have an almost comic-strip effect. One theory is that they were put there to offend the goddess of lightning, a prudish female, and so to encourage her to avoid the temple. Another theory is that they are a kind of manual for the performance of Tantric rites, communal sexual acts— still practiced, it is said, in parts of Nepal. One Nepalese commentator that I read speculated that the carvings had no special religious significance but were simply an expression of the joy and vigor of life. One of the chief characteristics of the carvings, though, is their very lack of joyousness and their strong sense of ritual.) Even the carvings and metal castings of animals, often half-human, have a savagery about them. It is as if the cruelties of the nature around the artists who created these works were being explained in terms of the cruelties of the unseen gods and goddesses.

It is not entirely clear what these religious symbols mean to contemporary Nepalese themselves. No week goes by in Nepal without some sort of religious festival. (One of the most remarkable is the Indra Jatra, an eight-day festival cele-brated to propitiate the rain god Indra. On the third day a "living goddess"—a young girl chosen in infancy by the priests of the Kumari Temple in Kathmandu, who then passes her life, until puberty, sequestered in a special apartment in the temple—is paraded through the streets of the city. Her only public appearances until the Indra Jatra are at a balcony window in the temple, where, dressed and made up almost like a costume doll, she will occasionally cast an aloof and languid eye on visitors assembled in the courtyard below. But during the Indra Jatra she is carried through the streets of Kathmandu in a chariot for all to see. After puberty she is free to marry—but it is thought that marrying her brings bad luck, even death, to the groom, so she is likely to spend her life a spinster.) Among the most beautiful Nepalese holidays is the Tihar, the festival of light, which occurs in the autumn, when the nights in Kathmandu are clear and quite warm. All of the houses are decorated with lights, usually oil lamps, and the entire city glows in a lovely flickering illumination.

The first night of the five-day festival is dedicated to the crows, which are offered food to placate them, since the crow is regarded in Nepalese mythology as the messenger of death. These festivals are a fundamental part of Nepalese life, and the obviously profound feelings that are associated with them are clear to anyone who has witnessed them. On the other hand, the temples—which at night are places of worship, and where Nepalese go who have come to Kathmandu from the countryside for a festival or to sell their agricultural produce and have no other place to stay, sleep, and eat—during the day become market bazaars. The bases of statues are covered with baskets full of fruits and merchandise—sandals, razor blades, shoelaces, kitchen utensils, herbs, and tea. Just below a statue of Ganesh, the elephant god, one may well find a Nepalese barber plying his trade. In the temples and religious sanctuaries in the countryside, often all but abandoned, one comes upon totems, carvings of figures half demon and half animal, whose religious significance now seems lost even to the Nepalese. These works of art, often remarkably beautiful and usually in a state of physical decay, lie in some sort of limbo between religious icons and secular museum pieces. Village life, with its endless swirl of animals, lively children, and farming activities, appears to flow around them as if they were not there.

In the last analysis, all of the endlessly complex and varied religious traditions of Nepalese life demonstrate the infinite and often beautiful ways that human beings have evolved to adapt to the realities of the world. As I have tried to indicate, these realities are in transition in Nepal as the Nepalese, and especially the rural Nepalese, increasingly come into contact with modern science and technology. Many of these changes, perhaps most of them, are for the better. Yet a traveler to Nepal, charmed by the people and the country, sometimes finds himself wishing that change could come about without destroying too much of what is so lovely in Nepalese life, and without importing too much of what appears to be destroying the beauty of Western environments like our own. Perhaps fulfilling this wish is impossible and, in making it, one is committing what has been called by Jacques Barzun "the fallacy of utopian addition"—the acceptance of technological progress without paying the price that goes with it. In any event, there are so many pressing, urgent problems in Nepal—problems that can be dealt with in terms of modern technology and that must be dealt with now if the country is to prosper—that it will be a long time before Nepal shares with us the problems of a civilization overburdened by its technology.

5

A Return to the Kingdom: Himalayan Journal, 1983

Friday, October 21: Roissy, France

It is six A.M. I have been at the Charles de Gaulle airport for about a half an hour. There is no one else in sight. Nothing is open. But now a trim-looking girl wearing jeans has gotten out of a taxi. She has a rucksack and is dragging a large duffel bag. I don't recognize her, but, given the ice ax, the duffel bag, and the rucksack, she must be one of us. She comes over to me and, as I suspected, she is part of the group of thirty-five of us who are about to go trekking in the Everest region of Nepal with Claude Jaccoux Voyages—an entity created by Jaccoux a decade or so ago. Our experience in Nepal in 1967 gave Jaccoux the taste for exotic travel. Over the years he and I have done a good deal of it together; overland to Pakistan from France; Kilimanjaro; and in 1979, a winter trip to Nepal where we did some river rafting but no trekking. This will be my fourth trip to Nepal and Jaccoux's nineteenth. He has been back to Solu Khumbu many times since 1967 and has told me about some of the changes there. I haven't been back and I am anxious to see for myself.

Jaccoux and I have been corresponding about this trip for several months. In one of his letters, written last July, he had informed me that we will divide into two groups "one strong and the other weaker." He has added, with not atypical irony, *"J'imagine que tu te battras pour être dans les forts!"* Be *that* as it may, he has also sent along a day-by-day detailed program of the proposed trek. The first thing that struck my wary eye upon reading it was the fact that we would be camped out for sixteen days at altitudes greater than eleven thousand feet. I have also noticed that the "weak" will cross something called Cho La at an altitude of about eighteen thousand feet, for which exercise crampons and an ice ax are advised. God knows what the "strong" will be doing. In preparation for all of this I have spent the summer tromping up and down a myriad of assorted Rockies near Aspen. But I have now been out of the high mountains for nearly two months and I have been assured by assorted experts that whatever conditioning I achieved during the summer is now worth nothing. *Tant pis.*

The blue-jeaned girl, it turns out, is a medical secretary from Strasbourg. This is, she says, her first *grand voyage.* She seems very nervous, so nervous that she can't eat the croissants we have ordered for breakfast at the airport cafeteria, which is now open. It seems from what she tells me that there are two essentially independent groups of us. One will be led by Jaccoux and the other by another mountain guide from Marseilles named Guy Abert, whom I have never met. The girl has climbed in Chamonix with Abert and will be part of his group. By this time the Lufthansa counter, to which we have returned, seems alive with people carrying ice axes, rucksacks, and duffel bags. In addition to our two groups totaling nearly thirty-five people, there is another contingent of about the same number from an organization called Nouvelles Frontières. They all look about sixteen and are, they say, headed for the Everest region. Seventy of us all going to Everest. When we were there in 1967 the Ministry of Tourism listed in its statistics three official trekkers—people who put "trekking" down on their visas as the reason for visiting the country—for that *entire* year. They must have been us. In thirty-seven days of trekking we saw about a half dozen Europeans or Americans and most of them were either in the Peace Corps or something like it. That year there were, exclusive of Indians, only a little over eighteen thousand visitors to the country in any capacity. In 1979 there were over twenty thousand official trekkers—people who had applied for trekking permits—and over two hundred thousand visitors. It's all become a big business.

I recognize Jaccoux. We had dinner last night but apart from that I had not seen him in two years. He turned fifty last May. I am fifty-three. He and Michele, who are divorced, have a daughter, Claire, who was married to a young filmmaker. They, in turn, had a daughter a year ago, making Jaccoux a grandfather. He is the most physically fit grandfather I know. He looks about the same as he did ten or fifteen years ago. His blondish brown hair seems unchanged and as copious as ever. From time to time he has written to me about some mountaineering accident or other that he has had but of those there is no apparent trace. He has been guiding all summer and has just come back from trekking in Ladakh in northern India. To boot he has given up smoking. He is obviously ready to go. I, on the other hand, have made a private decision to attempt to do the strict minimum on this trek. If I can get through *that* I will be well satisfied.

We will fly to Frankfurt, change planes, fly to New Delhi, change planes, and fly to Kathmandu. The duffel bags and rucksacks are loaded and we are on our way.

Saturday, October 22: Kathmandu

Before we left Paris I asked Jaccoux how long it would take to get from Paris to Kathmandu. He said about twenty-four hours. I thought he was crazy. How could it possibly take twenty-four hours of flying to get anywhere? He was wrong. It took twenty-seven hours. From Frankfurt to Karachi it was seven hours in the air, followed by about two hours on the ground while mechanics tried to figure out how to stuff an emergency slide that had somehow inflated and flown out one of the doors back into the plane. Since there was no way, they finally cut it off. It then took two hours to fly from Karachi to New Delhi, where we arrived at three A.M. local time. Jaccoux dealt with the flight in his usual way. He took some kind of sleeping pill, one probably strong enough to use during major surgery. He then covered his eyes with a blue eyeshade and was out of business until we reached New Delhi. I amused myself by variously reading, contemplating the map, and talking with my neighbors. My immediate neighbor was a very attractive Japanese girl, living in New York and married to an American she met in Japan. "He is a WASP," she explained in a charming Japanese accent. "In Japan we do not know WASP," she continued. "We only know Japanese and foreigners. I learn WASP in United States." She got off in New Delhi.

Now we are to take a Royal Nepal Airlines flight to Kathmandu, which leaves about seven thirty—four hours after our arrival in New Delhi. However, Jaccoux has made the ominous discovery that Royal Nepal Airlines has never heard of us. This is the height of the trekking season in Nepal and the flights are booked and even overbooked months in advance. I run into a pair of Americans who say they have been in the New Delhi airport for two days trying to get on a flight to Kathmandu. It does not look good. The Royal Nepal Airlines flight has gone its way and I have resigned myself to what seems inevitable when a mysterious Indian stranger appears and informs Jaccoux that we are set to go on the Air India flight that leaves at nine thirty. How *that* was arranged, God knows. When we leave, the sun is shining. It is a bright clear day which means that we will get a marvelous view of the western part of the Himalayan chain—Annapurna, Dhaulagiri, and the rest. Old hands on this flight know that one wants to be on the left side going up to Kathmandu. The mountains are on the left. I am on the right side, but, by bobbing and weaving, I can study those incredible peaks. They look like clouds floating above the earth.

The approach to Kathmandu always has for me a kind of magic carpet quality. The Kathmandu valley ranges between four and five thousand feet in altitude. Since Nepal is largely at the latitude of New Orleans, the country is hot and tropical in the lower altitudes—150 feet above sea level in the south. That is part of what gives the country its scenic fascination. The great mountains hover over the lush and often tropical lowlands. There is not much snow in the Himalayas—very little below seventeen thousand feet and none in Kathmandu. I have been in Kathmandu in mid-January and during the day it felt like Indian summer in New England. Skiing will never be developed in Nepal since all the resorts would be located at altitudes of something like the summit of Mont Blanc. On our arrival in late October, the valley is an incandescent green thanks to the summer monsoons.

We manage to clear customs rapidly and get on a bus that has come to the airport to take the thirty-five of us to our hotel. By the time we get to the hotel it is close to one P.M. Our plans now become somewhat ambiguous. This has to do with the way trekking and, indeed, tourism, has evolved in Nepal since 1967. In 1967 there were two treks possible in Nepal, and we did both of them. A limited area of western Nepal was open to foreigners, which enabled one to trek in the general region of Annapurna although not too close to the Tibetan border. Then there was the Everest trek, which followed the route used by the two Swiss expeditions in 1952. In 1967 one was expected to stick precisely to this route and this was enforced in a rigorous way by the Nepalese authorities. The reason for this was the very delicate relations the Nepalese had with the Chinese. Since 1967 there has been a general relaxation of relations with China—both ours and Nepal's. One corollary of this is that the Nepalese have opened up most of the frontier region around Everest to trekkers. It is now possible to crisscross various valleys by high mountain passes and to see at close range mountains like Cho Oyu, which at 26,750 feet is the eighth highest mountain in the world. (It was climbed by an Austrian group in 1954.) It is not far from Everest, but because other mountains blocked the view we never saw it in 1967. Furthermore, since 1978 the Nepalese government has opened up to trekkers the "trekkers peaks." These are peaks in the eighteen-thousand- to twenty-thousand-foot range, which range from very difficult to easy to climb and which are accessible to small trekking parties for a fee of slightly less than thirty dollars a person. Many Nepalese treks—including those of Jaccoux—offer, for those who are interested, the possibility of climbing one or more of these relatively modest Himalayan peaks.

In view of all of the new possibilities, very few trekkers want to spend the thirteen days it takes to walk to the Everest region. Most prefer to fly. This is a pity since one of the great satisfactions we got out of our 1967 trek was seeing so much of the Nepalese countryside. When one finally saw the mountains it was the culmination of days of hard work. One felt that one had earned the view. Moreover, by the time one arrived in Namche Bazar, one was well acclimatized to the altitude. This is why the climbing expeditions often still make the walk. In the Everest region altitude is everything. The nature of the experience one will have there depends on how one adapts to altitude. Regardless, most trekkers now fly from Kathmandu directly to the airfield at Lukla in the Sherpa country. Lukla is a day's hard walk from Namche Bazar. In 1967 we used this field—it was literally just that—to fly in the tiny light plane back to Kathmandu. Since most treks to Everest now begin at Lukla, air transport has become essential. This, in turn, has created all kinds of problems which Jaccoux, once checked in to the hotel, has gone off to deal with.

The first problem is to find us a plane. The basic plane that Royal Nepal Airlines uses to fly to Lukla is the Canadian-built Twin Otter of which the airline has two. This plane will hold about sixteen trekkers and climbers plus their gear. The flights begin operating about seven in the morning if there is no ground fog in Kathmandu. Often there is ground fog which does not burn off until perhaps nine or ten. The flights then operate until about noon when, very often, clouds begin closing in at Lukla. Visibility is absolutely essential to these mountain flights. One of the local pilots commented, "If in Nepal you encounter a cloud it usually has rocks in it." This means that there is a narrow time frame in which the Lukla flights—which take about forty minutes—can operate. On a good day, between the two Twin Otters, there might be four flights to Lukla, and on a *very* good day, six. This means that some eighty trekkers can be ferried to Lukla on a good day. Our group alone, which was one of dozens in Kathmandu all wanting to go to Everest, consisted of thirty-five people.

Jaccoux works with a large trekking and mountaineering organization in Kathmandu that supplies the Sherpas, tents, and food for the treks. This company, like all the large trekking companies in Kathmandu, has a man located in the Tribhuvan Airport in Kathmandu and another in Lukla during the trekking season whose full time jobs are to get the company's clients on flights to and from Lukla. Someone who simply shows up wanting to fly from one airport to the other will be in for a long wait—usually days. For this reason the first thing that Jaccoux does when getting to Kathmandu is to go to his agency to see when we can expect to leave. Before going he warns us that it may be as early as the next morning at seven, so we had better get our gear in order. I privately hope this will not happen since I am tired from the flight from Europe. Also I would welcome a few days to look around Kathmandu once again. But I spend the afternoon arranging everything so that I will be set to leave the next morning. I am relieved when Jaccoux shows up in the early evening to announce that there is no space for us on the next morning's flight so we have the day off. Finally I can get to bed.

Sunday, October 23: Kathmandu

Visiting Kathmandu has always reminded me of eating one of those very elaborate Christmas fruitcakes whose contents are full of surprises. To cushion the general culture shock I usually begin by going to the Durbar Marg, the avenue where the Annapurna Hotel and several of the airline and travel agency offices are located. In 1967 there were three good hotels in or near Kathmandu. The Annapurna, which was under Swiss management, and was owned by the royal family, was, and is, a conservative, orderly, carefully run European-style hotel. Then there was the Oberoi-Soaltee, also owned by the royal family, which was and is located outside of Kathmandu. It was one of the fanciest hotels in the Indian subcontinent, with its four restaurants, a casino, and a swimming pool. Finally there was the Royal. As far as I was concerned, this was the obvious place to stay in 1967 and I spent many happy weeks there. But the Royal Hotel is no more. In fact, by the time of my second visit to Kathmandu in 1969 it had closed and Boris was engaged in building a more grandiose hotel which was to be called the Yak and Yeti, the name of the noted bar in the Royal. The Yak and Yeti was built and is now one of the four five-star luxury hotels in Kathmandu, joining the Annapurna, the Soaltee, and the Everest Sheraton. Somehow Boris got himself dealt out of what had been his hotel. But by 1979 he had opened an elegant restaurant at the edge of town called simply Boris. We paid it a visit in 1979 and were greeted effusively by Boris, who plied Jaccoux and myself with innumerable free "yak tails"—tomato juice and vodka— and then treated us to a free lunch of snipe pâté and bekti, which is a fish from the Ganges. It was always very difficult for Boris to charge anyone he knew for anything, which was one of the reasons that various of his enterprises, including the restaurant, got themselves in financial difficulties.

For me the large visible changes in Kathmandu occurred between my visits in 1969 and 1979. That period marked the expansion of the tourism business, with the construction of new hotels, as I just mentioned. In 1969 no Westerner in his or her right mind would eat in any but the few hotel restaurants. At the present time there is an entire gamut of restaurants; a few featuring Western food, but most serving Indian, Chinese, Tibetan, or Nepalese cuisine. I, at least, would have no hesitation in eating in any of these places—being careful about eating salads and fruit. In 1967 there was one trekking outfit in Nepal, the one belonging to Colonel Roberts. A guide book to Nepal published in 1983 lists *thirty-four* such agencies in Kathmandu and is careful to note that these are only "some" of the agencies. In 1967 it was practically impossible to buy or rent mountaineering or trekking equipment in Nepal. Now there is a whole section of town—the Thamel—crammed with shops that rent and sell such equipment. Tourism is now the largest source of foreign exchange in the country and trekking is, by Nepalese standards, a very big business.

Given all of this it is tempting, and almost too easy, to forget what a genuinely poor country Nepal is. According to recent statistics, 4.5 million Nepalese, which represents about a quarter of the population, have a daily income of less than two rupees—about eight cents. Since Nepal is an agrarian country this number does not quite mean what it would mean in a more industrialized nation. But one can translate it into available per capita daily calories of food for this part of the population, which turns out to be about 1,750 calories while the minimal survival limit as I have noted is usually given as 2,256 calories. Despite this, one does not have the impression—as one does sometimes in India—of a starving, desperate population. On the contrary, there seems to be a genuine sense of goodwill among people on all levels of the economic scale. Each time I have come to Nepal I have—perhaps naïvely—come away with a sense that I was basically among a population of reasonably happy and often joyous people.

By changing blocks in Kathmandu one can still transport oneself back and forth over various centuries in a way that is almost unimaginable in a Western city. Apart from anything else, the community, which is largely Hindu, gives free rein to a plethora of sacred cows who wander unobstructed in the middle of the steadily growing vehicular traffic. At the same time there are now a number of English-language bookstores in Kathmandu, some of which have fairly advanced physics and mathematics textbooks in their windows indicating that Nepal is now producing a young generation of scientists and engineers. In one of the bookstores I asked if they still had my old book on Nepal—*The Wildest Dreams of Kew*—which, at least in 1979, one could get in Kathmandu in a British edition. The proprietor expressed great regret that it is no longer available and said I should write a new one. "It will sell like a hot cake," he assured me.

Finally I get back to the hotel in time to get ready for a party I have been invited to that evening. There is a note from Jaccoux saying that we don't go tomorrow and that the Abert group has not gotten off either. They will try tomorrow. But the party is a great success. Kathmandu has always attracted pretty and adventuresome girls from all over the world and many of them seem to be here this evening. Boris is also here. He tells me that he is now seventy-eight. He looks fine. His Yak and Yeti restaurant was closed, he informs me, but he expects to open another new one in a few weeks. He does not seem much changed and it is very good to see him. My old friend Elizabeth Hawley, one of the world's greatest experts on Himalayan mountaineering lore, tells me that prior to the fall of 1983, 135 different people from about thirty expeditions had climbed Mount Everest. She would know, since part of her job as a Reuters correspondent is to provide all of the mountaineering news from Nepal. She also tells me that as of just ten days ago there has been electricity in Namche Bazar, provided by a small hydroelectric generating project. Electricity in Namche—it is a different world. There are several people at the party from the trekking agencies and from them I learn an amusing tale. A few years ago, in one of their promotional stunts, the Canadian Club people buried a case of whiskey somewhere near the high pass that we are scheduled to cross. However, as a joke, a second group, which included a couple of Sherpas, dug the case up and reburied it farther north, near a higher pass between the same two valleys; a pass which, in fact, is called the Shangri La. (*Khangri*— or *changri*—means "peak" in the Sherpa dialect of Tibetan, and *la* means a pass. The Shangri La is a difficult pass of nearly nineteen thousand feet.) As far as anyone knows, the case is still there waiting for some hardy soul to dig it up. The second group offered it back to Canadian Club for a "ransom" but was refused. I get to my bed after midnight.

Monday, October 24: Kathmandu

Last night—or really early this morning—there was a violent thunder and lightning storm in Kathmandu. In the times I have been here I have never seen lightning. I ask Jaccoux if he remembers ever having seen lightning in these mountains and he doesn't either. Thunder over the Himalayas is very impressive and a little frightening. This morning one can see a good deal of fresh snow on the mountains. But the day is clear and the Abert group is able to fly to Lukla. Perhaps our day will come.

Tuesday, October 25: Kathmandu

One of the Twin Otters has broken down, so there will be no flight for us today. Jaccoux has arranged a bus trip for our group to the Dashinkali. About twelve miles from Kathmandu, in the countryside, there is a shrine that is dedicated to the Hindu goddess Kali—the terrifying goddess of death. At this particular shrine animal sacrifice is still practiced. I have, to put it mildly, no fondness for animal sacrifice, but the drive is one of the loveliest short excursions one can make from Kathmandu, so I go along. Besides, I have been so busy wandering around Kathmandu that I have not really spent any time with our group and it seems to me like a good idea to begin to get to know some of the people I am going to be trekking with—assuming we ever get to Lukla. I get down to the lobby of the hotel around seven and it is a polyglot mass of trekkers, some coming and some going. There is gear everywhere. Some of these people are going to western Nepal by bus, so at least they are not in competition for the spaces to Lukla.

As the bus leaves Kathmandu the road begins to climb and soon one has new and wonderful views of the Himalayas. We arrive at the Dakshinkali at midmorning. The atmosphere is that mixture of the sacred and the mundane that often seems to attend Nepalese religious ceremonies. When we get out of our bus we are inundated by beggars and hawkers of every persuasion. The business of children asking for things is something that seems to be of fairly recent origin in Nepal.

Jaccoux reminded me of something that I had forgotten from our 1967 trip. He had been struck that the only place that we visited where children asked for things like "bonbons" was the ancient and very interesting town of Kirtipur in the Kathmandu Valley. He was so taken by this anomaly that he looked into the matter and discovered that there had been an American film crew there the previous summer and they had distributed candy to the children. By the time we had gotten there, a few months later, the children assumed that any foreigner might give them candy. By now the phenomenon of children asking for money or candy, or in more remote areas for pens, is pervasive.

I struck up an extensive conversation with a lively kid who spoke English extremely well. He was selling lucky charms.

He told me, "Business is good luck—no business bad luck." I asked him how old he was and he said "Fifteen." I asked him if he was married and he said "Yes." I asked if he had any children and he said "Five." He added, with a huge mischievous grin, "And after one more year I want to marry a French girl." Of these we had a goodly supply in our group, but when I mentioned his interest to them there were no takers. I asked him how to say "I don't have any money" in Nepali. He told me that the phrase was *Paisa chhaina*. He made me pronounce it several times until I got it right. He then tried to sell me a charm. I said, "*Paisa chhaina*." He looked a little dumbfounded until he realized that he had been hoist by his own petard. He then broke into irrepressible giggles. I bought two charms.

On the way back we stopped at the Chobar Gorge. This is the place where, according to Nepalese legend, the Bodhisattva Manjusri cut, with a sword, a passage through a hill that released the water that was, the legend says, covering the Kathmandu Valley. The Bagamati River flows through this gorge. Until 1974 it was one of the loveliest places in all of Nepal. One could walk down the steep embankment to the river where there was a beautiful and ancient pagoda temple. Nearby, one of the first bridges built in Nepal—a footbridge constructed close to the turn of the century—crossed the river. I used to go there often just to sit and think. In 1974, with the aid of the West Germans, the Nepalese constructed a cement factory not far from the temple. It spews smoke into the otherwise crystal-clear atmosphere—smoke that can be seen all over the valley. The whole place has been transformed into an ugly mess. God knows the Nepalese need housing and therefore cement, but was it necessary to put that factory precisely in that place? In fact when I was in Nepal in 1979 I read that the factory was having difficulty finding the right kind of earth nearby to use in the manufacture of cement. The whole thing seems to me like something that could have been done better if it had been thought through more carefully. I was glad when our bus left to return to Kathmandu.

Wednesday, October 26: Kathmandu

Today we got as far as the airport. We woke up at four forty-five to be ready to leave with our gear at six. There were two flights for Lukla listed, the first one leaving about seven. Last night we almost gave up. Jaccoux said he could not be optimistic about our getting out at any specific time in the near future. He said we might consider another trek—to Langtang, which is due north of Kathmandu and for which no airplanes are involved, for example. We talked it over and decided that we would stick to our original plan and try to go to Everest. The airport appeared to be a total chaos of trekkers and Nepalese trying to get to various places. Somehow out of all of this Jaccoux managed to get six members of our group onto the flights to Lukla. They were called one at a time by name. Someone said that it was a little like the Last Judgment. At ten thirty-one, according to my watch, there was the sound of loud hammering. Someone said, "They are fixing the plane." At ten-forty those of us who haven't been summoned give up and go back to the hotel.

I spent part of the day visiting the extraordinary library that belonged to Field Marshal Kaiser Shamsher Rana, who died in 1964. On my first visit in 1967 the library, which was part of the field marshal's palacelike residence, was being cataloged prior to its being turned over to the general public. I wanted to see how this project had fared. On my walk to the library I passed the place where the Royal Hotel once was. The old Rana palace is still there but it looks as if it is in the process of being gutted. On the front lawn there is a large sign that reads ELECTION COMMISSION, so, one imagines, the Royal Hotel will now become part of the government. *Sic transit* . . . The library in the field marshal's house is now open to the general public. There were a few people who seemed to be using it. I wandered around the various shelves for a while and got the impression that nothing had been added since the field marshal's death. It is still a somewhat bizarre collection of books ranging from *The Wizard of Oz* to an entire cabinet devoted to sex. I noted that the stuffed tiger that had been shot by the field marshal and which on the occasion of my first visit was being nibbled on by a live deer, is still there although the deer seems to have disappeared.

Thursday, October 27: Namche Bazar

Dear Lord what a day! The hotel had been instructed to wake us at four forty-five—like yesterday—but for some reason they phoned all of us at three forty-five. By five we are ready to leave for the airport. A special flight has been arranged for seven o'clock, for those of us who did not get off yesterday. By the time the dust settles and we are loaded on with our gear, it is seven thirty. I manage to get a front seat just behind the pilots. Both of them are Nepalese although the pilot has on his black bag a decal in English that says "No More Mr. Nice Guy." While the flight from New Delhi to Kathmandu is beautiful this is surely the most spectacular mountain flight in the world. One flies close to the eastern range of the Himalayas. As one goes east the peaks get higher, finally culminating in the spectacular mountains around Everest-Lhotse, which at 27,923 feet is the fourth-highest mountain in the world, and a little farther away Makalu, which at 27,824 feet is the fifth-highest, along with an almost uncountable panoply of snow-and-ice covered summits of every imaginable shape and size. It is hard to make a choice of direction in which to look. From the air, the field at Lukla looks like a postage stamp. It is still a grass and dirt field and it is so small that the pilots land uphill in order to stop their planes. Conversely they take off downhill over a precipice that leads down at least a thousand feet to the Dudh Kosi River. It is not flying for the faint-hearted.

When I was last there in 1967 Lukla consisted of a field perched above a small Sherpa village. There was, needless to say, no tower, no airport hotel, and no coffee shop. In fact, while we were camped in this field, waiting to be flown out, our tents were visited at night by some kind of large cat—conceivably a snow leopard. One could see its eyes gleaming in a nearby field. The present Lukla has everything the previous one lacked. In fact it calls itself the Lukla International Airport. There are innumerable small innlike hotels of uncertain quality as well as a very substantial and comfortable hotel—the Sherpa Cooperative Hotel—with hot and cold running water. I doubt a snow leopard or other big cat has been seen in the vicinity of the airport for many years.

After we land, the first order of business is to rearrange our gear. We have worn our heaviest clothing on the plane so that it would not be weighed with the baggage. The weight limits on these flights are strict. At nine thousand feet it is pretty snappy at eight thirty in the morning, but not cold enough to justify wearing all that gear. We begin locating our Sherpas and porters, some of whom are at Lukla and some of whom have gone on ahead to Namche with the first six members of our group, who came in yesterday. That done, we eat breakfast—eggs and chapattis (unleavened bread)—and coffee and tea. Then Jaccoux explains the facts of life. The original plan that Jaccoux worked out in France assumed that we would be in Lukla on Monday. It is now Thursday, which means that we have lost three days. If we want to do the full program it means that some of the schedule will have to be revised. In particular, instead of going from Lukla to Namche in two days—the original plan—we will try to get to Namche today. This means first dropping six hundred feet to the river to a place called Phakding—which was to have been our first campsite—and then climbing up to about twelve thousand feet, which is the altitude of Namche, the entire exercise to take a minimum of eight hours. We all agree that, under the circumstances, it is the thing to try, and we set off at our various paces.

While still in Kathmandu I had purchased a wonderful new guide book to Nepal written by two professors at the Tribhuvan University in Kirtipur—Trilok Chandra Majupuria and Indra Majupuria. What I like about this guide is its candor and its accuracy. I am also very fond of how it is written since it captures the cadence of the way Nepalese often speak English. There is a paragraph called "While Trekking" that I have, more or less, committed to memory and whose advice I intend to follow. It reads, "By plane or bus you can reach your departure point for trekking. A new feeling can be experienced. Departure time should be usually early in the morning. Fix porters ahead of your schedule. Usually they are quite punctual. During trekking you should see that it is very important to maintain your trekking rhythms. It should be generally 300 m (984 feet) per hour on an upward slope and 400–600 m (1312–1968 feet) per hour for a downward slope." The Majupurias do not say so but this must refer to changes in altitude. If not, it seems incredibly slow to me.

In a definitive book on the effects of high altitude, *Going High*, the noted American climber and doctor Charles Houston suggests the following schedule. Take one "day" to reach five thousand feet. He doesn't say what a "day" is but six to eight hours is a normal to heavy trekking day. Then, says Houston, take one day for each two thousand feet up to ten thousand feet. Thereafter take one day for each seven hundred to one thousand feet of altitude change. This pace is much slower than the Majupurias and makes a good deal more sense to me. It was quite clear to me that our trek to Namche was going to violate both of these limits.

The Majupurias go on to say,

> Do not walk fast on the trail as it is harmful. Do not mind if any members of your group walks fast, you should be slow and steady at your normal pace. Porters like to walk quickly and stop frequently. Let them do so or ask them to keep pace with you, but you maintain your rhythm. Experience shows that you should not move very straight as it is tiresome. Another hint given by porters is that your pace should be crisscross. These hints will not make you feel tired during the trail. In the next morning, the sirdar or chief porter gets up early and offers you hot tea or coffee which can be repeated if you want. Early hours

begin with washing and cleaning. Take breakfast, pack up things and start trekking. It is advised that trekking should be done generally for 3 hours in the morning and 3 hours in the afternoon. During the mid-day, relaxing is suggested. Take care during the trek you should eat more. During trekking keep some distance with your friends otherwise you may discuss your own things. Enjoy the trail with your open eyes and ears. In the evening you can write in your diary if you want. Porters like to halt about 10-10:30 A.M. as they do not eat breakfast. They fill their plate with rice or *tsampa* [barley flour] and eat a good quantity. Smoke a bidi [a small cigar] or cigarette and become ready for the rest of the day's march. During the day you may want to have a wash in the sun or you may do so in the evening at your halting place or may not do so at all. There are several tea shops along the trail where you can enjoy hot tea. It is better to halt several times during the day as you have to get acclimatised and develop the habits. A camping site should be near the water and near a place which gives a good view. . . .

Apart from smoking the bidi it all seems like fine advice to me. On the way down from Lukla there is not much opportunity for "crisscross." Jaccoux told me that this part of the trail has been made into a kind of "super highway," because there is so much traffic to and from Lukla. Indeed it has. Every few minutes one meets up with trekkers, Sherpas, or trains of yaks or the lowland equivalents. (*Yak* is a word that has come to mean all animals that look like yaks. In fact *yak* refers to the male long-haired animal. The female is called a *nak*. Yaks are often crossed with cows to produce the *dazum*, the male version of which is the dzopchuk. The word, when pronounced, sounds to me something like "zop-cho." It is the dzopchuk that is usually used to transport things.) There are no wheeled vehicles here or in any part of the Everest region and it is difficult for me to imagine that there ever will be. It would be a very expensive proposition to build a road to Namche and beyond and there is the risk that it might be wiped out by a flood. Indeed in September of 1977 there was an avalanche which fell from Ama Dablam—the magnificent

22,350-foot Matterhornlike mountain north of Namche. The avalanche fell into a lake that was feeding the Dudh Kosi river. It created a thirty-foot wave in the river that washed away part of the trail we are walking on—including seven bridges. As far as I can see all of this devastation has been repaired, and if Jaccoux had not told me about it I don't think I would have noticed anything.

As we walk we pass a number of small hotels, tea shops, and restaurants. Some of the hotels advertise hot showers. All of this is completely new to me and none of it was here in 1967. Around noon we stop for lunch and then after lunch come to the small Sherpa community of Jorsale, part of which was also wiped out in the flood. Just beyond Jorsale is the entrance to what is known as Sagarmatha National Park. (Sagarmatha is the name in Nepali for Mount Everest. The Tibetan, and therefore, the Sherpa, name for the mountain is Chomolungma, sometimes translated as "Goddess Mother of the Snows," which is also the translation of the Nepali name.) This park, which was created in 1976 and comprises an area of 1,243 square kilometers, contains all the high mountains in the Everest region. It was created to preserve the area because the number of trekkers and climbers had simply become too large and their effects on the environment too destructive to let matters continue without some kind of regulation.

At the entrance to the park one is stopped by a uniformed park official. One must show one's trekking permit. This is a kind of internal passport issued for a fee by the Ministry of Home Affairs in Kathmandu. It bears one's photograph and one's passport number and states the precise regions that can be visited and for how long. Our trekking permits were good for about three weeks. It also stated "He/She must, however, keep twenty-five miles off the northern borders of Nepal." If one's trekking permit is in order then one must pay a fee of sixty rupees—about two and a half dollars—for an entry permit that allows one to stay in the park for the length of one's trekking permit. This permit, which is a pink paper, has on its back the park rules, and from them one can get a pretty clear idea of the kind of concerns that led to the creation of the park. Rules two and three are particularly instructive. Rule 2 reads: *"Trekking is an acceptable challenge. But* please do not litter, dispose it properly. Please do not remove anything from the park. Please do not damage plant. Please do not disturb wildlife. Please do not carry arms and explosives. Please do not scale any mountain without proper permission. Please do not scale any sacred peaks of any elevation. Please keep all the time to the main trek-routes."

I was told in Kathmandu that since the creation of the park there has been a resurgence of wildlife in the region, which suggests that there must have been hunting there before these rules went into effect. Wolves, snow leopards, various kinds of deer, and pheasants are coming back. The wolves have created a problem for the Sherpas, who now must protect their yaks more carefully.

Rule 3 reads: "Be self-sufficient in your fuel supply before entering the Park. Buying fuel wood from local people or removing any wood materials from the forest is illegal. This will apply to your guides, cooks and porters also."

This rule has to do with the fact that, between the trekkers and the local people, the forests in the Sherpa country, and indeed in much of Nepal, were simply being cut away. The corollary of this was a dramatic increase in land erosion. In a certain sense the Himalaya is being washed into the Indian Ocean. There are attempts at reforestation all over Nepal, but it is not clear that these do, or can, keep up with the destruction of the forests. It had been pointed out to me in Kathmandu that while these regulations against using wood for fires in the park are obeyed by the trekking companies— for example, we were packing in with us large cans of kerosene—they are not being obeyed by the local people, who have little or no contact with the park officials. Indeed, as I passed some of the little hotels and restaurants along the trail I noticed stacks of firewood, and, from time to time, I came across Sherpas carrying baskets of wood. If this continues soon all the accessible forests will be gone.

Not far after Jorsale the Dudh Kosi and the Bhote Kosi rivers join together. The trail bisects the distance between the two rivers and ascends about two thousand feet to Namche. Before we started climbing Jaccoux had given us a little lecture in which he suggested that to acclimatize we should walk for twenty minutes and rest for about ten even if we did not feel winded. The idea was simply to let one's body become accustomed to the new altitudes. I was quite happy to do this and, as we got higher, it became, as far as I was concerned, more like walking ten minutes and resting twenty. By the time I got to Namche it was dark. Because of the new electric lights I had no trouble finding my way. Namche is small but crammed with shops, restaurants, and little hotels. The houses are all of the classic stone Sherpa construction but I did notice that most of them now seem to have glass windows which were extremely rare in 1967. While I was wandering around the main street I ran into a couple of members of our group, and they showed me where we were all camped in a small field behind one of the hotels. That night we had a cheerful dinner in our communal "mess tent" which we topped off with a few generous libations of the expedition whiskey.

Friday, October 28: Kunde

In the Jaccoux itinerary this has been advertised as a "*Journée d'acclimatation,*" which I would freely translate as a day when Jaccoux intends to train the balloons off us. It has been a fairly cold night and I am sure that it is going to get colder. The Sherpas wake us up at seven thirty—rather late for a trekking morning—and by the time we get going it is nine thirty. The object of the exercise is to hike to Kunde, a lovely Sherpa village about a thousand feet higher than Namche, and then to climb a 14,500-foot peak behind the village. This will presumably enable Jaccoux to see what kind of shape everybody is in. Our group ranges in age from a sixty-year-old man who works for the French railways but whose hobby is climbing and skiing, which he does every week all year long, to a fellow in his twenties who works for the French space program and also climbs and hikes. In between there are several young women whom I would estimate to be in their early thirties. One of them is an ophthalmologist who practices in Lyons. She has spent a year practicing in general medicine in Africa. She will be our trek doctor. Two of the other women are nurses, so medically we should be all right. There is a smattering of engineers as well as an electronics technician from the physics laboratory in Orsay. Nearly all of these people—about half men and half women—are either dedicated climbers or have been on treks with Jaccoux before or both. I seem to be the second oldest and I intend to try not to slow things down.

The walk to Kunde is stunningly beautiful. One has the first views of the magnificent Ama Dablam. A sign not far from Namche warns trekkers about the effects of altitude, pointing out that one trekker in a thousand in the Everest region dies because of altitude-related disorders. (For Himalayan climbers the statistic is that one in forty dies climbing in the Himalayas, but that is another matter.) Indeed we had heard that the night before a seventy-four-year-old trekker had died following a heart attack at the Thyangboche monastery, which is at nearly thirteen thousand feet. I discussed this with Jaccoux and asked him why more people did not get into serious altitude problems when they climbed Mont Blanc, which is the highest mountain in Western Europe at an altitude of 15,771 feet. People simply come off the street in Chamonix and successfully climb Mont Blanc. Jaccoux thought that the reason was that when one climbs Mont Blanc one spends at most one night at something like 12,500 feet. One climbs the mountain early the next morning and, as a rule, is back in Chamonix by the afternoon. On the other hand the Everest trekker spends two weeks at altitudes well over twelve thousand feet and is often camping at altitudes substantially higher than Mont Blanc. The body either adapts to that or it breaks down. Jaccoux noted, "It's too bad that the most beautiful trek in Nepal is also the most dangerous."

The trail, which is as wide as a jeep road, leads over a pass at about thirteen thousand feet and then down into Kunde. Our first stop is the hospital that Sir Edmund Hillary built for the Sherpas in 1966 with money he raised from speaking tours and other contributions. In 1967 we spent a good deal of time here talking with John McKinnon and his wife Diane, who were from New Zealand. John McKinnon was the first Hillary doctor in the Kunde hospital, a post that he held for two years. He is now back in New Zealand practicing and we have corresponded from time to time. I was curious to see how some of his projects were faring sixteen years later, including his project to add iodine to the Sherpa diet. Sherpas had never eaten iodized salt prior to the arrival of the McKinnons, because it was not available, and didn't eat it now because they didn't like it. A consequence of this—and this was also true in the Alps, in the last century—was a very high incidence of goiter among the adult population. Even worse, parents with this disorder tend to produce cretinous children. I recall with horror that in 1967 we passed through a village not far from Namche in which every adult appeared to have goiter and every child appeared to be cretinous. (This problem was so severe in the Alps that Edward Whymper, the man who first climbed the Matterhorn, used to refer to these Alpine villages as places where, in the words of the missionary hymn, "every prospect pleases and only man is vile.") McKinnon was trying to figure out what to do about this.

The hospital is in a neat rectangular building with a magnificent view of the mountains. There is a long stone terrace in front of it and our group pulled up to it while I went in search of whoever might be inside. I knocked on the door and an amiable-looking bearded young man appeared who identified himself as Keith Buswell, the present New Zealand doctor. I told him of my friendship with the McKinnons. He said that, in fact, John McKinnon would be visiting the hospital in a few weeks, so we will have just missed each other. Buswell told me that he had only been in Kunde for two months but was planning on staying for two years. I asked him about the iodine matter and he told me that the problem has essentially been solved. There have been, as far as he knows, no recent cases of cretinous children born to parents with goiter. The therapeutic technique that was successfully used was injections of iodine—at least initially. Then an odd thing happened. Sherpas, like most farmers in the Indian subcontinent, use human waste as fertilizer. This waste now contains iodine in sufficient quantities—it appears—to iodize crops like the potato, which is a staple of the Sherpa diet. The net result is that in one way or another the iodine problem has been solved.

Buswell also sees relatively few cases of tuberculosis, which was another one of McKinnon's major problems—and those he does see he can treat. Smallpox, which used to ravage entire villages, has long been eradicated by inoculation. Buswell thinks that Sherpa longevity is now greater than that of the general Nepalese population in substantial part due to the better medical care Sherpas get. In all Nepal, according to the 1981 figure, there was one doctor for each 25,230 Nepalese. Buswell is, on the other hand, treating a population that is probably at most a few thousand. (It is estimated that there are twenty thousand Sherpas that live in the *entire* Solu-Khumbu region. Many of these people live several days' walk from Kunde, which is in Khumbu, and probably do not get to the hospital.)

Our medical women wanted to see what the operating room looked like and Buswell gave us a tour. They asked him if he could do complicated childbirths—cesareans for example. He said that he could, but that Sherpa women, if it is at all possible, want to have their babies at home. When we went outside to join the rest of the group it turned out that another woman had a problem she wanted to discuss with Dr. Buswell. She spoke only French, so I acted as interpreter. She had been taking a medicine for a thyroid condition and last night she had broken the bottle and lost the medicine. Our doctor and Buswell conferred, again with me acting as interpreter, to figure out how to replace her medication. It turned out that this was possible with medicine in the hospital, and we insisted on paying for both the medicine—which Buswell wanted to give us—and the established trekker's consulting fee, which is a hundred rupees (some five dollars). The hospital needs this money and we were glad to donate it. As we were leaving Buswell asked us not to give any candy to the Sherpa kids. "It's bad for their teeth," he said, "and there is no dentist in the region."

We climbed our peak with me bringing up the rear. By the time I got back to our camp in Namche it was dark. I managed to take a hot shower—the last for a while—using the hotel's primitive system in which hot water is poured into a bucket from which a pipe feeds into the shower when one opens a valve. It may be crude but it felt wonderful. I was asleep by seven thirty.

Saturday, October 29: The Phortse Bridge

At six A.M., as expected, the Sherpas woke us for tea. There is a good deal of packing up to do. Jaccoux ran into someone who told him that he had just been over our high pass in basketball shoes, which must mean there is less snow up there than usual. In any case I am jettisoning my crampons. One less thing to carry. I have, on the other hand, rented an ancient ice ax in Namche. It has a wooden handle, which makes it something out of the dark ages of mountaineering. But it looks perfectly adequate to me. On this part of the trip the heavy loads are to be carried by beasts—yaks—or dzopchuks or whatever they are. By the time the animals are loaded it is nine thirty. After that, the first stop is the police station just above Namche, where the trekking permit of each person in the group must be checked. Then we move out on the trail north and a bit east.

I was hoping we might get a view of the now-defunct Hotel

Everest View above Khumjung not far from Kunde. This was a sort of chimera constructed by some Japanese entrepreneurs—a luxury hotel at thirteen thousand feet. There was reportedly oxygen in every room in case one felt the need. To get there people flew in—when this was possible—to the STOL landing strip in Thyangboche. The hotel might have had a chance if the transportation there had been surer. It is difficult to imagine that they expected to make a living from passing trekkers.

In 1979 we visited an equally chimerical place also now defunct. Somewhat south of the Everest region there is a beautiful Sherpa village called Phaplu at just a little over nine thousand feet. Just before the time of our visit, a twenty-four-year-old Sherpa named Rinzi Lama, who came from an extremely wealthy and distinguished Sherpa family, had constructed in Phaplu a marvelous hotel, the Hostellerie des Sherpas. Rinzi had studied the hotel business in Italy. At the time we met him, he spoke Sherpa, Tibetan, Nepali, Hindi, English, and Italian. His uncle represented essentially the entire Sherpa community in the national parliament and his family had made what amounted to a fortune in local terms by trading in Tibet. The hotel cost him about thirty-five thousand dollars to build—an enormous sum in a country where the average daily wage is eight cents. He built the whole thing with local labor. It had magnificent Tibetan-style decorations and chandeliers with electric lights, which he ran from a special generator since there was no other electric power in Phaplu. It had a sign on front which read—and I preserve the original spelling:

"Hostellerie Des Sherpa"
Really Just Two & ¹/₂ Hours From Junbesi Through The Beautiful Coniferous
& Rhododendrons Along The Terribly Romantic River Valley
In The Sherpa Village Of Phaplu
Approximately (Ft. 8000 Mt. 2400 Telecommunications—Airstrip, Medical Facilities) *Middle of January 1976*

Opening of Surprising, Exciting & Unimaginable
"Hostellierie Des Sherpa"
Unique & Exceptional Hotel Capable of Arousing Full of
Amicable Feelings Built & Decorated in Smartest Sherpa
& Tibetan Style Six Luxirious Bed Rooms for Romantic
Explorers
Attach Bathroom *With Running Hot & Cold Water Bathtub*
Shower Watertap W.C. & Heater in Each Room & Bathroom
Plus
Six Three Beds in Each Warm Room for Expert Trekkers
Hygenic & Clean Environment
Laundry Work
Delicious International Cuisines
Mysterious Bar in Candle Light
Crazy Music In Discotheque
Six Gentle Horses for Quite Ride But Sorry No Daily
Newspaper & Any Drug
"Hostellerie Des Sherpa"
Unbelievable Discovery
For Your Holiday's Relax & Enjoyment, *For*
Acclamatisation of Your Trekking & Expeditions
For the Departure of Your Successful Adventure
Trust Us: Please Come to Have Drinks Together
All the Prices Are Very Fair
Waiting Your Pleasureable Visit
Sincerely, Rinzi Pasang Lama,
G. Manager

It was a marvelous place in a superb setting, but it failed since the only way to get there—apart from walking for a week— was to fly to the STOL strip in Phaplu in one of the Swiss Pilatus Porters that hold about six passengers. Given the premium on flights in Nepal it was simply not possible— especially during the trekking season—to guarantee transportation there. (We had visited in January when there are almost no trekkers.)

Our trail does not go by the Everest View, but follows the

classic route to Everest, the same route we took in 1967. After lunch we will take a different route that, at least to me, will be terra incognita. We are on our way to the Gokyo Valley near the base of Cho Oyu, an area that was completely closed to us in 1967. We begin by heading up a steep trail to the top of a ridge at 12,900 feet. (Jaccoux has brought along a very accurate altimeter which is good to 26,000 feet, from which he reads off the altitudes.) I am resting at a large *chorten*—a religious monument on top of the ridge—when along comes one of our Sherpani—as Sherpa women are called—following one of our beasts, whom she massages from time to time with a stick to indicate who is in charge. She has a beautiful, strong Asiatic face—a lovely-looking young girl. She must be carrying at least forty pounds on her back in a woven basket. She is wearing a long black dress, typical of Sherpa women, with a decorative necklace, also typical. The dress comes down to the well-worn pair of blue basketball shoes that she has on her feet. These shoes are a symbol of the new Sherpa prosperity which trekking has brought about. In 1967 all the Sherpas and Sherpanis except those who were going to high altitudes on snow, went largely barefoot on trails like this.

The Sherpani smells of smoke. There are not many chimneys in the houses in Solu Khumbu. There weren't in 1967 and there still aren't. Smoke from the interior fires used for cooking and keeping warm pervades the Sherpa houses. The place of honor in a Sherpa house is next to the fire, which, considering the temperatures inside these houses, is not very surprising.

As she walks along the Sherpani sings a mournful wordless song over and over. I am very fond of the melody and wish I had enough of an ear that I could sing it too. From time to time she says something like "*eeuk-eeuk*" to her beast. She and her beast are walking at a delightfully slow pace so I tag along. She occasionally meets a girlfriend on the trail and they have a giggly chat. The only thing I can think of asking when we are walking along together is "Yak?" pointing to the beast. "Dzopchuk," she says, giving the beast an affectionate tap on the rump. That exhausts my Sherpa and she does not know any English. We pad along the trail in our separate linguistic spaces. I wonder if she ever fantasizes about marrying a trekker or a climber. I know two cases where it happened. In 1979 the American climber Annie Whitehouse married the Sherpa Yeshi Tenzing. Tenzing had been a cook and Annie Whitehouse one of the climbers on the all-women's expedition to Annapurna the year before. A few years ago a Colorado climber—a friend of mutual friends—married a Sherpani from Namche. It was, I am told, tough sledding at first since neither spoke the other's language. Furthermore, the girl's family ostracized her for marrying outside the Sherpa community. The marriage did not go well and ended in divorce although she remains in the United States.

The Sherpani, her beast, and I pull in to a beautiful campsite near a bridge that crosses the Dudh Kosi river. A few hundred feet above the bridge is the village of Phortse, which at 12,600 feet is said to be the highest year-round community in all of Nepal. I can tell, as the sun sets, that it is going to be a cold night.

Sunday, October 30: Luza

As I suspected it *was* one cold night. Perhaps it is old age, but I can't seem to get myself warm enough at night even though I am wearing everything I can think of. The hot tea I had in my canteen to drink during the night has frozen solid—iced tea—and it remains half frozen for the whole day. On the other hand there has not been a cloud in the sky since we got here. When we were here about this time of year in 1967 it snowed almost every afternoon until we finally gave up the trek because of the snow.

The cold and the altitude begin to get on people's nerves. One of our married couples has been fighting all morning. She seems somewhat stronger than he does—or, at least, in better shape. And she is rubbing it in. The great French guide

Armand Charlet refused to take married couples climbing together because he was afraid that this sort of thing might happen. The nice thing about a trek like this is that by choosing one's pace one can walk by oneself or at least with compatible people. I have been walking by myself when suddenly there is the first spectacular view of Cho Oyu at the head of the valley. This is clearly *its* valley. The mountain, which was first climbed in 1954 by an Austrian group, looks like a giant snowy armchair. It is said to be the "easiest" of the eight-thousand-meter mountains. Lots of luck—it has killed its share of climbers. The trail leads straight to our next stop, the tiny summer village—a village that the Sherpas inhabit only in the summertime because of its altitude and inaccessibility in other seasons—of Luza, which is at 14,100 feet.

When we arrived at Luza in the late afternoon, the Abert group was already there, having spent a rest day. We had not seen the Abert group since they left Kathmandu for Lukla last Monday. It had been a perfect fall day—cold, but sunny and clear, with extraordinary views of Cho Oyu. We arrived at the campsite as the sun was beginning to set, and it was already getting quite cold. No sooner had we arrived when Abert found Jaccoux and told him that one of his party was missing. It turned out to be the young medical secretary from Strasbourg with whom I had shared a croissant in the Charles de Gaulle Airport and who had told me that this was to be her first *grand voyage*.

She had apparently gone for a walk by herself and had never come back. This was potentially a very serious matter, because she was not equipped to spend the night out in the subfreezing temperatures that were rapidly enveloping us. Exposure at altitude can turn a minor mishap into a fatal one. Jaccoux immediately organized a search party, consisting of himself, Abert, our doctor, and, as I recall, a Sherpa or two. We lent them the extra equipment they might need, such as extra flashlights. In an hour or so they were back. The worst had happened. They had found the young woman dead. She had apparently died in a fall, but how it happened no one could say. Her body was brought back and put in a small tent, by itself. I then participated in drawing up, with the aid of our doctor, the formal death certificate, which had to be in English. I learned, for the first time, how few words are needed to describe the cause of death. The fewer the better, our doctor said. We then were faced with the question of what to do next. Here the division of the expedition into two groups played a role. Some people from the Abert group, with whom she had been trekking, wanted to stop the trek right there. To our group she was a stranger. I may have been the only one in our group that had talked to her. Furthermore, in practical terms, it was not even clear what it would have meant to stop the trek. We were two weeks, by foot, from Kathmandu and, with the premium on air space from Lukla, to return before our scheduled day would have meant either waiting for up to ten days in Lukla, or walking back to Kathmandu. The only thing that made any sense was to continue on.

Abert took it upon himself to stay with the body of the young woman and to make whatever arrangements he could to notify her family via the French embassy in Kathmandu and, if possible—and if the family wanted—to bring the body back to France. It was at this point that we learned something about Nepal that I, at least, had not known. Despite the urging of the embassy and despite the family's stated willingness to pay for the transport down from Solu Khumbu by air, no plane could be chartered for the purposes of transporting a dead body. In Nepal planes are only for the living. One can see the logic of this from the point of view of a poor country with very few planes. On this matter there was no possibility of compromise. Hence it fell upon Abert to arrange with the local lamas to give the young woman a proper Buddhist funeral. Since the Sherpas cremate their dead, the young woman was cremated.

The sight of the small tent in which the young woman's body lay until the funeral has remained vividly in my memory ever since.

Monday, October 31: Gokyo

After a fitful night's sleep I get up with a sore throat. I take a gram of vitamin C and a tetracycline pill and decide that I am "cured." I have now evolved a trail philosophy. Since I like to walk slowly I start out before most of the group. That way I and they end up at the same place at about the same time. The trail goes sharply up for a bit and then moseys off in the general direction of Cho Oyu. After about three hours I encounter some of our Sherpas in what looks like a yak pen. They tell me that this is where we will have lunch. There is nothing to do but lie in the sun and wait, which is fine with me.

Next in view is Jaccoux, who has evidently moved up the trail like a deer. He informs me that not far behind him is a beautiful American girl who is not part of our group and is trekking by herself since her boyfriend, it seems, has ditched her. Jaccoux is usually reluctant to speak English but when it is a matter of a pretty girl he is willing to make the effort. Not long after we have this conversation, there, in fact, *is* a very pretty girl walking by herself. I say hello and invite her to join us for lunch. She has not seen a really square meal for a few days and is glad to accept. We get to talking and she confirms Jaccoux's report about her boyfriend. He had come to Nepal to "find himself"—one of those—and has decided that in this momentous search she was excess baggage. She had another three weeks to go on her trekking permit, and decided she would be damned if she was going home before she did all the trekking she could do. She is gutsy to be trekking by herself.

In their guide book the Majupurias comment about the young people who filled Nepal "finding themselves" not long ago. "In early sixties and seventies, Nepal had been very popular with the freak community for hemp. Smoking of ganja was tolerated. However, several Nepalese youths also started to smoke it heavily owing to their association with freaks. Therefore the government banned hashish smoking.

However it still continues. Smuggling of hashish is strictly prohibited. Owing to the ban of hashish, the socio-economic condition of the farmers of the hilly region of western Nepal has been badly affected." One thing that is evident even after a few days in Kathmandu, is that the hippie community—the "freaks" who were ubiquitous on my earlier visits—seems to have disappeared. Perhaps they have relocated somewhere else in Nepal or they have gone underground. There is still Freak Street in Kathmandu but the "freaks" seem to have moved on.

After lunch, the American girl goes her way and we go ours. The upper Gokyo Valley is one of the most beautiful places I have ever seen. It culminates at the tiny village of Gokyo itself, which is on the shore of a magnificent blue-green mountain lake. The thought occurs to me that if this place were ten thousand feet lower it might become the Lake Tahoe of Asia. At 15,800, we will be camping tonight twenty-nine feet higher than the summit of Mont Blanc.

Tuesday, November 1: Below the Cho La

Jaccoux has once again told us the facts of life. The first and determining fact is that we do not have enough porters. We do have the dzopchuks, but there is no way that those animals are going to get over the Cho La. It comes down to this. The dzopchuks and the Sherpanis will go back down the Gokyo Valley and then go back up, by the normal trekking route, to the village of Lobuche, which is at about 16,200 feet. It is a long way around the mountain and it will take them fully two days. Our Sherpas can carry enough tents so we can sleep four to a tent for a couple of nights. There should be just enough food. We will have to carry everything else—sleeping bags and the rest. That means that for the hardest day of the trek we will be carrying about double our usual load. The alternative is to go with the dzopchuks to Lobuche. Three of the group—including the bickering married couple—decide to do just that. They have had enough of the altitude.

We head down the Gokyo Valley trail and at a place which the Sherpas have no trouble in picking out, turn east. A little climbing brings us to the lower tongue of the Ngozumba Glacier, which, if one followed it north, would eventually lead, at least judging from the map, to the summit of Cho Oyu. From the map it looks like we cannot be any further than twenty-five miles from the Tibetan border. This part of the glacier is slightly slippery but not very icy. It is a morass, but the Sherpas seem to know where they are going. There are occasional cairns in the ice showing we are on the right track. Without much trouble we cross the glacier and find ourselves on a high sward just below the pass. From here the pass looks difficult but not impossible. Tomorrow will tell the tale.

Wednesday, November 2: The Cho La

After hours, in my tent, I have been reading by flashlight from a couple of paperback books I have carried along. One of them is the collection of essays by Camus called *The Myth of Sisyphus*. The title essay ends with the sentences, "The struggle itself towards the heights is enough to fill a man's heart. One must imagine Sisyphus happy." I don't think we know any of the details of the route that Sisyphus followed up his underworld mountain when he pushed the stone to the summit, but if it was like the Cho La it is difficult for *me* to imagine that he was happy. The terrain on the way up is not technically difficult. There is certainly no need for a rope. But it is steep and it is composed of that kind of unstable rock where one takes two steps up and slides one step back down. All of this is at an altitude of over seventeen thousand feet. The only virtue of the exercise is that it has enabled me to get to know, a little bit, one of our Sherpas.

In 1967 we were with a small number of Sherpas for several

weeks. There were only three of us and so we got to know the
Sherpas pretty well. In the end the Sherpa Ila Tsering had us
to his house in Namche for a couple of memorable feasts
complete with dancing. It was even suggested, as I recall, that
I marry one of the Sherpanis who was there. On this trip there
are seventeen of us and, perhaps, four Sherpas and two or
three Sherpanis. The *sirdar* seems to be a very nice man but
he is so unassuming and soft-spoken that I have never even
found out his name. There are just too many of us for anyone
to get to know anyone else. On the climb to the top of the Cho
La I am, as usual, bringing up the rear. The oldest Sherpa, a
man named Tashi, seems to have been given the job of seeing
to it that I keep going. He says every once in a while, "Now
slowly, slowly going." I grin at him to show that I am okay and
he grins back. He offers to carry my pack but I tell him that
that is not necessary. He cannot be much taller than five feet
three. He has a wizened face and is tough as nails. He re-
minds me of Ang Dorje, my friend from 1967.

I am going along like this with the snow-covered summit of
the pass getting ever closer. It is horribly tiring work and I am
constantly having to sit down and catch my breath. But
things don't seem, at least to me, impossible, or even desperate. I look up and see Jaccoux coming back down in my
direction. That is odd. The last time I saw him was at breakfast when he gave all of us something like a Mars bar to give
us an extra shot of glucose to get us over the pass. When he
gets above me I am sitting down on a small rock and he tells
me to come up where he is. I tell him that I am perfectly
satisfied with my rock and I don't see any reason to come up
to his. He says the reason that I should come up is that he is
going to take my pack. There is no arguing about this. He
puts it on and remarks that it seems incredibly light to him.
Thanks. He also remarks that I look my fifty-three years.
Thanks again. It is true that I haven't shaved in several days
and have a sort of white beard. It is also true that the various
sun blocks I have been using don't seem to have worked and
that my nose is peeling and the rest of my face is multi-

colored. I am trying to think of something equally insulting to say to him when I notice that we have reached the snowy summit. I also notice that the woman who had the thyroid problem is being, more or less, carried by two Sherpas. After she has been seated for a while she seems recovered. The rest of the group is sprawled out variously eating lunch in the bright sunshine. It is a magnificent place and if I weren't so beat I would enjoy it a lot more.

After lunch Jaccoux gives me some kind of a glucose pill and we head off on a wide track in the snow in a fairly gentle downward direction. The track becomes steeper. Here is where crampons would have come in handy. I begin to slide and Jaccoux takes an arm and in this somewhat ungainly fashion we get off the snow and ice and onto a rocky trail. After a while Jaccoux points to where we are eventually going—a place called Dzonghila at 15,900 feet. The trail has now broadened out and since there is no way I can break anything Jaccoux takes off for our camp at his usual pace. This leaves me alone in this vast valley with the sun beginning to set. I am very tired but I like the solitude. From time to time I look back where we have come from. From here it looks vertical. Going my own slow pace I manage to get to our camp just after the sun has set. I am asleep by eight. It has been a very long, tough day.

Thursday, November 3: Lobuche

This has been a relatively easy day, which is just as well because I am beat. This is the eighth day we have been at this without a rest. Our original schedule called for a couple of rest days but we lost them when we had our problems getting the plane to Lukla. The woman with the thyroid problem, and her husband, have gone back down toward Namche. The three people who left two days ago have also gone down. That leaves eleven of the sixteen plus of course Jaccoux. Lobuche, at 16,200 feet, was the highest place we camped in

1967. It was a pretty grim place then. It consisted of a few yak pens and, as I recall, one stone building with no windows and no doors. The town is now on the main trekking route to the Everest base camp. It is crawling with trekkers of every size, shape, and nationality. There are a few small hotels which sell, among other things, beer at fifty-five rupees—somewhat more than two dollars a bottle. Considering where we are, it seems like a bargain. I hear an American say, "We saw a lot of mountains from the ridge but I don't know what they are." Dear Lord! Everest can't be much more than five miles from here.

Friday, November 4: Periche

Some of the group have gone off to climb the Kala Pattar. It is just short of 18,200 feet and is a wonderful place from which to see the whole south side of Everest. We climbed it in 1967 and I have decided that I don't need to do it again, especially since we are not planning to camp tonight at Lobuche but farther down the valley at Pheriche. The Kala Pattar people are not expected to get into camp until nine, or so, tonight. I loaf a bit in the sun during the morning and then follow our dzopchuks—which have now rejoined us—down to Periche. Periche is practically in the lowlands at just under 14,000 feet. It is a substantial village and it has in it one of the most interesting institutions to have been constructed here since 1967, namely, the Trekker's Aid Post. So far as I can make out, this was the idea of a Peace Corps volunteer named John Skow. It began in 1973 in a hut in Periche in which Skow lived during the trekking season—the middle of September to the first week in December—and in which with the support of several of the large trekking agencies he performed various services for trekkers. However, in 1975 a hundred thousand dollars was raised to build a small hospital which could service the local community but whose main function was to give medical support to trekkers and climbers. By this time

enough people had gotten into serious trouble with the altitude that this was a welcome idea. The first doctor was a man
named Peter Hackett, who is now director of High Altitude
Research in the Department of High Altitude Studies of the
University of Alaska in Anchorage. That year he had 436
trekker patient visits and 503 Sherpa patient visits. The
Sherpas are treated free and the trekkers are charged.

At the present time the hospital is financed by a nonprofit
organization named the Himalayan Rescue Association and it
is located in a compact stone building. It normally has two
doctors on duty. When I called, one of them—a British doctor
named Patrick O'Sullivan—was out in the field. As part of
their job the doctors visit places like Gokyo from time to time
to see if there is anyone up there who is in trouble. The doctor
who was in was a thirty-two-year-old bearded American from
Iowa named Tony Waickman. He was in the process of making a chocolate cake since O'Sullivan was leaving and Waickman wanted to give him a farewell dinner. He told me that his
own medical specialty was cardiology, which must be useful
considering some of the likely trouble his prospective patients
can get into. He said that the physicians do this on an unpaid
voluntary basis and, in fact, are just in Nepal on tourist and
trekking visas. He said that they have seen as many as fifteen
hundred trekker patients in a season with all kinds of ail-
ments from skin diseases to pulmonary edema—a severe and
often fatal form of altitude sickness. He, and everyone else I
have spoken to, agrees that there is only one really effective
thing to do about altitude sickness—and that is to get the
patient down to lower altitudes. The "miracle cure" is to lose a
couple of thousand feet of altitude. Barring that, the best
things one can do include injections of diuretics, which cause
the body to lose fluid—fluid buildup in the brain and lungs is
the dangerous element of the edemas—or giving the patient
oxygen. But there is no substitute for getting down. Waickman told me that the one thing the doctors will not do is
mountain rescue. He said, "If their friends can't save them,
they will die." However, not long before, he was able to help

an injured climber on Ama Dablam who was close to the base of the mountain. Waickman told me that when he gets finished with his stint in Periche he wants to go back to Thailand, where he was working in a refugee camp. He is a very impressive young man.

By the time I left the hospital it was dark. The group that climbed Kala Patar began coming in around nine. Their feeling was that they were glad to have done it—*once*.

Saturday, November 5: Chukung

From Periche we head back up toward Tibet in a northeasterly direction, up the valley of the Imja Kola river. This valley was also closed in 1967. I have read and heard from friends that it is one of the most spectacular places in all of Nepal. This becomes apparent once one has climbed over a ridge that separates Periche from the higher village of Dingboche. At that point one can begin to see the mountains that flank the valley. On the right is Ama Dablam, so close that one can practically touch it. We looked through binoculars for an expedition climbing the mountain while we were there but couldn't find them. On the left is the south face of Nuptse and Lhotse. In front of us is a whole array of snow-covered peaks, some of them with fluted walls that look as if they have been carved by a sculptor. The great Italian climber Reinhold Messner, who has climbed Everest three times—once without oxygen—has stated that this wall is not for climbers of this century—maybe the next. It towers some ten thousand feet above the valley and is absolutely sheer and swept with avalanches. It is beautiful to look at from the safety of the grassy valley.

We get to Chukung—a small summer village at 15,500 feet—in midafternoon. Jaccoux announces that tomorrow we will split into two groups. There will be a climbing group which he and Abert will lead that will try Island Peak, a

20,000-foot, fairly difficult "trekker's peak." The other group will be a hiking group that can try a nearby ridge at 16,500 feet. I announce that I am planning to constitute a third group. I have been walking for nine days, without a rest day, at high altitude, and I am taking tomorrow off. Jaccoux makes some slightly disparaging sound but I have made up my mind.

Sunday, November 6: Chukung

A delightful day. I have a late breakfast in the sun and watch the ridge group go off. Our Sherpanis are doing their laundry and I decide to wash a couple of shirts in a nearby stream. I hang them on my tent to dry. When I look at them an hour later they are frozen stiff. At noon Jaccoux and Abert go off for the base camp of Island Peak. They have found three takers from our group plus the faithful Tashi, who is carrying the expedition tent. They disappear up a melancholy-looking ridge. I read and think and watch the snow blow off the summits of the great mountains until the sun sets. A big dinner, a glass of the expeditionary cognac, and early to bed.

Monday, November 7: Dingpoche

We are on our way out. It will take a few days to get to Namche and Lukla but that is our general direction. The first stop is Dingpoche, a large Sherpa village about a thousand feet lower than Chukung. Here we will regroup. When we leave Chukung the Island Peak people have not yet come back. It is an easy downhill walk to Dingpoche and we get there in the afternoon. The Sherpas have set up camp at the lower end of the village. Across the way there is a local restaurant—a pleasant, somewhat primitive place, in which the cooking is done inside over an open fire. The large room, which is also the restaurant, is full of Sherpas and the odd trekker drinking beer or the cognac-like local liquor *rakshi*. It has gotten very cold outside and it is nice to be in here. We order some potatoes which are fried in yak butter and taste fine. Near the fire is the dried carcass of some unidentified animal. From time to time the Sherpani who is doing the cooking cuts off a piece and cooks it. I think I will pass on that one. After the potatoes we wander back to camp. Our *sirdar* is there and since he has nothing else to do I decide to ask him a question about Sherpas that has been exercising me. I have never seen a Sherpa wearing eyeglasses—apart from glacier goggles. I had asked our ophthalmologist doctor about this and she said that she had noticed it also. Her conjecture was that the nearsighted ones fall down a cliff as children and are thereby weeded out of the population. Since the life expectancy is in the early fifties, the farsighted ones never need corrective glasses, and besides, the population hardly reads anyway. I ask the *sirdar*. This takes some doing since his English is not very good and, for a while, he thinks I am complaining about my own glasses, which I wear all the time. When we succeed in communicating he laughs and says Sherpas only need glasses "if some snow coming." As far as he is concerned this settles the matter.

The first of the Island Peak group to come down is Abert. He says only Jaccoux got to the top and that no one else got very far. Pretty soon Jaccoux comes along and says that they had a cold and miserable night at base camp. It appears as if Tashi performed heroically getting water for everyone. Jaccoux says the final summit wall was quite steep and that it was loose snow over ice—a rather dangerous business. Pretty soon everyone else comes along and we have a huge dinner to celebrate. In the middle of it a runner comes up from Periche with a note for Jaccoux. The woman with the thyroid condition is in the hospital at Periche and will be there for several days. From the note it is not clear what happened but Jaccoux and our doctor will head to Periche the first thing next morning.

Tuesday, November 9: Thyangboche

We have had a bad night. A yak has been loose near our tents and it was so cold no one felt like getting out of their sleeping bags and chasing it away. It snorted around the tents all night, making it all but impossible to stay asleep. In 1967 a yak actually carried away part of my tent while I was sleeping in it. I awoke when I noticed that snow was falling on my face. The yak had made off with the top of the tent, leaving the platform. The Sherpas managed to round up the yak and the tent, all of which they found terribly funny, and I guess it was—if it wasn't *your* tent. This morning the Sherpanis, who always come to the tents with morning tea, got us up at six. There is no apparent reason to be up this early. There is no sun and it is so cold that one has to eat breakfast with one's heavy gloves on. The group looks a little beat. It is time to be getting down.

We are now back on the standard trekking route. The lower we get the lusher the scenery becomes. It is as if life flows back into everything. It is odd to feel this way since we are still above twelve thousand feet but here, a couple of thousand feet can transform the vegetation. We stop at a small village for lunch. While we are sitting there a couple of trekkers dressed as if they have just stepped out of the L. L. Bean catalog come up and demand lunch in a hurry. They are a day out of Namche—going up. A couple of nights at fifteen thousand feet will calm them down. Jaccoux appears with our doctor. It turns out that the woman in the Periche hospital had phlebitis, a blood clot in her leg, probably altitude-related. This is a life-threatening condition, if it is not treated. It is very likely that the hospital in Periche saved her life. She is now out of danger and will be helicoptered back to Kathmandu as soon as a helicopter can be flown up to Periche which, I gather, can take forty-eight hours (and costs several thousand dollars). Jaccoux, like many people who organize difficult trips to out-of-the-way places, insists that all of his clients have a form of medical insurance that pays for this kind of thing, as well as emergency repatriation. It will pay for her helicopter flight.

Our destination for the day is the monastery at Thyangboche. I read recently that there is a committee that is at work trying to select a new version of the Seven Wonders of the World. If I were on that committee I would vote for Thyangboche. The monastery rests—almost floats—on a kind of mesa at 12,600 feet. The mesa is fringed by fir trees and rhododendrons. The gilded main temple was rebuilt in 1933 after it had been destroyed by an earthquake. This is the spiritual center of the whole Solu-Khumbu region—the religious center for the twenty thousand Sherpas who live there. Its spiritual leader is Nawang Tenzing Zang-Po, the reincarnated *rimpoche*—head lama. He is the same man we met in 1967. Then he blessed the members of our trek by giving us white scarves that he had touched to his forehead. I still have the one he gave me. He has written a small booklet on the monastery. This is what he says about the view:

"To the east is Ama Dablam, to the south Tamserku, to the north Taweche. To the northwest is the mountain god Khumbila, to the northeast Everest. The Emja river flows in the north, Dudh Khosi in the west, a small river in the east, and Nakding river in the south. In the lower areas there is thick forest, in the middle areas the forest is thinner, and in some places there is none at all. In the higher areas there is very thin forest. In summer and spring there are many flowers, and the smell is lovely. Everyone likes this place which is called Tengboche. . . ."

My great fear was that all the trekkers might have ruined the place. I am extremely happy to find that this is not so. In 1967 the only structure that was extraneous to the monastery was a small wooden shed that Hillary had built for trekkers and climbers. We had signed a wall along with every other expedition that had come through. The shed is still there but it is locked up, so I can't go inside and look for our names on the wall. In addition to the shed there is now a handsome trekkers' lodge which was built by a New Zealand group as part of the Sagarmatha National Park. There is very much the sense now that this place is a treasure which must and will be preserved. There are a couple of restaurants that are innocuous enough so as not to spoil anything. In one of them I ask if the *rimpoche* is here at present. I thought I would try to see him. I am told that he is away and, in fact, is engaged in some kind of negotiations to see if there is any way of bringing the Dalai Lama back to Tibet. I am also told that that very evening there is going to be a special service in the monastery connected with the new moon. We decide to go.

The interior of the monastery, where the thirty-five monks live, is open to visitors. The *ghompa*—the monastery building—is three stories high. In the first story is the main temple. Since there is no electricity in the *ghompa* its principal illumination comes from a gas lamp that casts strange shadows. The center of the temple is an open square, and it is surrounded by wooden benches. The exterior benches are for visitors and we are invited to sit on them. Shoes must be removed before entering the sanctuary and since the floor is stone, one's feet soon become extremely cold. Monks move in and out of the room in no apparent order. It is very difficult to understand what is happening. An elderly monk consults a book from time to time and a musician brings out a huge conch shell while another prepares a gong. Some of the younger monks come in and are instructed to take some special hats out of a case. To me the hats look like lunar crescents. The whole ceremony takes at least an hour to prepare. Finally the musicians begin to play and the monks walk around the square carrying various sacred objects, some of which they place on an altar. They also light oil lamps and drink something out of small beakers. I find it very moving but completely incomprehensible. One has the feeling of making some contact with a past that we have all but lost touch with. I cannot decide if this is good or bad. The musicians stop playing. The ceremony is over. We file out and go silently back to our tents.

Wednesday, November 10: Namche

The Sherpanis wake us up at five. This is their last day and they must be eager to get home. A bit later the sound of horns can be heard from the monastery. I think the festival is still going on. As soon as the sun comes up we begin the relatively easy walk to Namche. We have lunch on the way and arrive in midafternoon. I decide to do a little shopping and to try to find my old friends Ila Tsering and Ang Dorje.

Namche is crawling with shops. In some ways it is sort of a mess; too many people crowded into too small a space. I buy a long-sleeved cotton sweater and a few other things since I have about run out of even marginally clean clothes. I then try to locate Ila Tsering. I ask in a shop in which the Sherpani seems to speak good English. English is commercially advantageous here, so many more people seek to speak it than in 1967. I ask about Ila Tsering. She says there is no *I*la Tsering but there is an *U*lla Tsering. Perhaps they are one and the same. This Ulla, according to her, is an "old man." I explain that my friend "Ila" was a *sirdar* and had been a great climber. Yes, yes, her Ulla and my Ila are one and the same but now he is an old man whose business is "some yaks." I make a rapid calculation and conclude that Ila is probably a year or so younger than I am. In any case I get directions to his house. Then I ask about Ang Dorje. She has never heard of Ang Dorje. But she sends a Sherpa to show me the way to Ila's. It is a large house but it seems empty. We find someone who says that Ila has gone to Lukla with a train of yaks to bring in some trekkers. Since we are going to Lukla tomorrow perhaps I will meet him there.

Thursday, November 11: Lukla

Before I begin the long walk to Lukla I take a hot shower—the first in two weeks. It is marvelous. On the way to Lukla I keep trying to spot Ila. I pass several yak trains but there is no one leading them that I recognize. The walk to Lukla takes me about eight hours. When I get there the sun has set. I pass the various stores and in front of the Royal Nepal Airlines office I hear a trekker say that he is number eighty-nine on the waiting list for a flight back to Kathmandu. There are trekkers everywhere. I head for our camp, which is just above the Sherpa Hotel. I have privately decided that if we are stuck in Lukla for several days I will take a room there. I have had enough of tents and cold water. I meet our *sirdar* and he tells me that I must have crossed Ila going the other way. We simply did not recognize each other. Sixteen years is a long time.

That night we had a sort of a feast in which we had roasted goat meat, which was terrible. We gave the Sherpas presents. I gave Tashi a shirt and a pair of down slippers. He was the only one of the Sherpas I had gotten to know at all. We and the Sherpas drank to each other's health and then I spent what I hoped would be my last night for a while in a tent.

Friday, November 12: Airborne

When I woke up clouds had begun to gather over the mountains. The weather is changing. The *sirdar* said, "Some snow Khumbu side." There are four scheduled flights in and out today. Really three scheduled, and ours—the last—a special flight for our group. (The Abert people got out yesterday.) At seven we bring our gear up to the field. The clouds lift and the first flight comes in about eight. Trekkers come and go. I meet an American woman who has been leading trekking groups in Nepal for many years. I ask her how the Sherpas have changed. She told me that the young ones don't know the Sherpa dances anymore. She quoted something someone had said to her: "The Sherpas are going to become part of the modern world. They can't be kept up here in cages like animals in a zoo just to preserve them." That is certainly right, but one only hopes that much of what has been so valuable in that society will be saved.

Two more planes come in bringing more trekkers. Then finally our plane arrives. As it takes off and then gains altitude I can see Everest—the Goddess Mother. A plume of snow is blowing from her summit.

Epilogue

On the nineteenth of January, 1989, the main building and the courtyard of the Thyangboche monastery caught fire and burned to the ground. About eighty percent of the religious artifacts, including the library, were destroyed. The previous April electricity had come to Thyangboche and, it seems, an electric heater was to blame for the fire. Originally, it was thought that the use of hydroelectricity might save firewood. Even this does not seem to have been the case. It is said that, with the electric lights, people stayed up later and used even more wood since the heaters were inadequate. There is now a massive effort to rebuild the monastery. How much of that rebuilding will, one wonders, reflect the inappropriate use of Western technology? Perhaps there is some lesson in that terrible fire.

6

Nepal One More Time

In the fall of 1986 I returned to Nepal to trek with Jaccoux around the Annapurna range; a trek of some two hundred miles lasting about a month. It is one of the most beautiful treks in Nepal and, also, during the fall trekking season, one of the most popular. Air transport is not the problem here since one can, and we did, make the trip to western Nepal by bus. The problem is that there is essentially one circuit here that serves both for the trekkers and all of the local commerce, which is transported on the backs either of animals or of people. I would not be surprised if during the three-month high fall trekking season there are more than ten thousand people who do part, or all, of this circuit. The effect of this on the lives of the Nepalese in this region has been dramatic. On the positive side it certainly has improved the standard of living of the local people. The life expectancy of the average Nepalese is higher by some ten years since I first went there in

1967. Some people might feel that this settles the argument about whether this kind of mass tourism has been good or bad for Nepal. But the tourism has taken its toll in the spiritual lives of the Nepalese. To give some examples that struck me in my 1986 trip:

While I never did succeed in contacting Ila Tsering, I did meet his son in Kathmandu. (Ang Dorje, I learned, had died the year before.) Ila Tsering, as I mentioned in my account of our 1967 trek, had three sons. One, with whom I correspond occasionally, is a premedical student in the United States; a second is a monk in the Thyangboche monastery, and a third, the one I met, is in the trekking business. He told me that he sees the decline of the traditional Sherpa values in his own family. His children do not want to speak Sherpa, since Nepali is the language of Kathmandu, where they live. The only time he likes to go back to Namche is in the summer, when the tourists are gone. It is the monsoon season. Then he and the other Sherpa families get together to sing Sherpa songs.

Speaking of children: in the early years of my visits to Nepal the children were one of the delights. Now they are not, at least on the popular trekking routes. Playful begging for candy and other treats has turned into something else. When one goes through a village there is a chorus of demands for money and, in some cases, these demands become quite rough. One is torn between feeling angry at the children and trying to feel compassionate about the situation. After all, trekkers are *guests* of these people and may well be spending, over the course of a few days, more than an average Nepalese farmer earns in a year. It is little wonder that the children have come to feel almost a right to a part of the riches of these alien visitors.

Then there is the degradation of the environment. One should not be overly romantic about this. I can testify that in 1967, both in the villages and in Kathmandu, there was a manifest lack of hygiene. In the countryside even these traces of civilization disappeared. Now, at least on the popular treks, civilization is everywhere. On the Annapurna trek, for example, I ran across a restaurant serving allegedly Mexican food. The sound of the transistor radio is everywhere.

While I was having these somewhat pessimistic thoughts touring the Annapurnas, I kept running into people, mostly young, who had just returned from Tibet and who told me that traveling in Tibet, as far as they were concerned, was the same kind of pure adventure that traveling in Nepal had been in the early days of tourism. I have had a lifelong interest in Tibet, but with the Chinese occupation, I had given up any idea of going there. In fact I had not realized that in 1985 the Chinese began issuing tourist visas for border crossings into Tibet from Nepal, an enterprise that got underway in earnest in 1986. Suddenly, here were all these people on the trail around Annapurna, fresh back from Tibet. When I returned to Kathmandu I decided to look into the matter. The more I did, the more intrigued I became about the prospects of visiting Tibet. There was, however, a practical problem. How could I possibly swing two trips to this part of the world in a single year—financially and in every other way? I returned to New York.

Then an extraordinary thing happened. In the late fall of 1986 I learned that I had been selected as one of the five winners of the Britannica Award for 1987, an award given out by the *Encyclopaedia Britannica* for the "dissemination of learning"; in my case for writing about science for the general public. Apart from a gold medal and a handsome monetary prize, the award contained a remarkable provision; namely, that the awardee was to give a lecture on any subject of his or her choice anywhere in the world, the expenses to be paid and the arrangements to be made by the *Britannica*. Immediately a wild plan began to emerge in my mind. I would give my lecture at the Tribhuvan University in Kathmandu and use the occasion to go on to Tibet.

My first thought was that the people at the *Britannica* would think that the idea of lecturing in Kathmandu was absolutely mad. On the contrary; nothing could have pleased them more. Here was the dissemination of knowledge on the grand

scale. My second thought was that the officials at the Tribhuvan University would think that the idea of giving a lecture
there on the history of modern cosmology—my putative
subject—was equally mad. On the contrary, nothing could
have pleased *them* more. In fact that very spring there was
going to be a series of celebrations in Kathmandu to com-
memorate the fortieth year of United States–Nepalese relations, and my lecture would fit in with the rest of the events.
Thus it was that in April of 1987 I found myself once again on
my way back to Nepal.

This trip was a very revealing one for me. In the first place I
had never been in the country in the pre-monsoon season.
The leaden humidity and saunalike temperatures, at least
during the day, sap one's energy. I cannot imagine how the
business of the country gets done. In the second place I made
contact with the scientific establishment of Nepal. In 1967 I do
not think there *was* a scientific establishment. I recall suggest-
ing to Dr. Upraity, who was then the vice chancellor of Tribhuvan University, that it might be a nice idea to hold an
international physics conference in Nepal, since so many
physicists climb and hike in the mountains. He told me that
that might be nice sometime in the future, but that, for the
present, there was so little context that he didn't see that the
local people could get anything out of such a conference. I
have the feeling that that future time may be now. (Indeed,
such a conference took place in the spring of 1989.) There is,
for example, an active society of physicists, the Nepal Physical Society, working under very difficult economic conditions
to try to broaden the education of young people in physics
and to make it relevant to the practical problems of the country. They publish a journal and in one of the issues I ran across
an article by Professor S. R. Chalise entitled, "The Growth of
Physics in Nepal." Professor Chalise writes, "We scientists of
a poor country like Nepal, must always bear in mind that all
our knowledge and talent must be directed to improve the lot
of the common man. Science and technology must not be
utilized to make life comfortable for a small minority. It is

therefore very important that scientists take interest in the national issues, be involved in the total development process and direct their activities to those areas which will convince both the policy makers as well as the masses of their utility."

While I was in Kathmandu, an episode occurred which demonstrated, at least to me, how far along this scientific program had come. The incident began when it was alleged that some of the powdered milk sent from Poland to Bangladesh after the Chernobyl nuclear reactor accident had dangerously high levels of radiation. The rumor then spread that this powdered milk had come to Nepal from Bangladesh. This caused a panic. Without powdered milk there simply was not enough milk to meet Nepal's needs. Hence people stopped using milk: a nutritional disaster in a country like Nepal, where over a third of the population simply cannot get enough to eat. In 1982, King Birendra had established the Royal Nepal Academy of Science and Technology (RONAST), of which he is the chancellor. The function of RONAST is to coordinate all of the scientific development within the country. It has the capacity to mobilize scientists in Nepal to address an important matter, such as—in this case—the determination of the radioactive content of milk. This was done. On April 29, 1987, the *Rising Nepal*, Kathmandu's English-language daily newspaper, commented in an editorial:

> The government has done well to take into control all powder milk that has already arrived in the market and it has made clear that the milk will be released only when it is proven in tests that it is wholesome and safe for consumption. In order to conduct tests competently, a high level committee consisting of senior scientists and doctors has been set up by RONAST to ascertain the radioactivity level of milk and other foodstuffs and the panel is expected to submit its report within a week. It is very important that the maximum radioactivity level safe for the Nepalese people be determined; the level appropriate to any other country may not be proper to the Nepalese people and hence the crucial need to independently ascertain the acceptable limits for the Nepalese taking into consideration all

relevant factors. Second, the tests ought to be conducted in such a manner that no misunderstandings may develop among the consuming public. Since tests are conducted to determine the safety level, no compromise of any kind should be entertained and they should be such as to inspire the people.

By the time I left Nepal in May the tests had been carried out and it had been determined that no radioactive milk powder had been imported into Nepal. All of the work was done by the country's indigenous scientists; this in a country that until 1957 did not even have a university.

I gave two lectures while I was in Nepal. The first one, on the history of modern cosmology, the official Britannica Award Lecture, was given in the large lecture hall on the main campus of Tribhuvan University in Kirtipur, just outside Kathmandu. One can see the Himalayan range through the windows of the lecture hall. *Le tout Kathmandu* was there. I was very pleased to see Father Moran, now in his eighties but looking ageless. We discussed how much we both missed Boris. The lecture was a very formal affair with the pomp that is special to elite social functions in that part of the world. I was given three lengthy welcoming speeches and a concluding "few words from the chair" delivered by Dr. Ratna Shumshere J. B. Rana, the vice chancellor of RONAST, who congratulated me on my citations from the Upanishads. An Indian colleague of mine had been kind enough to point out some passages in the scripture that seemed to indicate intimations of the Big Bang cosmology.

The ambience of the second lecture was totally different and more familiar. The physics professors asked if I would give an informal lecture for students and faculty of physics, at the Amrit Science Campus in Kathmandu. This campus is located in the Thamel, the section of Kathmandu where all the mountaineering stores are, in a large nondescript building, on a busy traffic-burdened street. I must have passed this building a hundred times without ever realizing what it was.

The first problem I faced was what to lecture on and at what level. I had been given several issues of the *Journal of the Nepal Physical Society* and had noticed several popular articles on both cosmology and elementary particle physics; my specialties. I finally decided to lecture on something that would be an amplification of one of the articles I had read and to make the level match that of the article. The inside of the building, when I got there the afternoon of my lecture, turned out to be a warren of ancient-looking classrooms and teaching laboratories. I was very moved watching a roomful of young Nepalese boys and girls making measurements designed to reveal some of the properties of light. They were so absorbed, like young science students everywhere, although with a minuscule fraction of the facilities taken for granted in our colleges and even high schools. As I watched them at work and during my lecture I kept thinking of how far the country had come but also how far it had to go.

All of this took place on Thursday afternoon, April 30. On the morning of the first of May, I was on my way to Lhasa.

PART II

Tibet

7

The Past

When Alexandra David-Neel died in her home in Digne, France, on September 8, 1969, she was just six weeks short of her 101st birthday. Her father, Louis David, a French radical journalist, born in 1812, who had been forced into exile in Belgium, had not married until the age of forty. He then married a twenty-year-old Belgian schoolteacher, Alexandrine Borghmans, and their only child, Alexandra, was born sixteen years later. The marriage was not a happy one and, as a child, Alexandra frequently thought of running away from her parents' home. Many years later she wrote, "Ever since I was five years old, a tiny precocious child of Paris, I wished to move out of the narrow limits in which, like all children my age, I was then kept. I craved to go beyond the garden gate, to follow the road that passed it by, and to set out for the Unknown. But, strangely enough, the 'Unknown' fancied by my baby mind always turned out to be a solitary spot where I could sit alone, with no one near, and as the road toward it was closed to me I sought solitude behind any bush, any mound of sand, that I could find in the garden, or wherever else my nurse took me."

She continues, "Later on, I never asked my parents for any gifts except books on travel, maps, and the privilege of being taken abroad during my school holidays. When a girl, I could remain for hours near a railway line, fascinated by the glittering rails and fancying the many lands toward which they led. But again, my imagination did not evoke towns, buildings, gay crowds, or stately pageants; I dreamed of wild hills, immense deserted steppes and impassable landscapes of glaciers."

When Alexandra was five her family moved from Paris to Brussels, where she spent the next fifteen years. She was enrolled in the Bois Fleuri, a Carmelite convent school. In 1889, after a brief sojourn in England, she returned to Brussels and took up the study of voice. Even as a young teenager she had shown signs of vocal ability. Not long afterward she left home for good, moving to Paris, where she found inexpensive lodgings in the Latin Quarter with a local branch of the Theosophical Society. It was at this time in Paris that she found what became her true vocation in the Musée Guimet in Paris, a museum devoted to the Far East. She spent hours in a small reading room, near a statue of the Buddha, poring over books about the Orient. In her early twenties she inherited a small amount of money from a grandmother, which she used to finance her first trip to Asia, a long sea voyage to India and Ceylon. The money spent, and with no prospects of financial aid from her family, she again returned to Paris to earn her living. She was now a gifted, well-trained singer and for a period of several years around the turn of the century she sang both opera and operetta, even traveling to Indochina with a comic opera touring company. In 1900 she found herself in Tunis, where she met her future husband, a distant cousin named Philippe-Francois Neel, a thirty-nine-year-old railway engineer who worked in North Africa. They

were married in 1904 and, although they remained married until his death in 1941, they barely saw each other, let
alone lived together. Nonetheless, Neel regarded "Mouchy"—
her nickname for her husband—as her closest friend and
staunchest supporter.

Almost from her wedding day Alexandra made it clear that
she did not intend to have a conventional marriage. There is
no indication that she and Philippe ever had sexual relations.
A recent biography, *Forbidden Journey*, written by Barbara and
Michael Foster, credits Alexandra with a vivid sex life including premarital relations with Philippe. I remain skeptical. I do
not think the Fosters make a convincing case. While Philippe
continued to support her financially, to some degree, she
began an independent career as a journalist living mostly in
Paris and London, occasionally giving lectures in comparative
literature. Soon after they were married Philippe offered her a
trip back to Asia, but it was not until 1911 that she finally
went. The trip lasted fourteen years. At this time the thirteenth Dalai Lama (the present Dalai Lama is the fourteenth)
had, for political reasons, sought temporary refuge with the
British in India, and Alexandra got the notion that she would
travel to Darjeeling to interview him for a French publication.
As it happened, the thirty-seven-year-old thirteenth Dalai
Lama was a man of considerable sophistication who, unlike
his predecessors, had had a good deal of contact with Europeans. Thus, Alexandra became the first Western woman
ever to be granted a private audience with any Dalai Lama.
This interview, and the circumstances surrounding it, transformed her life. She loved the atmosphere of the Himalayan
frontier towns like Darjeeling, and she met a wide mixture of
people including the first Tibetans she had met. She was
greatly taken by the snow-covered mountains that float above
these towns like some sort of distant promise. The Dalai
Lama was very impressed by her general knowledge of Buddhist doctrine, and his final piece of advice to her was to learn
Tibetan.

About the same time she met, and favorably impressed,

Sidkeong Tulka, the crown prince of Sikkim, who invited her to visit Gangtok, the Sikkimese capital, a several days' horseback ride. The prince was also a lama and the two of them spent hours discussing the nuances of Tibetan Buddhism. After a brief and not very happy sojourn in Benares, she accepted the prince's offer of a small apartment in a monastery near Gangtok. Here she acquired a Tibetan tutor and, at age forty-four, began her study of Tibetan, a language she became fluent in. In 1914, after the death of his father, Sidkeong became the ruler of Sikkim. He gave Alexandra carte blanche to wander as she pleased in his country, accompanied only by an interpreter. She did manage to acquire, as an additional companion, a fifteen-year-old Sikkimese boy, who had entered one of the monasteries as a novice. His name was Yongden and, from 1914 until his death in 1955, he traveled with her constantly. Indeed, in 1925, the uncharacteristically recalcitrant Philippe agreed to sign adoption papers that made Yongden their adopted son. Not long after she had taken on Yongden as part of her retinue, she decided to visit Tibet. By this time the Thirteenth Dalai Lama had returned to Lhasa, the capital city, and Tibet had, as was characteristic of it, once again closed its borders to foreigners. For Alexandra a large part of the appeal of visiting it lay in the fact that for a foreigner, and especially a woman, Tibet was forbidden terrain.

In 1916 Alexandra made her first visit. She, Yongden, and a monk she hired to serve as a guide, all on horseback and accompanied by baggage-laden mules, crossed the Sikkimese border into Tibet, with no permission, and proceeded to the second-largest city in the country, Shigatse, some five hundred miles southwest of Lhasa. Then, as now, Shigatse was the seat of the Tashi, or Panchen, Lama. In the Tibetan hierarchy, at least until the Chinese occupied the country in 1959, the Dalai Lama was the supreme secular as well as religious authority, while the Panchen Lama was meant to be its spiritual symbol. Traditionally he presided over the monastery of Tashilhunpo near Shigatse; "a mass of white buildings," wrote Neel, "crowned with golden roofs that reflected the last dim rays of the sun." The Panchen Lama, as well as his mother, received Alexandra most cordially and after hours of talk with him she was awarded the red robe of a graduate lama; a considerable honor. Afterward she decided to return to India, where she received the unpleasant news that she was being fined and expelled from the country for having illegally crossed the border into Tibet. This made her all the more determined to visit Lhasa, but now the only route open to her was through China. In 1917 she arrived in Beijing with Yongden and set out on a seven-month, two-thousand-mile journey to the Kumbum monastery in Mongolia, where she and Yongden spent the next three years. She then began a series of nomadic trips along the frontiers of Tibet until in 1923, at the age of fifty-five, she began the adventure of her life, a journey to Lhasa.

Alexandra Neel's great travel book, *My Journey to Lhasa*, was written in English despite the fact that her mother tongue was French, and published in the United States first in 1927 by Harper and Brothers. This must certainly have reflected the favorable royalty terms which she extracted from an American, as opposed to a European, publisher. In a biographical sketch in the book *On Top of the World*, about women explorers in Tibet, Luree Miller reports that after Neel had passed her hundredth birthday, her English publisher, John Robinson, paid her a visit in her home in France. Miller writes, "He expected to find a wise old woman meditating and preparing for her death. Instead he found a canny bargainer familiar with every clause and percentage of her contracts. She wanted to negotiate with him to forego the royalties on the translations of her books and get instead a big advance immediately." And this when she was *a hundred!*

Photographs of her in her late eighties show her as a formidable white-haired lady. An earlier photo taken during her stay in Tibet and entitled, *Madame Alexandra David-Neel as the guest of the Tashi Lama's mother at the private dwelling of the Tashi Lama in the Tashilhumpo's Monastery,* shows Alexandra in a robe and a Tibetan hat, with what appear to be wings on it, towering over the Tashi Lama's mother and staring at the camera with grim determination. Another entitled, *Madame Alexandra David-Neel with two Tibetan ladies*, shows her again robed but wearing an enormous Tibetan good-luck necklace. The "ladies" are wearing costumes that pale by comparison. My favorite shows Alexandra and Yongden in robes, Yongden wearing eyeglasses—rare in that part of the world—with a pleasant, intelligent-looking face, while Alexandra reveals the trace of a smile.

Her 1923–1924 trip to Lhasa with Yongden all but defies comprehension. Their route, a giant looping detour away from the direct caravan route from Beijing to Lhasa, began in the Gobi Desert. For seven months they traveled southwest until they reached the Tibetan border in October of 1923. It was here that the *real* trip began. Up to this point there had been no need for disguise, and Alexandra and Yongden had been able to use porters. Now, however, they were proposing to enter Tibet, moving westward toward Lhasa, for which they had no permission. Alexandra's notion was that they should travel away from the trade routes disguised as a pilgrim lama—Yongden—and his Tibetan mother. To this end, she and Yongden

discarded the only pieces of spare clothing we had kept. Nothing was now left us except the clothes we were wearing. We had not even a blanket, although we knew that, during winter, we should have to cross high, snowy ranges, passes of over 18,000 feet. . . . We had only one aluminum pot, which was our kettle, teapot and saucepan, all in one. There was also one lama wooden bowl for Yongden, an aluminum bowl for myself, two spoons, and a Chinese travelling case containing one long knife and chopsticks, which could be hung by the belt. That was all. We did not intend to indulge in refined cooking. Our meals were to be those of the common Tibetan travellers: that is to say, *tsampa* [a barley flour, which is the staple of the Tibetan diet] mixed with buttered tea, or eaten nearly dry, kneaded with butter. When circumstances would allow, we would make soup. Forks were useless with such a diet, and even our two cheap spoons could not be produced freely, as they were of a foreign pattern such as only affluent Tibetans possess. *Arjopas* (pilgrims travelling on foot and often begging their food), as we pretended to be, have none.

Alexandra attempted to disguise herself. She wore a hairpiece made out of jet-black yak hair and, "in order to match that color I rubbed a wet stick of Chinese ink on my own brown hair. I hung large earrings on my ears, and they altered my appearance. Finally I powdered my face with a mixture of cocoa and crushed charcoal to obtain a dark complexion. The 'make-up' was rather strange, but suppliers to the theatrical trade, from whom I could have obtained better ingredients, have not yet opened branches in the Tibetan wilds!" Hidden away beneath her robes, she carried a small compass, some maps, a watch, some gold and silver, and a revolver. Alexandra would certainly have used the latter, if necessary—the Tibetan trade routes were swarming with bandits. On an earlier trip she had not hesitated to break up a fight involving armed men, using a bullwhip. But displaying any of these things would have immediately revealed that she was a *philing*, a foreigner, and that news would very quickly have reached the authorities, who would have thrown her out of the country—or worse.

When possible, Alexandra and Yongden traveled at night to avoid people. Sometimes, to beg food—they were afraid to buy any since they were supposed to be moneyless pilgrims—they were forced to spend the night in villages. This experience gave Alexandra a unique insight into the way common Tibetans live, but it had its drawbacks. As she writes, "In a country where everything is done in public, down to the most intimate personal acts, I was forced to affect peculiar local customs which embarrassed me terribly."

One local custom that she practiced was something she had learned in her years in the monastery. Known as *thumo re-skiang*, it is the apparent ability of Tibetan mystics to control their body temperature through a kind of special meditation, and, in particular, to will themselves into feeling warm. She writes that during one winter, while living at thirteen thousand feet, she deliberately spent five months dressed in nothing but a thin cotton garment practicing the *thumo* discipline. On one bitterly cold night during their trip, Alexandra and Yongden discovered that the flint and steel they used for making fires had gotten wet and was useless. Alexandra sent Yongden to collect twigs and dry yak dung, a common fuel in Tibet, while she put herself into a *thumo* trance with the wet flint and steel next to her body. By the time Yongden returned, she writes, she had dried the fire-lighting materials and had a small fire going. In her book, and in a sequel, *Magic and Mystery in Tibet*, these matters are described straightforwardly with no apologies to the skeptical.

As far as I am concerned, the greatest mystery of all was her ability to travel for hundreds of miles on foot, and in the dead of winter, in this most austere land. Once one sets foot on the Tibetan plateau it is difficult to find anyplace that is much less than 10,000 feet in altitude. Lhasa is at 11,830 feet and Shigatse is at 12,800 feet. Today one can drive in a matter of hours from the Nepalese border, a few thousand feet above sea level, to a 16,000-foot-high plateau from which a vast sweep of the Himalayan range rising to the summit of Mount Everest at 29,108 feet can be seen to the south. Most of Tibet is above 15,000 feet. Winds sweep across the lunar surface of this great plain and, at first sight, one's impression is that nothing can possibly grow there. Nonetheless, great herds of yaks and sheep roam these plains, along with the odd enormous jackrabbit loping along, and one is led to wonder whether these remarkable animals have found a way of metabolizing rocks. It was not difficult to keep unwanted foreigners out of Tibet. All one had to do was to deny them permission to buy food in the widely spaced villages where there was food. In this sere and naked land, in the dead of winter, Alexandra and Yongden marched day after day west toward Lhasa.

The Potala Lhassa. (*Photo courtesy of R.N. Griffith*)

View of Ghanste Fort. (*Photo courtesy of R.N. Griffith*)

Monks outside Jokhang. (*Photo courtesy of R.N. Griffith*)

A Tibetan dentist in Lhasa. (*Photo courtesy of R.N. Griffith*)

A Tibetan family on the road from Lhasa. (*Photo courtesy of R.N. Griffith*)

Monks at the market in Thimpha. (*Photo courtesy of R.N. Griffith*)

The airport in Paro. (*Photo by Jeremy Bernstein*)

Two views of the Tigers Nest monastery. (*Photo by Jeremy Bernstein*)

The Tashichadjong Thimpu. (*Photo by Jeremy Bernstein*)

Everest from Tibet. (*Photo by Jeremy Bernstein*)

To the high camp of Everest from Tibet. (*Photo by Jeremy Bernstein*)

The Bhutanese countryside. (*Photo by Jeremy Bernstein*)

In the late winter of 1924, some four months after they had entered Tibet, they got their first view of the Potala, the fortress-cathedral home of the Dalai Lama, then the administrative nerve center of Tibet. The massive structure set high on a hill above Lhasa seems to float in midair. Alexandra became the first European woman to see it. She wrote, "As we advanced the Potala grew larger and larger. Now we could discern the elegant outlines of its many golden roofs. They glittered in the blue sky, sparks seeming to spring from them their sharp upturned corners, as if the whole castle, the glory of Tibet, had been crowned with flames." She decided that she would continue with her disguise to try to explore Lhasa. As she wrote,

I was in Lhasa. No doubt I could be proud of my victory, but the struggle, with cunning and trickery as weapons, was not yet over. I was in Lhasa and now the problem was to stay there. Although I had endeavoured to reach the Tibetan capital rather because I had been challenged than out of any real desire to visit it, now that I stood on the forbidden ground at the cost of so much hardship and danger, I meant to enjoy myself in all possible ways. I should really have felt ashamed of myself had I been caught, locked up somewhere, and taken back to the border, having only had a superficial and brief glance at the exterior of the palaces and temples. This should not be! No! I would climb to the top of the Potala itself; I would visit the most famous shrines in the vicinity of Lhasa, and I would witness the religious ceremonies, the races, and the pageants of the New Year festival. [The Tibetan new year usually begins in February, although some years it begins in March. Of the vagaries of the Tibetan calendar, more later.] All sights, all things which are Lhasa's own beauty and peculiarity, would have to be seen by the lone woman explorer who had had the nerve to come to them from afar, the first of her sex. It was my well-won reward after the trials on the road and the vexations by which for several years various officials had endeavoured to prevent my wanderings in Tibet. This time I intended that nobody should deprive me of it.

For two months Alexandra and Yongden wandered undetected around Lhasa and its environs. She then decided that she would leave the country, traveling southward into British India. Since the Tibetan authorities had little interest in people *leaving* Lhasa, she left it in style; riding horseback accompanied by Yongden and a servant. In August of 1924 she arrived at the town of Gyantse, then the third-largest in Tibet, and, for reasons I will later explain, the headquarters of a resident British trade agent. The usual trade route from Tibet to India passed through Gyantse. The astonished British Resident, David Macdonald, received her and gave her permission to stay in the mission's rest house. Although Macdonald was disappointed that Alexandra was not more forthcoming with details of her trip—she was saving the better anecdotes for her book—he was gracious enough to provide her with a brief handwritten document:

To all Whom it May Concern

This is to certify that Madame Alexandra David-Neel visited at Gyantse while she came through Lhasa from Eastern Tibet.

D. Macdonald 21/8/24
British Trade Agent
Yatung, Tibet

After a sojourn in Sikkim and India, Alexandra decided to return to France with the intention of resuming—in some sense or other—her marriage with Philippe. However, he balked at the idea of her moving in with him with her vast collection of books on Asia, to say nothing of Yongden, and after a brief reunion in France he returned to Africa. They never made any further attempt to live together, although Philippe generously provided money for her, to say nothing of storing her Tibetan artifacts, until in 1927, with his help, she purchased a house on a hill in the south of France near Digne. She named it Samten Dzong, Tibetan for "Fortress of Meditation," and lived in it, when she was in France, for the rest of her life, sharing it with Yongden until his death in 1955. Her books and articles made her famous, which she enjoyed immensely. She remained tough, lucid and shrewd into her hundredth year. It was typical of her that when she was eighty she made a deal with the community of Digne agreeing to bequeath to Digne the posthumous royalties on her books provided the community would exempt her from taxes for the rest of her life. It was unlikely that anyone expected her to live for another twenty years.

While Alexandra David-Neel was the first Western woman to enter Lhasa, she was not the first Western woman to enter Tibet. Luree Miller's book, *On Top of the World*, describes the exploration of Tibet in the late nineteenth and early twentieth centuries by women. In 1872 Elizabeth Sarah Mazuchelli— "Nina"—the wife of a British army chaplain stationed in India, was carried in a device called a Barielly dandy, a sort of portable armchair, in the general direction of Tibet, followed by her reluctant husband Francis. In *My Journey to Lhasa*, Alexandra makes no mention of her predecessors, including the redoubtable Annie Taylor, who in 1892 became the first European woman to actually enter Tibet. Annie Taylor was an English-born missionary stationed in China. In 1887 she made her way to the Kumbum monastery in Mongolia, the very place where thirty years later Alexandra Neel was to spend three years studying. Taylor presented a large number of biblical text cards, written in Tibetan, to the bemused monks.

During her sojourn at Kumbum, Annie acquired a liking for Tibetans who were studying there, and gradually she conceived a plan to bring the Word to the interior of Tibet— that is, to travel to Lhasa. Like Alexandra Neel, Annie found a young boy, a Tibetan from Lhasa named Pontso, who became her traveling companion for the next twenty years. Luree Miller reports that one evening in March of 1891, while Annie was in Darjeeling, she heard a voice commanding her to go to China: a preliminary to entering Tibet. In time she assembled a group of five Asians, including Pontso, and six horses, and this unlikely caravan set off from Tauchau in China a year later to make a dash to Lhasa. Within days they were beset by robbers who made off with nearly everything, including four of the horses and two of the Asians. Nonetheless she continued on, sleeping in the open. On Christmas Day, 1892, she reported in her diary that she had stumbled on an old campsite with plenty of yak dung for fuel. She writes, "We are resting in our pleasant hiding place. A nice Christmas Day, the sun shining brightly. I had fellowship in spirit with friends all over the world. Quite safe here with Jesus." However, on January 3, 1893, she was arrested and ordered to leave the country by the same route that she had used entering. As it happened, she was then only three days' march from Lhasa. Arguing that if she were forced to repeat her march without an escort she would die on the road, she managed to persuade the authorities to give her ten soldiers to accompany her for eleven days, after which she was on her own. In April she arrived back in China, having made a thirteen-hundred-mile round trip in seven months. Eventually, Annie Taylor settled in Gangtok, the capital of Sikkim, always with an eye to returning to Tibet. But sometime after 1907—the precise date is not known—she returned to England and, historically speaking, vanished.

Besides their extraordinary courage and stamina, these women had in common the notion that they were visiting, or attempting to visit, a proper country, Tibet, with a well-defined boundary and government. The historical chronology of how this came about is made somewhat complicated by the peculiarities of dates in the traditional Tibetan calendar. Tibetans employ a lunar calendar, which would in theory assign to each month $29\frac{1}{2}$ days. Since the solar year is $365\frac{1}{4}$ days, each lunar year—twelve lunar months—is 11 days too short. To make up for this, every three years an additional month is added. However, like wild cards in a poker game, the extra month can be added anywhere in the Tibetan calendar year, the position being determined by an astrological forecast indicating what would be the lucky place to add the new month. Actually, even this is a slight oversimplification. In practice Tibetans round off the lunar month to exactly thirty days, but then they go ahead and add the extra month every three years anyway. To make up the difference, certain days of the month—again decided by the official astrologers—are simply eliminated, or, if some days are thought to be particularly fortunate, they may be doubled. At the end of each year the official astrologer presents the calendar for the following year. Until then, there is no future calendar. The new year begins in February, except in those years that begin following an added month, when the year begins in March. Hence when modern historical writers on Tibet indicate that some event occurred, say, in April of 619 A.D., it gives one pause for thought.

The days of the Tibetan week—seven in number—are named after the sun, the moon, and the five visible planets; Mars, Mercury, Jupiter, Venus, and Saturn. *Sa* is the Tibetan word for "planet" and the seven days are thus named: *Sa Nyima, Sa Da-wa, Sa Mik-mar, Sa Lhak-pa, Sa Phur-bu, Sa Pa-sang* and *Sa Pen-pa*. Until the eleventh century, a twelve-year calendar cycle was used; each year being named after one of the following animals: mouse, ox, tiger, hare, dragon, serpent, horse, sheep, ape, bird, dog, and hog. In the year 1027 A.D.— one hopes the historians have made the correct conversion— the Tibetans began a sixty-year cycle as advocated in the Kalacakra-Tantra, a Sanskrit religious text that was translated into Tibetan that year. To make up the sixty-year cycle, the twelve animals are combined with five elements: wood, fire, earth, iron, and water. Thus the years have colorful names like Fire-Mouse or Iron-Ape. Tibetan historical documents contain phrases like "On the thirteenth day of the eighth month of the Water-Tiger year . . ." One is reminded of what Alfonso X of Castile said when the notion of planetary epicycles was explained to him: "If the Lord Almighty had consulted me before embarking upon the Creation, I should have recommended something simpler."

Assuming that the historians have done the conversion

correctly, the first date in modern Tibetan history is 617 A.D., the year that Songtsen Gampo, who can be regarded as the founder of the modern Tibetan state, was born. Prior to that time there had been a homogeneous race of people with black hair, brown eyes, and brown skin, and often strongly resembling American Indians, who lived in a land that was variously called Bod (by the Tibetans), Bhot (by the Indians), Tobet (by the Mongols), and Tufan (by the Chinese). They practiced a shamanistic religion called Bon, one of whose symbols was a reversed swastika, which can still be found as a decoration on some of the monasteries. They spoke a Tibeto-Burman language with roots in both Chinese and Thai, which had no written counterpart. The country, a collection of fiefdoms, had no national capital. It was apparently not uncommon for the son of a local ruler to take over for his father at age thirteen. (One would imagine that the average lifespan of these people was in the twenties or early thirties. As late as the 1960s the average lifespan of the Sherpas living in similar conditions, and related racially, was about thirty-five.)

Apparently Songtsen Gampo became ruler of his local domain at thirteen. He must have been a remarkable man. He succeeded in unifying Tibet and established Lhasa as its national capital. He sent one of his ministers, Thon-mi Sambhota, to India to devise a script to use for written Tibetan. A version of Kashmiri Sanskrit was chosen and remains in use. People who try to learn Tibetan say it is difficult to make the oral and written languages correspond; the language is so unphonetic. This surely has to do with the artificial way the written language was grafted onto the spoken one.* Thon-mi

* My own knowledge of Tibetan, meager as it is, has been acquired by reading books such as *A Cultural History of Tibet* by David Snellgrove and Hugh Richardson. I have therefore tried to adopt the spelling of Tibetan words as they are used in this book. To give some notion of what is involved, the letters g,d,b,m,r,s,l, and the apostrophe (') can appear at the beginning of words and are not pronounced. Thus, as an example, the systematization of the Buddhist texts that was done around the fourteenth century which is transliterated into English as *bs Tan-'gyur*, or "translation of the treatises," is pronounced "Tenjur." Alexandra Neel used the spelling *thumo* for

Sam-bhota also brought back Buddhism from India and Nepal and this, eventually, was grafted onto Bon to produce the special form of Tantric Buddhism that is practiced in Tibet.

Songtsen Gampo had at least two wives; one Nepalese and one Chinese. These wives, who have become canonized in the Buddhist tradition as the Green and White Taras, are credited with completing his conversion to Buddhism. The Chinese wife—the White Tara—was, according to Tibetan historians, a sort of war prize. During much of its early history, Tibet more than held its own militarily against its neighbors, including China and Nepal. According to tradition, both wives brought, as part of their marriage dowries, statues of the Buddha, and each was given a newly constructed temple built around her statue. The White Tara's temple was built in Lhasa over a small lake which the Tibetans filled in with logs and earth. This temple, now known as the Jokhang, still stands, having been restored many times, most recently after its desecration in the late 1960s by the Red Guard in the course of China's Cultural Revolution. At this point a visitor to the Jokhang would be hard put to say which of the statues and frescoes are the originals and which are total or partial restorations. Many Tibetans say that the statue given to Songtsen Gampo by the White Tara still stands in its original form. This statue, in the heart of the Jokhang, is the most sacred object of Tibetan Buddhism.

After the death of Songtsen Gampo, his descendants ruled until the end of the ninth century, when Tibet became a chaos of local chiefs and religious leaders, each with his own domain. In the early thirteenth century the Mongols dominated Tibet. The Tibetans, separately or united, were no match for

---

the yogic power to raise one's body temperature. The word is pronounced "tumo." Finally, the ancient name for Tibet, *Bod* is pronounced "Po." In the next life I would like to return as a master of the Tibetan language. In this one I beg the indulgence of readers more knowledgeable than I for inconsistencies in these transliterated spellings.

the Mongols and in 1207 they worked out an arrangement with Genghis Khan according to which they agreed to pay a certain amount of tribute to him in return for being left alone. This agreement was honored until Genghis Khan's death twenty years later, after which the Tibetans stopped paying ransom. In 1240, however, Godan, the grandson of Genghis, amassed an army which invaded Tibet, looting several towns and villages. Then Godan did a very strange thing, as recounted by the Tibetan diplomat and historian Tsepon W. D. Shakabpa in his book *Tibet: A Political History.* Godan decided that he needed instruction in the Buddhist doctrine, and, having learned that the most religiously learned man in Tibet was Kunga Gyaltsen, the abbot of the Sakya monastery in eastern Tibet, he wrote the following remarkable letter, translated and quoted in Mr. Shakabpa's book. It reads:

I, the most powerful and prosperous Prince Godan, wish to inform the Sakya Pandita, Kunga Gyaltsen, that we need a lama to advise my ignorant people on how to conduct themselves morally and spiritually.

I need someone to pray for the welfare of my deceased parents, to whom I am deeply grateful.

I have been pondering this problem for some time, and after much consideration, have decided that you are the only person suitable for the task. As you are the only lama I have chosen, I will not accept any excuse on account of your age or the rigors of the journey.

The Lord Buddha gave his life for all living beings. Would you not therefore, be denying your faith if you tried to avoid this duty of yours? It would, of course, be easy for me to send a large body of troops to bring you here; but in so doing, harm and unhappiness might be brought to many innocent living beings. In the interest of the Buddha's faith and the welfare of all living creatures, I suggest that you come to us immediately.

As a favor to you, I shall be very kind to those monks who are now living on the west side of the sun . . .

This was hardly an offer that the Sakya Pandita was in position to refuse. And so he became the religious tutor to

Godan. As Mr. Shakabpa puts it, "Sakya Pandita instructed Godan in the teachings of the Buddha and even persuaded him to refrain from throwing large numbers of Chinese into the nearby river," a method used by the Mongols to keep down the population. With the Sakya Pandita there began a relationship between the Mongol rulers and certain lamas of Tibet, who were provided protection and patronage as a reward for religious counseling. It was just this relationship that became the foundation of the Tibetan theocratic state. Kublai Khan, Godan's son, provided civil muscle for the theocratic rule of the Sakya Pandita's nephew, Phagpa, and the matter was formalized in the late sixteenth century when Altan Khan created the institution of the Dalai Lama. The great monastery of Tashilhunpo near Shigatse, the second-largest city in Tibet, was founded in 1447 by a monk named Gedun Truppa. It eventually housed three thousand monks. After Gedun Truppa died, his successor, Gedun Gyatso, who was born a year after Gedun Truppa's death, was chosen because he was thought to be Gedun Truppa's reincarnation. The notion of successive religious figures being reincarnations of their predecessor is a tenet of Tibetan Buddhism that appears to have evolved from the Bon belief in divine kingship. The abbots of the important monasteries in Tibet, as well as certain monasteries in Nepal and elsewhere, are taken to be reincarnations.

When Gedun Gyatso died, he, in turn, was succeeded by a reincarnation named Sonam Gyatso. Sonam Gyatso became the religious tutor to Altan Khan and, indeed, converted the khan to Buddhism. Out of gratitude the khan in 1578 conferred the title of Tale (Dalai), Mongolian for "ocean," implying that Sonam Gyatso's knowledge was as deep as the ocean. Since Sonam Gyatso was the third incarnation of Gedun Truppa he became, therefore, the third Dalai Lama. The present Dalai Lama, Tenzin Gyatso, is the fourteenth. When referring to any of his predecessors the present Dalai Lama uses the term, "The previous body."

For the third and fourth Dalai Lamas the title was little more than an honorific. This changed with the revelation of the fifth—the Great Fifth, as he is known—Lozang Gyatso, in 1622. The Mongol ruler then was Gushri Khan, and on the fifth day of the fourth month of the Water-Horse year, corresponding to year 2186 after the death of Buddha, i.e., 1642 A.D., in a ceremony in Shigatse, he conferred the spiritual and temporal power to rule Tibet on the Dalai Lama, who then designated Lhasa as his capital. Three years later, the Great Fifth ordered the beginning of the construction of the Potala, his palace, one of the architectural marvels of the world. (It was rumored to be scheduled for destruction by the Red Guard, but, again according to rumor, was saved by the intervention of Chou En-lai and the regular Chinese army.)

The Potala is really two palaces—the White Palace, completed during the Great Fifth's lifetime, and the Red Palace, completed after his death. The whole structure comprises over a thousand rooms. Its thirteen stories are set on a hill that rises a thousand feet above Lhasa. As Alexandra David-Neel discovered, and as anyone who has visited Lhasa can confirm, it is the first thing one sees as one approaches the city and it is visible everywhere in Lhasa. The remains of eight Dalai Lamas are entombed there in golden stupas, or rounded tombs. The stupa of the Great Fifth rises more than three stories. It is built of sandalwood and covered with over eight thousand pounds of gold.

The Dalai Lama's rule is not hereditary in the usual sense of the term. Dalai Lamas belong to the Gelugpa, or "Yellow Hat" (as opposed to the "Red Hat") Buddhist sect, in which the lamas are celibate. A Dalai Lama can come from any segment of Tibetan society. The present Dalai Lama, who was born in 1935, came, for example, from a peasant family from the Amdo region of Tibet, which is now part of the Chinese province of Tsinghai. The selection process by which the Dalai Lamas are chosen is mysterious. Heinrich Harrer, the Austrian alpinist who was interned by the British just before the Second World War in India, and who escaped by walking into Tibet and later wrote his classic *Seven Years in Tibet*, became a kind of tutor to the present Dalai Lama. He asked the Dalai Lama how he had been discovered. The Dalai Lama himself, Harrer reports, did not remember the event, but he put Harrer in touch with the then commander in chief of the Tibetan army, Dzaza Kunsangtse. Kunsangtse recalled that before the thirteenth Dalai Lama, the present Dalai Lama's predecessor, died in 1933, he gave "intimations" regarding his rebirth. Harrer writes, "After his death, the body sat in state in the Potala in traditional Buddha-posture, looking towards the south. One morning it was noticed that his head was turned to the east. The State Oracle was straightway consulted, and while in his trance the monk Oracle threw a white scarf in the direction of the rising sun. But for two years nothing more definite was indicated."

Since it was recognized that a Dalai Lama, a child, would be unable to govern for many years, the interregnum power was held by a regent appointed by the previous Dalai Lama. In fact, during much of the recent history of Tibet the country was really ruled by the regent. As Hugh M. Richardson (Richardson served for nine years in Lhasa as the head of the British mission until the takeover by the Chinese) points out in his book *Tibet and Its History*, during the one hundred and twenty years between the death of the seventh Dalai Lama in 1757 and the birth of the thirteenth Dalai Lama in 1876, actual authority was held by a Dalai Lama for only seven years. During this period only the eighth Dalai Lama reached maturity—the others dying mysteriously before they could take power from the regent—and the eighth Dalai Lama effectively abdicated to the regent.

It was the responsibility of the regent to locate the reincarnate of the thirteenth Dalai Lama. He went on a pilgrimage to a lake and on its surface, he reported, he saw the vision of a three-storied monastery near which stood, in Harrer's words, "a little Chinese peasant house with carved gables." It is a misconception that the reincarnate must have been born at the instant of the Dalai Lama's death. Indeed, in principle, years may pass. In this case the serious search did not begin until

1937, four years after the death of the thirteenth Dalai Lama. By this time, the matter had become the urgent concern of the entire country, since without a Dalai Lama Tibetans then, as now, felt bereft of divine protection. One of the search parties went to Amdo and there found the house with the carved gables near a three-storied monastery with golden roofs. What happened next is described by Harrer.

"Full of excitement [the search party] dressed themselves in the clothes of their servants. This maneuver is customary during these searches, for persons dressed as high officials attract too much attention and find it hard to get in touch with the people. The servants, dressed in the garments of their masters, were taken to the best rooms while the disguised monks went into the kitchen, where it was likely they would find the children of the house."

Harrer goes on,

> As soon as they entered the house, they felt sure they would find the Holy Child in it, and they waited tensely to see what would happen. And sure enough, a two-year-old boy came running to meet them and seized the skirts of the Lama, who wore around his neck the rosary of the thirteenth Dalai Lama. Unabashed the child cried, "Sera Lama, Sera Lama!" It was already a matter of wonder that the infant recognized a lama in the garb of a servant and that he said that he came from the Monastery of Sera—which was the case. Then the boy grasped the rosary and tugged at it till the Lama gave it to him; thereupon he hung it around his own neck. The noble searchers found it hard not to throw themselves on the ground before the child, as they had no longer any doubt. They had found the Incarnation.

For reasons involving the intricate question of Chinese "suzerainity" over Tibet, which I will discuss later, that part of Amdo region had a Chinese governor whose permission had to be sought before the emigration of the child was allowed. The Chinese governor charged the Tibetan government the equivalent of $92,600, an enormous sum by Tibetan standards, to allow the departure of the child. It was only after he was well within Tibetan territory that it was publicly announced that the fourteenth Dalai Lama had been discovered. The actual coronation of the child as a Dalai Lama with full administrative and religious authority did not take place until 1940. In the meanwhile, the young incarnate had impressed everyone with his intelligence and serene religious vocation. In this sense, he was quite a contrast to the successor of the Great Fifth, the sixth Dalai Lama, who was known as a poet and a womanizer and whose poems are still recited and sung in Tibet.

Alexandra David-Neel notwithstanding, Tibet seems to have attracted few Westerners. Even Marco Polo never visited Tibet. The first known Western visitor was a religious missionary, the Jesuit John Grueber, who arrived in 1661. He was followed by the Capuchins, Father Giuseppe d'Ascoli and François de Tours, who arrived in the capital in 1707. The Capuchins established a mission, which was closed in 1745. They left behind a bell inscribed "Te Deum Laudamus," which hung, for at least two centuries, in the Jokhang palace above the passageway leading to the White Tara's statue of the Buddha. The bell seems to have disappeared. I made a considerable effort to find it when I visited the Jokhang in May of 1987. One of the older monks identified a bell, which indeed looked very different from the other bells hanging in the passageway. Much to the amusement of a line of Tibetans waiting to worship at the statue, I clambered around with a flashlight trying, unsuccessfully, to find the Latin inscription. Heinrich Harrer, in the successor volume to *Seven Years in Tibet, Return to Tibet,* reports that he too made an attempt to find the bell and was told it was locked up with other historical relics. One hopes it is safe.

By the eighteenth century, with the firm implantation in India of the British East India Company—the "United Company of Merchants trading in the East Indies," to give it its full name—it was inevitable that some contact would be made between the Tibetans and the British. This occurred thanks to the Panchen Lama. The institution of the Panchen Lama was established by the fifth Dalai Lama, the Great Fifth. He had a beloved teacher, Lobzang Chokyi Gyaltsen, whom he appointed to be the abbot of the Tashilhunpo monastery near Shigatse. Additionally, he pronounced that this abbot would continue to undergo reincarnation, with the title of Panchen Lama. The Panchen Lamas were meant to occupy themselves with things of the spirit. The Dalai Lama, as both spiritual and temporal leader of the country, could not devote himself fully to spiritual contemplation and study, while the Panchen, free of earthly cares, could. Since the Dalai Lamas after the Great Fifth rarely ruled the country, the Panchen became a second (or third, if one counts the regent) center of political power. The Panchen often became, and still is, a tool of the Chinese in their attempts to reduce the authority of the Dalai Lama and widen their influence in Tibet. Indeed, the most recent Panchen Lama, who died in 1989, lived in Beijing and visited Tibet from time to time. Some Tibetans regarded him as a Quisling who sold out his country to the Chinese, while others gave him credit for engineering whatever occasional liberalization there has been in Tibet since the occupation.

On March 29, 1774, Warren Hastings, the governor general of Bengal, received a remarkable letter from the Panchen Lama. Hastings had just sent a small army in pursuit of some Bhutanese who had attempted to unseat the raja of Cooch Behar in Bengal. Having discharged its duty, the army had continued moving northward into the Bhutanese hills close to the Tibetan border. At that point the Panchen Lama wrote,

Having been informed by travellers from your quarter of your exalted fame and reputation, my heart, like the blossom of spring, abounds with gaiety, gladness, and joy; praise that the star of your fortune is in its ascension; praise that happiness and ease are the surrounding attendants of myself and family. Neither to molest nor persecute is my aim; it is even characteristic of my sect to deprive ourselves of the necessary refreshment of sleep, should an injury be done to a single individual.

But in justice and humanity I am informed you far surpass us. May you ever adorn the seat of justice and power, that mankind under the shadow of your bosom, enjoy the blessings of happiness and ease.

Contrast this with the Panchen's remarks about the ruler of Bhutan, one Deb Juhur. "As he is of a rude and ignorant race (Past times are not destitute of instances of the like misconduct, which his own avarice tempted him to commit.) it is not unlikely that he has now renewed those instances; and the ravages and plunder which he may have committed of the skirts of the Bengal and Bahar provinces have given you provocation to send your vindictive army against him."

Cutting through the rest of the rhetoric, it is clear that the Bhutanese had been thoroughly alarmed by the use of British power and had appealed to the Tibetans to use their diplomacy to bring an end to the hostilities before they got out of hand. This served the Tibetan interest, since it established a dependency on the part of Bhutan and it also kept the British army out of Tibet. However, to Governor General Hastings, the Panchen's unexpected letter seemed a wonderful opportunity both to expand trade into new terrain and to learn about a remote and hitherto unknown country, Tibet. Indeed, it had been thought for some time that Tibet might prove a useful route to China. There now came into the scene one of those wonderful figures who make reading about the history of this part of the world such a delight, namely George Bogle.

Bogle was born in Scotland in 1746 and, at age twenty-three, went to India where he joined the British East India Company. Bogle seems to have made a favorable impression on everyone he came in contact with, including Hastings, who assigned to him the task of traveling to Tibet to open diplomatic relations with the Panchen Lama. Bogle was just twenty-eight when his expedition set off for Shigatse on the thirteenth of May, 1774. Bogle's account of the expedition, along with a biography of Bogle and other items, can be found in a book called *Narratives of the Mission of George Bogle to Tibet,* edited by Clements R. Markham and published in 1879. The book is now a collector's item, but I had the good fortune of coming across a copy in a private library in Kathmandu. All the quotations are from that edition. In particular, Mr. Markham reproduces the *private* commission Bogle received from Hastings, which shows the extent of Hastings's fascination with Tibet. He asked Bogle to do the following:

1. To send one or more pair of the animals called tus, which produce the shawl wool. If by a dooley, chairs, or any other contrivance they can be secured from the fatigues and hazards of the way, the expense is to be no objection.
2. To send one or more pair of the cattle [yaks] which bear what are called cowtails.
3. To send me carefully packed some fresh ripe walnuts for seed, or an entire plant, if it can be transported; and any other curious or valuable seeds or plants, the rhubarb and gensing especially.
4. Any curiosities, whether natural productions, manufactured paintings, or what else may be acceptable to persons of taste in England. Animals only that may be useful, unless any that may be remarkably curious.
5. In your inquiries concerning the people, the form of their government, and the mode of collecting their revenue, are points principally meriting your attention.
6. To keep a diary, inserting whatever passes before your observation which shall be characteristic of the people, the country, the climate, or the road, their manners, customs, buildings, cookery, etc., or interesting to the trade of this country, carrying with you a pencil and a pocket-book for the purpose of minuting short notes of every fact or remark as it occurs, and putting them in order at your leisure, while they are fresh in your memory.
7. To inquire what countries lie between Lhasa and Siberia, and what communication there is between them. The same with regard to China and Kashmir.
8. To ascertain the value of their trade with Bengal by their gold and silver coins, and to send me samples of both.

9. Every nation excels others in some particular art or science. To find out this excellence of the Bhutanese.
10. To inform yourself of the course and navigation of the Brahmaputra River, and of the state of the countries through which it runs.

Bogle, it appears, took to heart Hastings's injunction to take a notebook and his *Narratives* are the result. As a few entries will show, they are a delight.

Of polyandry, then widely practiced, he notes: "The elder brother marries a woman, and she becomes the wife of the whole family. They club together in matrimony as merchants do in trade. Nor is this joint concern often productive of jealousy among the partners. They are little addicted to jealousy. Disputes indeed, sometimes arise about the children of the marriage; but they are settled either by a comparison of the features of the child with those of its several fathers, or left to the determination of the mother."

Of the oracles he notes, "The Tibetans have great faith in fortune telling, which indeed seems to be common to all mankind, except our European philosophers, who are too wise to believe in anything."

He marveled, as has every traveler to Tibet, at the forbearance of the Tibetan people. "They have none of the markets, fairs, churches, and weddings of England; they have none of the skipping and dancing of France; they have none of the devotion of the lower people in other Roman Catholic countries; they have none of the bathings, bracelets, etc., of the Bengali; and yet I know not how it comes to pass, but they seem to bear it all without murmuring." It is clear from this entry that despite Bogle's keen sense of observation, the role of religion in Tibet was beyond him. Indeed, as he writes, "The religion of the Lamas is somehow connected with that of the Hindus, though I will not pretend to say how."

Nevertheless, Bogle got on famously with the Panchen Lama and his family. This seems to have led to one of the most remarkable elements in the whole episode. It would appear that, while in Shigatse, Bogle *married* one of the Panchen Lama's sisters. I say, "it would appear," because one can search the entire 1879 edition of the *Narratives* in vain to find any reference to this singular event. The source is Richardson's book, *Tibet and Its History,* which states, "In 1775 [Bogle] reached Tashilunpo and, before long, had won the friendship of the Third Panchen Lama and had cultivated a close intimacy with his family. He married a Tibetan lady, described [by whom Richardson does not say] as a sister of the Panchen Lama, by whom he had two daughters. The girls were later educated at Bogle's ancestral home in Lanarkshire and there each married a Scottish husband. All reference to Bogle's Tibetan wife seems to have been suppressed when his papers were edited for publication; but his descendants, of whom several survive in Britain, now look back to that ancestry with pride." Bogle, whose career seemed so promising, died of a fever in Bengal in 1781. He was only thirty-four.

It is in Bogle's *Narratives* that we also find the first intimation of the "Great Game," an expression that seems to have first appeared in print in Kay's *History of the War in Afghanistan* (1843), referring to the sometimes clandestine and sometimes overt power struggle among the Russians, the British, and, at least in Tibet, the Chinese, for the right to have the dominant influence in Central Asia. Bogle first ran across it when he tried to get permission to visit Lhasa. The Panchen was willing, but he did not have the authority to issue such a permission. The Dalai Lama had not reached his majority so the nominal head of the country was the regent. But it was Bogle's impression that the regent could do nothing without the permission of the emperor of China's representatives in Lhasa, the so-called Ambans, usually two in number. Bogle writes, "Two Chinese viceroys, with a guard of a thousand soldiers, are stationed at Lhasa, and are changed every three years. The Emperor of China is acknowledged as the sovereign of the country; the appointment to the first offices in the state is made by his order, and, in all measures of consequence, reference is first had to the Court of Peking; but the internal government of the country is committed entirely to natives; the Chinese in general are confined to the capital, no tribute is exacted, and the people of Tibet, except at Lhasa, hardly feel the weight of a foreign yoke."

The early eighteenth century had been a period of civil unrest in Tibet, and in 1720 the Manchu emperor K'ang Hsi had sent a strong force to Lhasa to restore order. It was he who created the institution of the Ambans. From that time, until the full Chinese takeover in 1959, the issue of Tibetan independence from China, or lack of it, was a constant source of irritation between the two countries. Compounding the situation was Tibet's sometimes stormy relationship with its southern neighbor, Nepal. In the eighteenth century, after the Gurkha kings succeeded in unifying Nepal by force, they turned their attention northward, and invaded Tibet. In 1788 they were met by a mixed Tibetan and Chinese army, and finally defeated in 1792. The fact that Chinese soldiers had helped to defeat the Gurkhas became one of the principal arguments of the Chinese that Tibet was not an independent country. Indeed, as Bogle noted, all the foreign affairs of Tibet were then decided by the Ambans. In particular, they concluded that the British might have had a hand in the Gurkha invasion and they decided to seal off Tibet from foreign influence. In return, the Chinese would defend the country if and when it was invaded. This "patron-lama" relationship remained viable so long as the Chinese had the power to fulfill their side of the equation.

But in 1854 the Gurkhas again invaded Tibet in force, and this time the Chinese were unable to come to the aid of the Tibetans. The Tibetans were forced to conclude a humiliating treaty with the Nepalese in 1856, the second clause of which indicates that the Nepalese had decided to take over the role of the Chinese. It reads, "The States of Gorkha and Tibet have both respected the Emperor of China up to the present time. The country of Tibet is merely the shrine or place of worship of the Lama, for which reason the Gorkha Government will in future give all assistance that may be in its power to the Government of Tibet, if the troops of any other 'Raja' invade that country." Treaty or no, the Nepalese did not lift a finger when in 1903 Tibet was invaded by the British, and indeed, the invading force consisted largely of mercenary Gurkhas.

In the half century between these two events Tibet acquired its reputation as a land of mystery. The only systematic exploration of the country was made clandestinely by a group of Indians in the employ of the Survey of India. These spies became known collectively as the Pundits, and the first of them, Nain Singh, entered Tibet in 1866. Their job was to map the country. They used a variety of methods to keep track of the miles. Nain Singh, for example, had a rosary which looked like the traditional Tibetan rosary with its 108 beads, except that in Singh's case the number had been rounded off to an even hundred, which he used to count off distances. Others used such devices as compasses hidden in prayer wheels. The Pundits got as far as Lhasa, where their glimpses of the Tibetan capital seemed to add to its intrigue.

The fullest, and certainly the most savorous, account of the 1903 British invasion is to be found in Peter Fleming's book *Bayonets to Lhasa*. The key player in his inning of the Great Game was Lord Curzon, the man who in 1899 became the Viceroy of India. As Fleming points out, Curzon's attitudes, if not formed on the playing fields of Eton, were formed in its debating society. As a schoolboy he participated in a debate on the question, "Are we justified in regarding with equanimity the advance of Russia towards our Indian frontier?" in the debating society's minute book he summarized his position, namely that "The policy of Russia was a most ambitious and aggressive one. It dated its origin from the time of Peter the Great by whom the scheme or conquest had been first made. He did not imagine for a moment that the Russians would actually invade India, and were they to do so, we need have no fear for the result; but . . . a great question of diplomacy might arise in Europe in which the interests of England were opposed to those of Russia. It might then suit Russia to send out an army to watch our Indian frontier. In such a case as this England's right hand would obviously be tied back." The notion that the sinister hand of Russia could be perceived constantly at work in Tibet, and elsewhere on India's northern frontier, formed an important part of Curzon's thinking throughout his tenure in India.

Friction between the British and the Tibetans was caused by the poorly demarcated frontier between Sikkim and Tibet. Indeed, the Tibetans did not accept that the British had any right to sovereignty over Sikkim. Curzon attempted to communicate with the thirteenth Dalai Lama by letter on these matters and, much to his exasperation, the letters came back with every indication that they had never been read, at least by the Dalai Lama. One can only wonder what the history of this part of the world would have been like if the Dalai Lama had humored the British by entering into a correspondence over a remote boundary in a region that was frequented only by the occasional yak herder. Curzon's anger at what he regarded as both a personal and official slight was compounded by the matter of Aharamba-Agyan-Dorjieff, a Russian monk of Mongolian origin, who had somehow gotten himself into the good graces of the Dalai Lama and became a sort of representative of the Tibetan authorities in St. Petersburg—to what end, if any, was never entirely clear. As far as Curzon was concerned, the comings and goings of Dorjieff were proof that the Russians were expanding their influence into Tibet. Curzon was now looking for an excuse to send an armed mission into Tibet and he soon found one.

In November 1903, some Nepalese yak herders wandered into Tibetan territory and were confronted by a party of armed Tibetans who proceeded to scare off the yaks with rattles. This inspired Curzon to send the following telegram to his superiors in London: "*Tibetan Affairs.* An overt act of hostility has taken place. Tibetan troops having, as we are now informed, attacked Nepalese yaks on the frontier and carried off many of them." This in turn inspired the Home Office to issue the following directive.

In view of the recent conduct of the Tibetans, His Majesty's
Government feel that it would be impossible not to take action,
and they accordingly sanction the advance of the Mission to
Gyantse. They are, however, clearly of the opinion that this step
should not be allowed to lead to occupation or to permanent
intervention in Tibetan affairs in any form. The advance should
be made for the sole purpose of obtaining satisfaction, and as
soon as reparation is obtained a withdrawal should be effected.
While His Majesty's Government consider the proposed action
to be necessary, they are not prepared to establish a permanent
mission in Tibet, and the question of enforcing trade facilities
in that country must be considered in the light of the decision
conveyed in this telegram.

Fleming comments, "Although it laid down firmly what the
Government of India was *not* to do, this directive was both
vague and inconsequent in its more positive aspects. What
was meant by 'obtaining satisfaction' and 'obtaining reparation'? What was meant by 'enforcing trade facilities'? Taken
literally, these expressions seemed to imply that a diplomatic
mission with a specific purpose was now regarded in London
as a punitive expedition with undefined objectives."

In the event, the man chosen by Curzon to lead this ambig-
uously construed expedition was Francis Edward Younghusband. Younghusband, who was born in 1863, had the Indian
subcontinent and Central Asia in his bones. He, his father,
four uncles, and two brothers were all to serve in the Indian
army. But Younghusband was an explorer as well as a soldier,
and by 1893, when he was stationed as Political Officer in
Chitral, on the northwest frontier between what was then
India and Afghanistan, he had made several fantastic overland trips to Central Asia. While in Chitral he had met
Curzon, who was also a great traveler. Additionally, he encountered and favorably impressed the Honorable Charles
Granville Bruce—known as Bruiser—a Gurkha officer, who
got the notion of teaching mountain warfare to the Gurkhas,
something that was to come in useful in Tibet. Bruce and
Younghusband found that they had a common interest in

mountain climbing and, indeed, they teamed up to climb the Ispero Zorn near Chitral. They also discussed the possibility of climbing Mount Everest, at least in the abstract. Nothing came of this notion for some thirty years. After his service in Chitral, Younghusband's career, which alternated between journalism and diplomacy, never really got anywhere until 1903, when a telegram from Curzon summoned him to Simla to organize the mission to Tibet.

The Younghusband mission was a mismatch; the feudal and antique Tibetans wanted only to be left alone, while the full weight of the British Empire, with all its ambiguous goals and motivations, stood behind Younghusband. The unfairness of it seems to have impressed the British public. Fleming reproduces a cartoon from the November 25, 1903, edition of *Punch* that shows a fully armed British lion confronting a goatlike animal dressed in a headpiece. The caption reads:

Forced Favours

THE GRAND LAMA OF TIBET. "Now, then, what's your business?"
BRITISH LION. "I've come to bring you the blessings of free trade."
THE GRAND LAMA. "I'm a protectionist. Don't want 'em."
BRITISH LION. "Well, you've got to have 'em!"

Fleming also reproduces a paragraph taken from the *Report on the Supply and Transport Arrangements with the Late Tibet Mission Force*. It speaks volumes.

Animals	Number Employed	Casualties
Mules	7,096	910
Bullocks	5,324	910
Camels	6	6
Buffaloes	138	137
Riding Ponies	185	24
Pack Ponies	1,372	899
Nepalese Yaks	2,953	2,922
Tibetan Yaks	1,513	1,192
Ekka Ponies	1,111	277

In addition, the expedition employed some ten thousand porters or coolies, of whom eighty-eight died. The expedition began with about eleven hundred soldiers with weapons, especially Maxim machine guns, which ultimately were the tools of conquest. At the frontier between Sikkim and Tibet, Younghusband encountered the first of many Tibetan emissaries whose messages were all essentially the same; namely that the British should go back to India. Younghusband's invariable answer was that while he had no intention of resorting to force unless attacked, he did have every intention of pressing on into Tibet. The expedition wintered in a village called Tuna and in March 1904 headed for Gyantse via a nearby village called Guru. It was here that the first armed skirmish took place. The Tibetans with their antiquated arms vastly outnumbered the British, and they more or less sat in the middle of the road and refused to budge. The British decided to disarm them. Fleming describes the situation:

> It is, as the world has learnt to its cost since 1904, difficult to disarm by mutual agreement; to disarm men without mutual agreement is possible only when they recognize that they have no alternative but to lay down their weapons. The Tibetan army had no alternative but did not recognize the fact. It had never seen a machine gun before; it understood only dimly how frightful was the menace of the Lee Metfords trained silently on the confined space, roughly an acre in extent, in which it was corralled; and the superstitious peasants in its ranks were sustained by a sort of half-faith in the charms, spells and other mumbo-jumbo which were supposed to render them invulnerable. They were in a death trap, but they did not know it.

The inevitable happened—the hand-to-hand skirmishing turned to slaughter. The Tibetans simply turned their backs and walked slowly to cover while they were mowed down like so many game birds. Nearly half of their original army of fifteen hundred were massacred.

Younghusband sincerely hoped that this lesson would be

absorbed by the Tibetans and that the army could now march on to Lhasa unmolested. What they were to do when they got there was not entirely clear. But in April the mission reached Gyantse, which had been its original authorized destination. The Tibetans were unwilling to discuss any of the diplomatic matters that had exercised the British until the latter left Tibet, which of course the British were unwilling to do. The Tibetans massed what remained of their army on a high pass that blocked the way to Lhasa and, although Younghusband had no authority to go beyond Gyantse, the decision was taken to clear the pass. Before this maneuver could take place the Tibetans made an ill-advised surprise attack on the British positions in Gyantse with the same result as the slaughter at Guru. A general stalemate followed, which lasted until July when a reinforced British column successfully stormed the great fort at Gyantse. The road to Lhasa now lay open. The question of what to demand once the army reached the Tibetan capital now took on considerable urgency.

The debate hinged on whether or not the British should demand from the Tibetans the right to station a British agent permanently in Lhasa. Younghusband categorically favored this, and Curzon agreed. However, by this time the Russians—who it turned out, despite the comings and goings of the mysterious Dorjieff, had never been a factor in Tibet—had begun to be seriously concerned about the British incursion. They had been given general assurances that, barring the unforeseen, the British intended to leave Tibet with no agent in place. These views were relayed to Curzon. In the meanwhile Younghusband and his army had reached Lhasa. The first official person he encountered was the Chinese Amban, Yu-t'ai. Yu-t'ai entered the British camp "preceded by ten unarmed servants clad in lavender-blue, edged and patterned with black velvet. Immediately behind them came forty men-at-arms similarly dressed in cardinal and black, bearing lances, scythe-headed poles, tridents and banners; after them came the secretaries and servants." He thought he could use the British presence in Lhasa to restore Chinese prestige, which at the time was at a low ebb. So he acted as a go-between for the British and Tibetan authorities.

By this time the thirteenth Dalai Lama—the very one who a few years later would be urging Alexandra David-Neel to study Tibetan—had departed Lhasa with Dorjieff for Outer Mongolia, leaving the regent behind to negotiate on his behalf. On the seventh of September, a day that the Tibetan oracles had decided was propitious, a treaty between Tibet and Britain was signed in the Potala. Most of the clauses had to do with trade and were perfectly innocuous. However, to the main treaty Younghusband had attached a separate signed agreement. It gave the British agent at Gyantse the right to visit Lhasa "to consult with high Chinese and Tibetan officials on such commercial matters of importance as he has found impossible to settle at Gyantse." In other words Younghusband had succeeded, or so he thought, in sneaking his agent in through the back door. This did not pass unperceived by Whitehall and, by the following October, Younghusband's career in the foreign service was essentially over, and he had been publicly reprimanded. He was given a sort of sinecure in Kashmir and in 1910 resigned from service with the government of India. He turned his interest to religion, and to the Royal Geographical Society, whose president he became after the First World War. As president of the Royal Geographical Society he helped to advance the cause of climbing Mount Everest. He died in 1942 at the age of seventy-nine.

The aftereffects of the Younghusband mission were complex, and many analysts argue that they determined Tibet's future. Article 9 of the treaty Younghusband signed with the Tibetans stated that "Tibet was to have no dealings of any kind with any Foreign Power without Britain's consent." The Chinese later used this clause, along with the fact that the Amban had acted as a sort of middleman in the negotiations, to argue that Tibet was not an independent country. Both the British and the Tibetans recognized that China had what was termed "suzerainity" over Tibet. This term was never defined in any treaty signed by all parties. Curzon expressed the

British view in a letter written in 1903, "We regard Chinese suzerainity over Tibet as a constitutional fiction—a political affectation which has only been maintained because of its convenience to both parties."

In 1910 the Chinese invaded Tibet. The Dalai Lama, who had returned to Lhasa from Outer Mongolia a few years prior, fled to British India, using the same route that his successor would take in 1959. The Dalai Lama was welcomed in the border town of Yatung by the British trade agent, David Macdonald, who had been with Younghusband in 1904 and who was to welcome Alexandra David-Neel twenty years later. From there he proceeded to Calcutta, where he was graciously received by the Viceroy. Meanwhile the Chinese attempted, as they would again after 1959, to replace the Dalai Lama by the Panchen Lama. Then, as now, the Tibetan people would not accept the change.

In 1911 Sun Yat-sen led the revolution in China which overthrew the Manchu emperor, and the Tibetans successfully rebelled against the Chinese occupation. In 1913 the Dalai Lama returned to Lhasa. He initiated wide-ranging reforms in the feudal land system, which many Tibetans regarded as unfair. In his own way, he attempted to bring Tibet gently into the modern world. (For example, he introduced both postage stamps and paper money to Tibet.) He never forgot his cordial treatment at the hands of the British and, when the Great War broke out in 1914, despite the fact that Tibet was still fighting the Chinese in the east, the Dalai Lama offered a thousand of his best troops to help the British fight the war. The Political Officer of Sikkim responded to the offer, noting that "the British Government was deeply touched and grateful to His Holiness, the Dalai Lama, for his offer to send one thousand Tibetan troops, to support the British Government. Please inform his Holiness that the British Government will seek the support of Tibet whenever the need arises." As Tsepon Shakabpa writes in *Tibet: A Political History,* "The Dalai Lama took the Political Officer's letter at face value and, in spite of his preoccupation with the troubled areas of Kham [an area of Tibet whose inhabitants often rebelled against central authority], kept one thousand of his best troops in readiness for helping Britain 'whenever the need arises.' " When the war ended, the troops were still in Lhasa, waiting to be called.

8

The Present

My interest in Tibet goes back to my childhood. In 1941, when I was eleven, my father gave me the then newly published book *High Conquest* by James Ramsey Ullman. It is a history of mountaineering written in the grandly romantic style that was characteristic of much of the writing about mountain climbing before World War Two. With the drier eyes of middle age, I can see all of its flaws, but to an eleven-year-old, with a vivid imagination, it was wonderful. The tenth chapter is called "Summit of the World: The Fight for Everest." It describes the unsuccessful attempts to climb Everest—all of them from the Tibet side—that had been made prior to the writing of the book. All the expeditions began in the Indian hill town of Darjeeling, then toiled through the jungles of Sikkim, and then upward onto the Tibetan plateau, which is at an average altitude of fifteen thousand feet. Seen by a flying crow the distance is only a hundred miles, but the terrain is so broken up by peaks and gorges that the actual walking distance is three times that. Ullman describes the progress of the first expedition, in 1921, which, like all the rest, was basically British. He writes,

Day after day they pushed northward and westward across as savage country as exists anywhere on the earth's surface— through sandstorms and raging, glacial torrents, across vast boulder-strewn plains and passes 20,000 feet above the sea. At night they camped under the stars or enjoyed the primitive hospitality of Buddhist monasteries and village headmen. Their passports from the Tibetan authorities in Lhasa assured them kindly and courteous treatment, but the announcement of the purpose of their journey elicited only a dubious shaking of heads and a solemn turning of prayer wheels. To those devout and superstitious orientals, Everest was more than a mountain. Chomolungma, they called it—Goddess-Mother-of-the-World. It was sacrilege, they believed, for mere mortals even to approach it.

Then there came a paragraph which stuck with me for decades and, even as a child, gave me the idea of visiting Tibet. Ullman writes,

At last in late June, the expedition arrived at the Great Rongbuk Monastery, where an isolated colony of priests and hermits dwelt, some twenty miles due north of Everest. And from here, at last, they saw their mountain head on, in its titanic majesty—the first white men ever to have a close-up view of the summit of the world. "We paused," wrote Mallory [George Leigh-Mallory, who was to die on the mountain in the expedition of 1924], "in sheer astonishment. The sight of it banished every thought; we asked no questions and made no comment, but simply looked. . . ." At the end of the valley and above the glacier Everest rises, not so much a peak as a prodigious mountain mass. There is no complication for the eye. The highest of the world's mountains, it seems, has to make but a single gesture of magnificence to be the lord of all, vast in unchallenged and isolated supremacy. To the discerning eye other mountains are visible, giants between 23,000 and 26,000 feet high. Not one of their slender heads even reaches their chief's shoulder; beside Everest they escape notice—such is the pre-eminence of the greatest.

Ullman was very good at this sort of thing. What he did not do was to explain how the British—the only foreigners who were able to do so—had gotten permission to enter Tibet at all, let alone to try to climb Everest. This, as we have seen, can be traced to the sequence of events beginning with Young-husband's expedition to Lhasa.

Younghusband had actually been considering the possi-bility of climbing Mount Everest as early as 1893, so it was not surprising that on his return from Lhasa, in 1904, he sent a small reconnaissance party to look at Everest. One of its members, Captain C. G. Rawling, having seen the mountain from a distance of sixty miles, even suggested a possible climbing route on it. Curzon also believed that Everest was climbable and that it should be climbed by an Englishman. He favored tackling the mountain from the Nepalese side (later Mallory, who looked over a ridge onto the Nepalese face, argued that it was unclimbable from that side) and offered to ask the Nepalese authorities for permission. That never came until 1950, when the Rana regime in Nepal was overthrown, and when Tibet was definitively closed. The mountain was in fact first climbed to the summit from the Nepalese side in 1953.

After Curzon left his post as viceroy of India, the British Everest efforts in Tibet were held up for several years because the secretary of state for India, John Morley, decided that any incursions by the British into Tibet would be contrary to a British-Russian understanding concerning the neutrality of that country. Hence he blocked all attempts to get permission to climb Everest from the Tibetans. After the Russian Revolu-tion the British decided that they no longer had an obligation to the Russians to stay out of Tibet and hence the Dalai Lama was approached for permission to mount an expedition to explore the Everest region. The British did not know how to get to the base of the mountain, let alone what the climbing routes might be. In 1921 the first British expedition entered Tibet armed with the following document signed by the regent—the prime minister of Tibet—and addressed to anyone the expeditionary party happened to come across:

> You are to bear in mind that a party of Sahibs are coming to see the Cho-mo-lung-ma mountain and they will evince great friendship towards the Tibetans. On the request of the Great Minister Bell [Charles Bell was the Political Officer in Sikkim who had welcomed the Dalai Lama when he fled Tibet] a passport has been issued requiring you and all officials and subjects of the Tibetan Government to supply transport, e.g., riding ponies, pack animals and coolies as required by the Sahibs, the rates for which should be fixed to mutual satisfaction. Any other assistance that the Sahibs may require either by day or by night, on the march or during halts, should be faithfully given, and their requirements about transport or anything else should be promptly attended to. All the people of the country, wherever the Sahibs may happen to come, should render all necessary assistance in the best possible way, in order to maintain friendly relations between the British and Tibetan Governments.

Mallory was a member of the 1921 expedition. He represented the new generation of Himalayan climbers who began to replace the many British climbers who had been killed or wounded during the war. His letters to his wife and various friends give a vivid description of the Tibet he was discovering. One of them will have familiar overtones to anyone who has traveled in the Tibetan countryside. As he wrote to his wife, ". . . But in the evening light this country can be beautiful, snow mountains and all: the harshness becomes subdued; shadows soften the hillsides; there is a blending of lines and folds until the last light, so that one comes to bless the absolute bareness, feeling that here is a pure beauty of form, a kind of ultimate harmony."

Then he adds, and this also will be only too familiar to the

Tibetan traveler, "Our great enemy, of course, is the wind. On the best of days it is absolutely calm in the early morning, chilly at first and as the sun gets up quite hot. (The sun is always *scorching* and threatens to take one's skin off.) Any time between 10:00 and 12:00, the wind gets up—a dry, dusty unceasing wind, with all the unpleasantness of an east wind at home. Towards evening it becomes very cold, and we have frost at nights. . . . The real problem for comfort now is to get a tent pitched so as to have some shelter when the day's destination is reached."

(A fuller account of these letters and the early Everest expeditions can be found in the fine book on the mountain, *Everest,* written by Walt Unsworth.)

The 1921 party did not try to climb the mountain. But they made a complete exploration of its lower extremities and discovered what the following year became the climbing route via the East Rongbuk Glacier. The leader of that expedition was the very Brigadier General Charles G. "Bruiser" Bruce who had discussed with Younghusband the possibility of climbing Everest in 1893. The 1922 expedition did not climb the mountain to its summit, but they set a new altitude record in climbing—27,235 feet. The 1922 expedition also had the first fatalities on the mountain. Seven porters were killed in an avalanche. The British were back in 1924, and it was on this expedition that Mallory and his protégé Andrew Irvine disappeared, perhaps having climbed the mountain, and perhaps not. The publicity following the deaths of Mallory and Irvine was the ostensible reason that the Dalai Lama withheld permission to climb the mountain for the next nine years.

On the 1924 expedition E. F. Norton reached 28,126 feet, and Mallory and Irvine may have climbed higher. The 1933 expedition reached about the same altitude and, furthermore, as I have noted recovered an old ice ax that could only have belonged to Mallory or Irvine, thus deepening the mystery of where, and how, they disappeared. There were British expeditions in 1935, '36 and '38, but none of them got as high as their predecessors.

In a curious way, the political history of Tibet since the 1920s is reflected in the climbing history of Mount Everest. As I have explained, that the British got permission at all to attempt the mountain from the Tibetan side was due to the close relationship the thirteenth Dalai Lama had with British officials like Charles Bell. That permission to enter Tibet was withheld for the nine years from 1924 to 1933 is also, perversely, related to the same relationship. While the thirteenth Dalai Lama, like his predecessors, was in theory the absolute ruler of Tibet, he had to take into account the attitudes in the monasteries. Before the Chinese occupation of Tibet, it has been estimated, there were between a quarter and a half million people—mostly men—in some six thousand monasteries in a Tibet which had a total population of less than two million people. This was a constituency which a Dalai Lama, himself a product of the monastic system, could not ignore. In addition there was the Tibetan National Assembly, led by the regent, often a man much older than the Dalai Lama, whose views could not be ignored either. These people tended to be very conservative, and this limited the thirteenth Dalai Lama's ability to modernize Tibet. In addition, he was strongly criticized for his close relationship with the British. It was in response to this criticism, and not to the deaths of Mallory and Irvine, that he closed the border to British climbing expeditions until 1933. At that time a far greater concern developed; namely deteriorating relations with China and Nepal, both of whom seemed to have territorial ambitions in Tibet. Against these the British could be a useful counterweight. Hence from 1933 until the Second World War, the British received regular permission to climb Everest despite the thirteenth Dalai Lama's death, at age fifty-eight, in 1933.

The last prewar British expedition was in 1938. If one knew nothing else about modern Tibetan history except that the next climbing expedition to Everest from the Tibetan side, which was in 1960, was Chinese, it would not be difficult to infer what had happened to Tibet between 1938 and 1960. To try to sort out the legalistic aspects of the Chinese occupation of Tibet would be like solving Rubik's cube. It is also sadly irrelevant. Depending on what year one began the argument, one could "prove" that parts of Tibet legally belong to Nepal, and vice-versa, and parts of Tibet belong to China and vice-versa. Be that as it may, it is clear that from 1911 to 1940 Tibet was a de facto independent, self-governing country. In 1914 the British had tried to normalize the situation by calling the so-called "Simla Conference" with China and Tibet. The British representative, Sir Henry McMahon, attempted to resolve the Chinese-Tibetan impasse over territorial claims by introducing the notion of "Inner" and "Outer" Tibet. Outer Tibet was the traditional Tibet, including Lhasa, which was to have been self-governing, subject to the vague constraint of Chinese "suzerainity," while Inner Tibet, which bordered both China and Burma, and was Tibetan in the sense that a substantial Tibetan population lived there, but which had Chinese governors, would continue to have them. The Chinese refused to sign the Simla convention, which left the British and the Tibetans free to negotiate the boundaries. McMahon drew up boundaries—the McMahon Line—which ran along the crest of the Himalayas and separated Tibet from the northeast corner of India. These boundaries were not recognized by the Chinese. Until 1933, the Chinese were kept out of most of Tibet—Outer Tibet—including Lhasa. However, in 1933 the Chinese asked permission to send a delegation to the funeral of the thirteenth Dalai Lama. This permission was granted and the attending Chinese delegation never left. They installed a wireless radio. The British then installed a wireless, over Chinese objections, arguing that if the Chinese would remove *their* wireless the British would do likewise. The wireless remained in place. It was during this period that the British had almost carte blanche permission to try to climb Everest.

If there was one thing the Chinese Nationalists and Communists agreed on, it was the annexation of Tibet. In 1947 Chiang Kai-shek put forth the theory that the Hans, Mongols, Manchus, Tibetans, and Tungans were all parts of a single

Chinese race. This is something that the Chinese Communists would certainly agree to, but they would, of course, add the Taiwanese. During the Second World War, the Tibetans had maintained a posture of neutrality, which was compromised when Chiang Kai-shek attempted to build roads across Tibetan territory despite Tibetan objections. There were troop movements on both sides, but the Chinese, who were heavily engaged in fighting the Japanese, backed off, avoiding an actual confrontation.

It is important to understand, when discussing Tibetan resistance, that there were at least two kinds of armed forces in Tibet. Some of the monasteries had their own armies. Indeed, these constituted the major military force in the country. In addition, the government had its own army, which it was never able to build up since the monasteries did not want to see their military importance diminished. In addition the so-called Khampas—tribal residents of the province of Kham in eastern Tibet—had their own army, if one wants to call it that. Khampas, at least Khampa men, are easily recognized in Lhasa. They wear high boots and their long hair, done up with a swirling flash of red yarn, makes them seem taller than they actually are. They walk with the confident swagger of cowboys in the Old West. They are also a pretty wild bunch, and during much of Tibetan history made their living as bandits preying on caravans of traders. They were never very enthusiastic about the central government in Lhasa, although religiously they were devoted to the Dalai Lama.

The central government, under the Dalai Lamas, was feudal. Tibetan society was divided between serfs and nobles and, in theory, the state owned all the land. Large parcels were given to monasteries and individual landowners and these were worked by the peasantry in return for small parcels of land for personal use. Social mobility came through the monastic orders. The Dalai Lamas, for example, frequently came from peasant stock, as did many of the other religious leaders. It also has to be stated that, in enforcing its mandate, the theocratic state could be brutal. Until the thirteenth Dalai Lama put a stop to it, serious crimes were punished by dismemberment and a traitor to the state could lose his eyes. One of the places in the Potala palace that visitors are not shown is the so-called Cave of Scorpions in which enemies of the state were interned and from which few emerged. Even after the Dalai Lama's mandate against mutilation as a punishment, flogging, which could lead to death, was still practiced. This kind of medieval feudalism led some observers of Tibetan society to feel that the Tibetans would be better off altogether without their central government. For example, Alexandra David-Neel, who, since she was traveling in the disguise of a mendicant pilgrim, probably got to know the ordinary Tibetan of the 1920s as well as any foreign observer, wrote in her book *My Journey to Lhasa*, "Tibetans have lost much in parting with China. Their sham independence profits only a clique of court officials. Most of those who rebelled against the far-off and relaxed Chinese rule regret it nowadays, when taxes, statute labour, and the arrogant plundering of the national soldiery greatly exceed the extortions of their former masters." Alexandra Neel lived, as we have noted, past her hundredth year—until 1969. By this time whatever pretense there had been of "far-off and relaxed Chinese rule" had turned into a nightmare. What Alexandra Neel could not have imagined is that the Chinese would attempt to cut the heart and soul out of Tibetan life by destroying its religion.

On the seventh of October, 1950, the Chinese army, supported by some Khampa irregulars, invaded eastern Tibet, while a second force of Chinese launched an invasion from the west. Since 1947, when the British had granted independence to India, the Indians had taken over the British treaty responsibilities to Tibet, including those of the Simla conference. Hence the Indian government made an appeal to the Chinese to respect the independence of Tibet. They were told, in no uncertain terms, that the invasion of Tibet was a purely internal Chinese matter. On November 11, 1950, Tsepon

Shakabpa—the author of *Tibet: A Political History,* but then an official of the Tibetan government—cabled the following appeal to the United Nations: "The armed invasion of Tibet for the incorporation of Tibet in communist China through sheer physical force is a clear case of aggression. As long as the people of Tibet are compelled by force to become part of China against their will and consent, the present invasion of Tibet will be the grossest instance of the violation of the weak by the strong. We therefore appeal through you to the nations of the world to intercede on our behalf and restrain Chinese aggression."

The government of El Salvador attempted to raise the matter of the invasion of Tibet before the secretary general, but got nowhere. Every major power, including Britain and the United States, supported an adjournment of the question, and it was not debated for the next nine years, by which time there was nothing left to debate. After the appeal to the United Nations failed, the Dalai Lama, then sixteen, and who, although the normal age was eighteen, had been invested with the full powers of his office, was moved from Lhasa to close to the Indian border. (In 1959 he fled to India.) The idea was that so long as the Dalai Lama remained out of Chinese custody there was some chance he could at least exercise a moral influence over the affairs of the country. This is the reason why, despite his personal feelings for his homeland, the Dalai Lama has, so far, refused to return to Tibet. On May 23, 1951, a Tibetan delegation in Beijing signed, under duress, a treaty with the Chinese which, if its provisions had actually been adhered to by the Chinese, might have made the occupation of Tibet bearable. The treaty, a seventeen-point Agreement on Measures for the Peaceful Liberation of Tibet, opens with a prologue that rewrites history. The treaty itself—if it was ever meant seriously—contained several provisions that would have meant the continuation of something like traditional Tibetan life.

It is not clear whether the Chinese ever intended to abide by the agreement. In the beginning, the Tibetans thought so, and the Dalai Lama returned to Lhasa on August 17, 1951. He made an attempt at land reform that was, curiously, opposed by the Chinese. Perhaps this was part of their plan to reduce his authority. Despite a clause in the agreement stating that the central authorities would not alter "the existing political system" in Tibet, the attempt to reduce the Dalai Lama's authority began almost at once. Although, at first, the Chinese took no direct action against the monasteries—that would come later—they made little secret of their contempt for the religious side of Tibetan life, which Mao Tse-tung referred to as a "poison." What transformed the situation was the havoc the Chinese wreaked on the fragile Tibetan economy. As anyone who has ever visited the country can testify, the opportunities for agriculture in Tibet are very limited. While there are over thirty-two million acres of grazing land, there are not much more than a half million acres of arable land. Most of Tibet is a desert with a population of something like one person per square kilometer. While the Tibetan diet, which consisted largely of *tsampa* (barley), often taken in a thick tea—with occasional yak meat—was spartan, there was no starvation in the country. The population and the food resources were in a delicate equilibrium. This was destroyed when the Chinese began moving in thousands of troops and settlers from heartland China—Han Chinese—and taking food resources from the Tibetans to feed them. This was the beginning of widespread starvation in Tibet. In addition, the Chinese began a program of road building—strategic roads to enable rapid movements of troops—and many Tibetans, many of whom lost their lives in the process, were pressed into road construction gangs. Some of the country's gold and silver reserves were "borrowed" by China and shipped out of Tibet. By 1954, much of the road building was completed, and the occupation began in earnest with a shameful Indo-Chinese pact—a pact that no Tibetan was a party to—agreeing that Tibet was an integral part of China, thus removing any paternal constraints, moral or otherwise, on Chinese behavior in Tibet.

By the spring of 1956, in response to ever-tightening Communist control, including the execution of some lamas, armed resistance began in earnest in eastern Tibet. The Khampas, some of whom had fought with the Chinese, now began a campaign of sabotage and guerrilla warfare. As H. M. Richardson points out in his book *Tibet and Its History*, this led to terrible reprisals. He quotes from a report published in 1960 by the International Commission of Jurists: "Eye-witnesses have described how monks and laymen were tortured and many killed, often in barbarous ways [the Dalai Lama, in his book *My Land and My People*, written in 1962, reports that some were 'beaten to death, crucified, burned alive, drowned, vivisected, starved, strangled, hanged, scalded, buried alive, disembowled and beheaded']: women raped and others publicly humiliated; venerated Lamas subjected to brutal and disgusting degradations; other monks and Lamas compelled to break their religious vows; men and boys deported or put to forced labour in harsh conditions; boys and girls taken from their homes, ostensibly for education in China; children incited to abuse and to beat their parents; private property seized; monasteries damaged by gunfire; and sacred images, books and relics carried off or publicly destroyed." All of this incited the Khampas to even fiercer guerrilla activities, and by February of 1957 Mao Tse-tung, Richardson reports, "announced that Tibet was not yet ready for reforms and that their introduction would be postponed for at least five years." All of this only stiffened the Tibetan will to resist, and in the autumn of 1958 the guerrillas wiped out a Chinese garrison with some three thousand men.

Four kilometers west of the Potala Palace there is a park. In this park the seventh Dalai Lama, in 1755, began construction of a summer palace—the Norbu Lingka ("Precious Jewel Island"). Each spring he and subsequent Dalai Lamas were carried in a gilded, curtained palanquin, or rode a mule, from the Potala to the Norbu Lingka. It was a great occasion with a long procession of lamas and nobles as well as a "police" guard of specially chosen, very tall monks armed with long, thin saplings, which they used to clear the crowd from the path of the Dalai Lama. During her illicit visit to Lhasa in 1924, Alexandra David-Neel witnessed that year's parade. She wrote, "At intervals, somebody ran along shouting orders. The arrival of the Dalai Lama was announced. All, women included, had to take their hats off, and those who delayed were soon acquainted with one or another of the lamaist policemen's weapons. Thanks to my short stature, I escaped thumps and thrashings during the hours I stood there. When danger threatened, I always managed to find shelter among a group of tall Tibetans who acted as a protecting roof over my head."

She continues, "The [thirteenth] Dalai Lama passed at last, riding a beautiful black mule, and accompanied by a few ecclesiastical dignitaries, all like himself dressed in religious robes—dark red, yellow, and gold brocades, half covered by the dark red toga. They wore Mongolian round hats of yellow brocade edged with fur. The Commander-in-chief rode before them, while some horse guards clad in khaki led the van and brought up the rear."

In early March of 1959 the fourteenth Dalai Lama made his accustomed pilgrimage to the Norbu Lingka. On the ninth of March he received an invitation from the Chinese commander in Lhasa to come to the Chinese barracks to witness some sort of cultural performance, but to come without his usual escort. Whatever the motive of the Chinese commander, once the people of Lhasa heard about this invitation, they concluded that the Chinese intended to seize the Dalai Lama. During the next few days some thirty thousand people formed in front of the Norbu Lingka to prevent the Chinese from entering it. On the seventeenth of March the Chinese fired two shells into the grounds of the palace, and that night the Dalai Lama left, in secret, for India, and an era of Tibetan history came to an end. For two days neither the Chinese nor the Tibetans surrounding the palace knew the Dalai Lama was gone. During the day of the nineteenth the Chinese began shelling the Norbu Lingka—the shells coming closer and closer to the palace buildings. Then, that evening, it was announced that the Dalai Lama had fled. With this news, the thousands of Tibetans who had been guarding the palace turned their anger on the Chinese garrisons themselves and in the resulting melee several thousand Tibetans were killed or taken prisoner.

With the flight of the Dalai Lama to India, the Chinese established a military government, backed up by as many as a half a million troops. (At present, it has been estimated that there may be as many as three hundred thousand troops and special police units in Tibet, not counting the thousands of troops that are stationed on the southern Tibetan frontier in a continuing confrontation with India over the borders established by McMahon in 1914.) As the Dalai Lama stated in 1959, "Wherever I am, accompanied by my government, the Tibetan people recognize us as the government of Tibet." In this spirit, the matter of Tibet was debated in the United Nations in the fall of 1959. It was one of those surrealistic UN debates that result in a vaporous statement endorsing human rights; this one passed by forty-five votes to nine with twenty-six abstentions. Among the abstainers were India, Nepal, and Great Britain.

For the next three decades the Chinese attempted to destroy the traditional culture of Tibet. In our century there has been so much cultural destruction that one has almost become numb to it. Although it is almost impossible to compare one such act with another, there is, in my view, something especially grotesque about what the Chinese have done in Tibet. The Tibetans were, and are, a basically kindly people, living largely for the rewards, and perhaps the sorrows, of the next life. They were, for better or worse, untouched by most of modern life. There were essentially no radios, no cars, no electricity, and to this day there is no railroad. Some forty-eight percent of the population were nomadic herders living in small self-contained units in black yak-haired tents, which can still be seen dotting the Tibetan countryside. These people had virtually no contact with modern technology at all.

Like most Tibetans they were illiterate. What they wanted most of all was to be left alone to practice their religious life—which, for Tibetans, is everything. The noted Tibetologist Giuseppe Tucci, in his book *Tibet: Land of Snows*, written in 1967—Tucci had been visiting the country regularly since 1927—described the confrontation of this antique way of life with Chinese Communism as well as anyone has. He wrote,

> Deep religiousness, capable of mystical raptures, but pervaded too by a magical *Angst*, and expressed in varying symbols—genial or grotesque, tranquil or obscene, often hard to understand in their apparent strangeness—precisely on account of these contradictions cannot long, I fear, withstand the new ideas forced upon it by foreign domination. The encounter between Marxist rationalism and the Tibetan's ingenuous blend of myth, fantasy and magic brings two entirely different conceptions face to face: an inflexible abstract scheme, all figures and duties, on the one hand, and on the other the fundamental anarchy of invisible presences that control us but which we can dominate, if we know their secret. Facts on the one side; imagination on the other. The life of man confined within time and space, in the service of a community which seeks economic and social betterment at the cost of individual freedom, with the new ideology; affirmation of the personality through its dialogue with the transcendent world of the divine, belittling of the real in comparison with the invisible, transcendence overriding time and space, with the Tibetan spiritual tradition.

He concludes, "Millennia of religious experience, supported by the innate archetypes of the Tibetan spirit, are hard to root out; but the very complications of a great deal of Lamaism, the bizarreness of some of its symbols, cannot long, I think, resist the disenchanted cold-bloodedness of the new principles." What Tucci did not know—which no one outside Tibet really knew—was that by the time these words were written, in 1967, as a manifestation of the Chinese Cultural Revolution, only some ten out of a total of 6,254 monasteries in Tibet had escaped total, or partial, destruction. Among the monasteries that had been totally destroyed was the great Rongbuk Monastery, where the seven prewar British climbing expeditions to Mount Everest had sought and received the blessing of the abbot.

Nineteen sixty-seven was when I first realized my childhood dream of seeing Mount Everest, but from Nepal. Tibet was closed and, indeed, Nepal had banned climbing from 1964 to 1969. The Nepalese were having their own problems with the Chinese, which they did not want aggravated by unauthorized transgressions of the border. In fact, in 1960, the Chinese had claimed all of Mount Everest, extending to the Sherpa community of Namche Bazar. The Nepalese had countered by also claiming all of Mount Everest, extending to the Rongbuk Monastery. The matter was settled in April of 1960 when Chou En-lai came to Kathmandu and agreed that the boundary between Nepal and Tibet would run across the summit of Everest. By 1967, some twenty thousand Tibetan refugees had fled to Nepal, and perhaps five times that many to India. It is a tribute to both of these desperately poor countries that these refugees were welcomed and given whatever facilities were available, to begin new lives. In the trek I made in 1967 from Kathmandu to the base of Everest I encountered newly arrived Tibetan refugees. They would try to sell us even their most precious religious possessions, for money to live on. One of my most striking memories, as I wrote earlier, was going into a small monastery not far from the Everest region and encountering an abbot recently come from Tibet. Before he would talk to me he insisted that I take off my sunglasses. He wanted to look at my eyes to make sure I was not Chinese.

We were allowed to approach within some ten miles of the Tibetan border. We could see what appeared to be distant mountains in Tibet over passes like the Lho La and the Shangri La. In a 1979 trip I actually went to the Tibetan border. I hired a taxi in Kathmandu and took the five-hour drive to the border along what is known as the Chinese Road, the one built by the Chinese and completed in 1967. It is a continuation of the road in Tibet that leads from Lhasa to the frontier.

The taxi was able to go as far as the border check post in Kodari. From there the so-called Friendship Bridge spans the Sun Kosi river (the Po Chu in Tibet) over to Tibet. One could see, on a distant hill, the Tibetan border town of Zhangmu (Khasa, to the Nepalese). By 1979, organized guerrilla activity in Tibet had stopped. From the time the fourteenth Dalai Lama fled to India, in 1959, until the 1972 Kissinger-Nixon visit to China, the Khampas, aided by the CIA, in some murky operations involving CIA agents posing as mountaineers and trekkers, continued to fight the Chinese. One of the conditions the Chinese laid down for diplomatic relations with the United States in 1972 was that we stop aiding the Khampas. At the same time, they put pressure on the Nepalese government to disarm the Khampas who were operating from western Nepal. It finally took the Nepalese army, and a good deal of bloodshed, to disarm them, and with that, organized resistance in Tibet came to an end.

To someone like myself, who had followed both the climbing history of Mount Everest and the political history of Tibet, it was clear that something had happened in Tibet when, in 1980, it was announced that a *Japanese* climber, Yasuo Kato, had climbed Everest from the Tibetan side. By this time Tibet had for some time been an "autonomous region" of China, a status it had had since 1964. It was, however, governed by a Chinese general, Ron Rong. Three years after Mao's death in 1976, General Ron Rong was dismissed in disgrace and replaced by another military man, Yin Fatang. Yin Fatang began something of a program of liberation. Part of this program was the development of tourism in Tibet. The first tourists I encountered who had been to Tibet in the early 1980s had gone there as part of various package tours to China. These tours had begun to include brief flying visits to Lhasa. Chengdu—the capital of Sichuan Province in China, adjacent to eastern Tibet—a city of over a million people, is accessible from all the major cities in China and it is a two-hour flight from Chengdu to the Lhasa airport in Gonggar, some fifty miles from the city. Chengdu is 413 feet above sea level while Lhasa is at an altitude of some twelve thousand feet, which means that the average tourist who arrived in the city in this way, breathless, was probably not in much of a position to do a great deal of sightseeing. As fascinated as I was with Tibet, this kind of visit did not appeal to me at all. I decided that if there was not another way of visiting the country, I was simply not going to go there.

In 1985 there was a dramatic change in the situation. The Chinese announced that they would now issue visas to tourists to cross the border into Tibet from Kodari, the very border town in Nepal I had gone to by taxi in 1979. This opened up the prospect of driving from Kathmandu to Lhasa, and back, with a side trip to the base of Mount Everest, which is, in a manner of speaking, along the way. The road to Lhasa is blocked by snow during the fall and winter—the average altitude is close to fifteen thousand feet—so tourist travel really began in earnest in the spring and summer of 1986. In fact, in April of 1986, an Australian, Michael Buckley, and an Englishman, Robert Strauss, published *Tibet: A Travel Survival Kit*, a delightfully irreverent travel guide written, one gathers, for the young, marginally solvent traveler who is willing to try a bit of anything. Here, for example, is their review of the Tasty Restaurant in Lhasa: "The Tasty Restaurant . . . is a lively place with the usual system where you go into the kitchen to choose ingredients from bowls of scallions, garlic, peanuts, green beans, tinned bamboo slices, eggs, diced yak meat, tinned mushrooms and greens. [Nearly all this, the authors point out, had been trucked from China.] A large meal will cost about Y3. [The yuan is the basic unit of Chinese, and hence Tibetan, money. There are two kinds of money used in China: *Renminbi*, the common street currency and *FEC*, Foreign Exchange Certificates, which, at least theoretically, are the only money that a foreign visitor to Tibet is allowed to use. It is the only money which can be legally exchanged into dollars. The current exchange rate is about thirty three cents per yuan.] The dumplings are good if they are fresh. Tea is brought round to tables."

This sounds promising, but then the authors go on, "The one problem with this place . . . is that you eat your meal amidst what can only be described as a circus. Beggars scrounge the scraps which are scraped into bowls—some of them are obviously pilgrims from remote places who have made it to Lhasa but run out of funds. Kids beg for pens by making a scribbling motion in the palm which becomes obnoxious when thrust between your chopsticks and your face. Meanwhile cripples will hunch over your table intent on swiping an empty beer bottle to get the deposit back, whilst beneath the table, snapping away between your feet, are dogs of all shapes and sizes. Once you've finished though you can have fun watching how the others react under attack." Quite.

The authors also have a section on visiting the Everest region, which, needless to say, caught my eye. I was struck by the fact that, with a suitable four-wheel-drive vehicle, one could drive up to base camp. In fact "base camp" was defined to be, as far as I could make out, the last place one *could* drive to. This, the guidebook noted, was some seven miles closer to the mountain than the old Rongbuk Monastery and was at an altitude of something over seventeen thousand feet. One would still be quite far from the mountain and at this point, the guidebook goes on to say, "From here on, you need proper mountaineering equipment. You would be most unwise to proceed any further unless you're in tip-top shape, have mountaineering experience, and know what you're getting into. Without a guide or a medic you could get into serious trouble, and no one is about to rescue you." Since going beyond base camp was the very thing I had in mind, if I ever managed to get to Tibet, I decided that I had better talk to someone who might tell me how to go about arranging such an expedition.

Over the years, Colonel Roberts's Mountain Travel has become a vast enterprise called Tiger Mountain, since it now also operates jungle trips to Tiger Tops, a lodge in southern Nepal, and nearby wildlife camps. Roberts himself lives in semiretirement in western Nepal, where he raises pheasants.

But still active in the company is my old friend Elizabeth Hawley, whom I first met in 1967 in Nepal, where she had lived since the early 1960s. Elizabeth Hawley is undoubtedly the world's greatest expert on the contemporary history of Himalayan mountaineering. No expedition comes through Kathmandu without talking at least once to Elizabeth, and if they do something spectacular, or get in trouble, she is the one who reports on such matters for much of the world's press. She is also one of the shareholding directors of Tiger Mountain. So when I was in Kathmandu in the fall of 1986, I asked her if there was a way in which I could drive from Kathmandu to Lhasa, visiting as much of the intervening countryside as possible, and trek into the base of Everest from the Tibetan side. In short order she produced a mimeographed itinerary under the Tiger Mountain logo which was entitled "16 Day Lhasa/Everest Base Camp." It was one of a spectrum of trips that Tiger Mountain has been offering to Tibet since the summer of 1986—a spectrum that ranges from fairly simple overland sightseeing tours to fantastic, month-long expeditions which go overland all the way from Kathmandu, through Tibet, finally emerging in the Karakoram range in Pakistan. The sixteen-day Lhasa/Base Camp trip looked perfect for me since it involved some days of camping and trekking in the Everest region as well as several days in Lhasa. With the various side trips in Tibet the whole excursion would cover nearly two thousand miles. The only problem, apart from the cost, which is considerable, was that Tiger Mountain required a minimum of five people to make the trip. I returned to the United States and set about trying to recruit at least one volunteer for the trip while the people in Kathmandu began doing likewise. Our tentative date of departure was to be the first of May, 1987.

During the winter I began receiving various communications from Tiger Mountain. The first one, under the rubric "Preparing for Tibet/China," began, "Tibet is an uncomfortable, remote and hard destination. It also offers glimpses into one of the most fascinating old civilizations and one of the most dramatic mountain lands. It is truly one of the last frontiers for discovery and exploration. All trips are of expeditionary nature but if you travel with an open mind Tibet will be a truly unique and rewarding experience."

Under "Food and Beverages," I came across the following. "Please note that the Chinese meals in Tibet are of a much lower standard than elsewhere in China and often served cold. On the 12 and 15-day Lhasa tours the meals served are generally good except in Xegar but on the treks/expeditions and particularly at the end of long drives expect rough and ready meals. It is advisable to bring items such as cheese, crackers, some favourite canned food, nuts and chocolates. Now that we will have Sherpas for support on 'treks' and most 'expeditions' who will be providing and preparing the food when away from hotels, we are happy that food standards will improve considerably."

The fact that we would have Sherpas was certainly *very* good news. Besides their other virtues they are, as I have mentioned, of Tibetan origin. The Sherpa language, which has no written counterpart, is fundamentally a dialect of Tibetan, and the Sherpas also regard the Dalai Lama as their spiritual leader. For the Sherpas a journey to Lhasa is also a religious pilgrimage. And I had found a recruit; Bil Dunaway. Dunaway is the owner and publisher of the *Aspen Times*, in Aspen, Colorado, and used to own *Climbing* magazine. He has climbed mountains all over the world, has been a downhill ski and automobile racer, and each Saturday, during the past ten summers, we have hiked together in the mountains around Aspen. Dunaway, who is in his early sixties, had, surprisingly considering his interests, never seen the Himalayas. The trip would be a pilgrimage for him, too. By February, we were informed that Tiger Mountain had found at least three additional recruits, so the trip was on.

But the cost was formidable. The authors of *Tibet: A Travel Survival Kit* estimated that living on the cheap one could get around Tibet for ten dollars a day, not counting Lhasa, which is considerably more expensive. However, once one gets into the matter of organized tours and expeditions, all of which must use the services of the China Tibet Tourism General Corporation, a government organization which started operating in 1985, and which has a monopoly on these matters, prices jump exponentially. It is possible to find tours that go, more or less, directly from Kathmandu to Lhasa by bus, or, if one is lucky, by Land Cruiser—a four-wheel-drive vehicle that seats five or six and is much better adapted to the Tibetan "highways," which are rarely paved. The most direct route is 1,004 kilometers (about 620 miles) long and can be done in three days of *very* hard driving. Round-trip economy tours were advertised in the newspapers in Kathmandu for something less than $800. If one wanted to combine this with an expedition to the Everest base camp, however, the price jumped exponentially again. Tiger Mountain, which is generally regarded as the top-of-the-line operator for expeditions like this, has a sliding scale of prices depending on the number of people. For five people—that is, five tourists, the accompanying staff is enormous—the price in 1987 for the Lhasa/Everest trip was $3,257 each, falling to $2,273 for fifteen or more people. When the Chinese opened the Nepalese border to tourists in 1985 it was only for tourists who were with an organized tour. One of their motivations must have been the realization that with an organized tour one could control the *minimum* people pay. The readers of *Tibet: A Travel Survival Kit,* who are encouraged to hitchhike—something that is both illegal and at the present time almost impossible—or take the occasional public bus, are not likely to leave in Tibet a large package of foreign exchange—an immensely valuable commodity to the Chinese. As the authors of the *Survival Kit* remark, wryly, "Tibet once held claim to being the most expensive destination in the world to visit. In the Victorian era the price was probable death—meted out either by the elements or by bandits; by the 1980's the price was reduced to a group tour arm and a leg." In 1986 the Chinese began issuing visas for *individuals* to cross the Nepal-Tibet border, but in May of 1987 they thought better of it, and at the present time only tours can cross from Nepal to Tibet. The people at Tiger Mountain told me that the base price the Chinese charge them for such a tour is so high that, as far as they are concerned, running trips to Tibet is practically a nonprofit service.

Toward the middle of April I headed back to Kathmandu. I managed to squeeze the necessary time away from my lecturing duties in Kathmandu to prepare for the trip. The preparation included a formal "briefing." Since Tiger Mountain was founded by an ex-Gurkha officer and has various ex-military people working for it, a certain amount of soldiering terminology is used in its operations. Thus on Wednesday, the twenty-ninth of April, at fifteen hundred hours sharp, we were all instructed to appear at Tiger Mountain headquarters, just outside Kathmandu, for the briefing. By this time Dunaway had arrived from Aspen, but neither of us had met the rest of the group. At the briefing, we were met by what seemed to be a small platoon of people. There were our three co-travelers who turned out to be young American petroleum engineers. Two of them worked in Saudi Arabia, and the third in London. All three had been on several treks in Nepal and looked bearded and hardy. There were four Sherpas, unbearded and *very* hardy. In addition, Tiger Mountain's office manager, Sonam Gyalpo, was to go with us. That was a fortunate piece of news, since Sonam is a Tibetan, born in Kalimpang, in West Bengal, where his parents were, until 1959, engaged in trade with Tibet. (*Sonam,* incidentally, is the Tibetan word for "merit" and many Tibetans and Sherpas have this first name.)

Sonam's family is a microcosmic illustration of the extraordinary ability of Tibetans to land on their feet in adversity. His older brother, for example, somehow managed to go to the University of Hawaii, where he studied computer science. He now lives in Vienna where he works as a systems analyst and is married to an Austrian. Sonam's mother tongue is Tibetan, but his English is absolutely fluent.

To round out the group was a very droll ex-British army helicopter pilot named Garry Daintry. Daintry specializes in iron-man feats like multi-day bicycle rides through deserts. He was coming along to get an idea if it would be possible to organize bicycle tours in Tibet.

The briefing lasted for about an hour and several salient points stuck out in my mind. First and foremost, there was the matter of the landslides. The region had been drenched with unusual pre-monsoon rains. This had resulted in two landslides near the Tibetan border, which had cut off the border town of Zhangmu from the roads that lead to it from both Tibet and Nepal. Under the best of circumstances we should have driven in a Nepalese bus to the Friendship Bridge, where we would have been met by a Chinese bus— no foreign cars are allowed in Tibet—which would have taken us up the fifteen-hundred-foot rise to Zhangmu and then, the next day, onward in the general direction of Lhasa. As things stood, we were going to be dropped at the border, where we would hire porters for the two-hour walk up to Zhangmu. The next day we would hire more porters who would take us under the second, and more recent, landslide, and then go to where the Chinese bus would, hopefully, be waiting. This brings up the matter of Chinese drivers and Tibetan hotels.

I learned at the briefing that there was only one hotel in Tibet where there is running hot water and that is the Holiday Inn in Lhasa. (The Tibet Guesthouse in Lhasa, which was under construction, also has modern plumbing.) Most of the rest of the hotels and guesthouses offer cold-water taps and outdoor latrines. Since we were going to have tents anyway for the Everest base-camp portion of our trip, it struck me that from every point of view, hygiene included, we would be much better off sleeping in our tents, away from civilization, than in a dubious hotel. The group agreed, and it was decided, or so we thought, that until we reached Lhasa we would camp out. That discussion brought up the matter of the Chinese drivers.

The China Tibet Tourism General Corporation employs only Chinese drivers to drive its buses and Land Cruisers.

This is a manifestation of the secondary role that Tibetans play in tourism in their own country. The key to any overland trip in Tibet is the performance of these drivers, which, we were warned, can border on the impossible. In particular, we were told, the drivers do not like the idea of camping out and, despite previous understandings, are perfectly capable of depositing their passengers, willy-nilly, in the nearest hotel. Finally, there was a laconic caution from Sonam. "With all the changes," he said, "don't expect Tibet to look like what you see in the pictures." With that, we were told to have our gear ready in the lobbies of our various hotels Friday morning at seven, when we would be picked up by a minibus. During the day, I made a few last-minute purchases in Kathmandu and, when the bus arrived on Friday, I was ready to go.

The drive to Kodari was the one I had made nearly a decade earlier by taxi. The one change that is evident, even to a passerby, is the population explosion in Nepal. If something is not done about it, the country will breed itself, despite its apparent floral luxuriance, into starvation. In the villages we passed, children seem to be everywhere. Halfway to Kodari the rickety bus broke down—par for the course—and was put back together skillfully by the driver and his assistant— also par for the course. With the delays, we arrived in Kodari in the early afternoon; that is, early afternoon in *Nepal*. It turned out that all of China, including Tibet, was on one time—Beijing time—which meant that the minute we stepped across the border it would be three hours and fifteen minutes *later*. One consequence of this inane arrangement was that, for the next sixteen days, we would get up in the pitch black and go to bed long before the sun had set. Now our problem was to get to the Zhangmu Hotel—a stiff two-hour climb sharply uphill—where we were to meet our Chinese guide and begin the next part of the trip, which, in theory, was to take us to our first campsite.

This part of Tibet is quite low—some six thousand feet— and the hills are forested with pines. The trail, which was boulder-strewn—during workdays the Chinese had been blasting above the trail in an effort to reopen the road and some of the debris had come down on the trail—was a living stream of porters carrying everything from pieces of plywood to wool—mainly wool. The major export from Tibet is wool—yak, sheep, and goat. Yak wool is very strong and a bit coarse for sweaters. It used to be widely used in the West for Santa Claus beards. Much of the wool goes into the manufacture of "Tibetan" carpets. With the flight of the Tibetans from Tibet, the carpet industry also left the country. Now all the high-quality Tibetan carpets are made out of wool, from Tibet, in Nepal and India. The Chinese have been trying to tempt emigrants, like the carpet weavers, back into Tibet by offering them special advantages if they are willing to set up a business in Tibet. However, to get these advantages the Tibetans must acknowledge that they are "Overseas Chinese," that the Chinese have a sovereign status in Tibet. For the most part, the carpet weavers refuse to do so. Thus "Tibetan carpets" continue to be made elsewhere. Fortunately for us, our arrival in Tibet coincided with May Day, and the Chinese were not blasting, so we could climb to the border check post without worrying about rocks coming down on our heads. Huffing and puffing, I arrived at the border station.

We had all been issued Chinese visas. (The visa form included the odd entry "Religion and political party.") We showed these to a border guard, a Chinese soldier. In the briefing we had been warned that at the border we would have to declare all of our watches and cameras down to the last lens, and that we had better have the same items with us when we left Tibet. With all of the formalities we arrived at the Zhangmu Hotel about four o'clock Nepalese time—seven fifteen local time. The lobby is a semimodern, cavernous place. I got a momentary feeling of homesickness when I looked over the registration desk to see an array of clocks, one of which was, more or less, set to New York time. Our Chinese guide was waiting for us, a diminutive, pink-cheeked eighteen-year-old girl named Kun. She was, or so we thought, to lead us under the second landslide and up to the road where the Chinese bus and an accompanying truck would be waiting for us. The truck was crucial since it would be carrying all the tents and other camping equipment as well as the food. Without the truck there would be no camping. "Unfortunately," Kun began in her musically accented but very serviceable English—I would learn that all the bad news always began with "Unfortunately"—"the truck is broken down." Freely translated, this meant there was no truck and that, very likely, there had never been a truck. Put somewhat differently, what this meant was that until we headed for Everest in the Land Cruisers—nearly ten days hence—we would be sleeping in the dreaded Tibetan hotels. This one was a multilevel warren, dimly lit, but basically clean. There was no running hot water—as was to have been expected—and the dining room was some floors below where we were to sleep. The only utensils on the table were a porcelain spoon for the soup, and chopsticks. Since I stubbornly refused to use the latter, I navigated an indifferent Chinese meal with the former. By seven o'clock Nepalese time—ten fifteen local—and, in broad daylight, I was fast asleep.

We had been warned that the next day would be brutal. It began about six A.M.—three in the morning, Nepalese—in the pitch darkness. We staggered around the hotel using our flashlights and after a breakfast of brown bread and tea we headed out in the direction of the landslide. Whatever a typical Tibetan village may be, Zhangmu is not it. The population looked to me as if all the races of Central Asia had been put in an urn, shaken up, and drawn out at random. Since Zhangmu is low and relatively tropical, people seemed to be living almost out of doors. The odd snow-covered mountain that one can see through the trees is in striking contrast to the hodgepodge squalor of the town. The place is set on the side of a steep hill—ergo the landslides—and to get out of it one walks up a series of terraces to what was the road. At one point the road simply disappeared. The beginning of the slide was signaled by a display of white prayer flags; some-

thing that Tibetans always put up to attract favorable attention from the gods. In the middle of the slide there was the
shell of what once must have been a substantial building. (On
our return visit to Zhangmu I saw a boulder the size of a
Volkswagen detach itself and in a series of explosive rebounds
move down in the general direction of the slide. That sort of
thing must have been what did the building in.) Because of
the recent rains, the middle of the slide was oozy mud which
seemed to suck at one's feet as one tried to move, as fast as
possible, to get to the other side, once again signaled by
prayer flags. Then, it was steeply uphill for about an hour to
where the road was still in one piece.

With the landslide, this road head was the terminus for all
the traffic moving from Tibet to Nepal, and vice-versa. There
were buses and trucks everywhere. Since the Chinese had not
yet put in their ban on individual travelers—that would come
at the end of May—there were all sorts of people wandering
from bus to bus trying to hitch rides. In the general chaos we
located our bus—a new and comfortable-looking Mitsubishi
with a Chinese crew of two. With all the gear, we fitted in
snugly but comfortably. Our destination was Shigatse, Tibet's
second city and the home of the Panchen Lama, on the rare
occasions when he visited Tibet from China. We had been
told that it would take about twelve hours to get to Shigatse—
a distance of a little over three hundred miles. There was
nothing for it but to settle in and watch the scenery go by.

For the first few hours the scenery was perfectly spectacular. The road is perched on the side of a profound gorge that
has cut, like a knife, through the Himalayas. Waterfalls make
their way from somewhere in the snows. In the eighteen miles
from Zhangmu to the nearest town, Nyalam, where we were
to have camped, the road rises five thousand feet. Nyalam is
at 12,300 feet and was about as low as we would be until we
left Tibet. The road is, of course, dirt and gravel, but it is a
marvel of construction. One can see why it cost a good many
lives to build. It hangs over the Po Chu River like a tightrope
walker. After Nyalam we were to be on the Tibetan plateau,

where we would remain for the rest of the trip. Today it was not at its best. Although, generally speaking, Tibet is dry—it averages about eighteen inches of precipitation a year—the usual April rains in Nepal had produced dark menacing skies over the Tibetan desert. We had been promised spectacular views of the mountains, including Everest and Shisha Pangma, the only one of the thirteen eight-thousand-meter mountains entirely in Tibet. Where the mountains should be, there were only clouds. However, on our return trip the skies were clear and the resulting mountain scene was mind-boggling. Out of the hazy green and brown Tibetan desert the mountains rose like giant icebergs. The vision was so surreal that one expected it to vanish like a dream.

The road wound inexorably. The winds were now howling outside the bus. I tried to imagine Alexandra Neel walking day after day in this semi-desert, in the winter, and failed. We could see the odd black nomad's tent dotting the landscape and the inevitable collection of grazing animals—grazing on what, I cannot imagine. My thought was, How can anyone—Chinese or anyone—*control* this country? and just as I was thinking this we came to the military check post near Xegar. Since we had all the necessary documents and were part of a tour, passing this post should have been routine. However, our young guide began what seemed to be a cheerful flirtation with some of the soldiers at the post. One of them had a batch of pistols on a wire—hopefully empty. Kun was offered one of them and began pointing it at various of us and pulling the trigger playfully. To put it mildly, we were not amused. Even less amused was an American I met a few days later who had been on a similar tour. At the same checkpoint his teen-age guide was given a pistol to shoot with *live* ammunition. After she had scattered a few shots around, the American had had enough, and picked her up bodily and put her back into the bus as she protested, "This is my country and I can do anything I like." When they got to Lhasa he and his companions complained and were given another guide. The Chinese must be aware of a growing number of tourist complaints about their guides and drivers, because while we were in Tibet an item came over the news that a certain number of them had been summoned to Beijing for "autocriticism."

After playing with the guns for a while, Kun seemed ready to get back onto the bus. She then asked us if we would "mind" if we gave a Chinese soldier a ride to Shigatse. There wasn't much room and, very shortly, the one soldier became two soldiers. Before we had a chance to complain Kun said, "Unfortunately, we have no choice." Someone in the group remarked that, if we were not careful, the soldiers could simply commandeer the bus and leave us at the checkpoint. They got on, young and unsmiling, with their gear, which included the brace of pistols and a guitar. Nothing was heard from them for the rest of the trip. Hour after hour went by until the sun began to set. The itemized list of things to bring on the trip included dust masks and now we could see why. Dust seemed to come into the bus from all sides even with the windows closed. We all had our dust masks on, giving everyone an oddly surgical look. To add to the general ambience the bus driver apparently had one tape, which he played over and over. It included, among other things, the theme music from the film of *Love Story*. As far as I was concerned, it was a new and much more effective version of the ancient Chinese water torture. Finally, not long before midnight, we pulled into the Shigatse Hotel, were fed a lukewarm midnight meal, and sent to bed with no warm shower.

Shigatse, a town of some forty thousand, is a microcosm of everything that has happened to Tibet since the Chinese takeover. It is, in the first place, the home of the Panchen Lama, that unfortunate soul who thought at first that the Chinese occupation was a "wonderful" thing for Tibet. After having been asked to denounce the Dalai Lama, and refusing, he was brought to trial and beaten into a state where he was once again able to see the merits of the occupation. He lived in Beijing, and was reported to have married. He died on January 29, 1989, of an apparent heart attack at the age of fifty, while on a visit to Tibet. His status with the Tibetan people was, perhaps, best reflected in the matter of the pictures. Before coming to Tibet we were told to go into the bazaars in Kathmandu and get as many photographs of the Dalai Lama as we could lay our hands on. Among us we must have had well over a hundred—many too few. Every Tibetan, it seems, knows how to say something that sounds like "Dalai Lama pichu," meaning that they want a photograph of the Dalai Lama. There is relatively little begging in Tibet, and much of what there is is for pictures of the Dalai Lama. By the time we left, all our pictures were long gone and we could have given away ten times the number we did. No one ever asked us for a picture of the Panchen Lama.

Then there is the city itself. The Tibetan quarter, if one can find it, near the entrance of the Tashilhunpo Monastery, the traditional home of the Panchen Lama, is completely dwarfed by the ugly Chinese city that surrounds it. The whole thing looks like a military camp, with concrete-block house after concrete-block house, most of them with ugly tin roofs. Apart from the Tashilhunpo and the ruins of an old fort demolished in the Cultural Revolution, I could not find a single redeeming bit of architecture. To boot, and this is common in Tibet, people in the city ride around wearing surgical masks to protect themselves from the dust that blows in from the surrounding plains. The Friendship Store—the local department store—is depressing in another way. It is filled with ill-made objects like plastic toy tractors, which I got the impression that Tibetan children could not afford to buy. They would stand staring at them until someone would kick them out of the store. I didn't have the heart to buy anything.

The Tashilhunpo Monastery is also a microcosm of what has happened to the monasteries. As with all monasteries in Tibet, the affairs of this one are run by the Bureau of Religious Affairs. This governmental bureau decides how much money shall be allocated to the restoration of any monastery. The Tashilhunpo suffered considerable destruction during the Cultural Revolution but, perhaps because of the Panchen Lama's association with it, it now seems fairly well restored.

The Bureau of Religious Affairs also decides how many monks there will be, and what they will do. Very few monks are now allowed to practice a purely contemplative life. The rest work—in monastic farms, for example—so as not to become "parasites." In the monasteries I visited I made it a point of asking how many monks were present now and how many had been there before. I came to the conclusion that there must be about a tenth of the monks there were before the Chinese occupation. This means that now, in Tibet, there may be some twenty-five thousand monks. In the Tashilhunpo, where there were four or five thousand monks, there are now around seven hundred. The Bureau of Religious Affairs also sets prices. Monasteries are the principal tourist attraction in Tibet.

Tourism is rapidly becoming big business in Tibet. In 1986 there were an estimated twenty thousand visitors, spending an average of six days in the country, four in Lhasa and two in Shigatse, where there is one thing to see: the Tashilhunpo Monastery, well worth seeing for its wonderful Tibetan religious art. In 1987, there were an estimated forty thousand visitors, and they were the main source of foreign exchange in the country. (Because of the unrest in Tibet in 1988 and '89 it is not clear, at this writing, what the present status of tourism is. It is certain to be much more tightly controlled than at the time of our visit.) The monasteries, as a rule, charge nominal entry fees. Where the money is made is in photography. Even I, who had never taken a picture in my life, and was notorious on all my previous travels for cadging photographs from people who did, took a camera to Tibet. One gets imbued with the sense that this is a once-in-a-lifetime experience, and that one must have a record of it. The better-known monasteries charge about twenty yuan—seven dollars—per camera—*per room*—to take photographs. This means that in a large and magnificent monastery, like the Tashilhunpo, a determined photographer can easily spend close to a hundred dollars to take pictures.

None of us were sorry, the next morning, to leave the Shigatse Hotel. The meals and cold water apart, there was the matter of the keys, which is tied to the general question of hotel service in these provincial hotels. Maybe it is part of the communal spirit, of which I have inordinately little, but none of us was allowed to have our own keys. If one locked the room by setting the latch, then to get back into the room one had to persuade one of the women at the service desk on one's floor, if one could find one, to let one back in. When one finally located her, she was carrying the keys to all the rooms on the floor on a giant ring. She was annoyed, and we were annoyed, at going through this ritual several times a day. Why we each couldn't have our own keys is one of those small mysteries.

From Shigatse to Lhasa is some two hundred miles, but we expected to be all day at it. There are two routes, each involving crossing passes of over sixteen thousand feet. The northern route, which we would take on the return trip, goes through some spectacular mountain scenery and links up with the road to central China. The southern route, which we took on our way to Lhasa, goes by Lake Yamdrok, which is the third largest lake in Tibet and on a sunny day looks like a turquoise scorpion. On this overcast and cold day, the lake was sea-bird gray. This route also goes through the town of Gyantse, which is linked by road to India via Sikkim. The storming of the fort in Gyantse on July 6, 1904, by the Young-husband mission, was the key to opening the way to Lhasa for the British.

It is only about sixty miles from Shigatse to Gyantse, but when we got there, Kun announced, "Boys, we will have a half hour to see the monastery and the fort." The "boys," who ranged in age from their mid-thirties to their mid-sixties, made it quite plain that they intended to spend as much time as they wanted examining these monuments. Kun went off in a teenage sulk, and we spent an hour or so looking at Kumbum—a house of worship consisting of many interlocking chapels, with their striking, and often demonic, decorations, which one can see as one works one's way up to the gilded roof.

As we drove around Lake Yamdrok we encountered a bicycle tour, supported by its own flotilla of vehicles, wending its way painfully in the direction of Shigatse. By late afternoon the desert gave way to cultivated land and the road had become, miraculously, paved. It was clear that we were nearing Lhasa. Lhasa is set in a kind of amphitheater of mountains and, from a distance, has just the aura of mystery and romance one hoped it would have. First one sees the gilded roofs of neighboring monasteries and then, fulfilling every expectation, the haunting vision of the Potala itself. It is only when one begins driving through the city that it becomes apparent what has happened. The Chinese have turned Lhasa into a lumpen provincial capital. Of its some 150,000 inhabitants, the vast majority are Chinese. There is also a large Moslem population, presumably a relic of the times when the Tibetans and the Mongols were in contact. It is interesting that the sense of disappointment one feels in actually setting foot in Lhasa seems to be a common denominator among most of its foreign visitors. In their own irreverent way the authors of the *Survival Kit* comment, "If you are disappointed with Lhasa, or feel cheated of the mystique you had expected, you won't be the first. The eccentric English traveller Manning delivered his verdict in 1812, and it still rings true: while he found the Potala extraordinary, he found the rest of the place a dump. In 1904, the invading English under Younghusband found their triumphal march into Lhasa impeded by piles of refuse, stagnant pools of water, open sewers and various rabid animals foraging for putrid scraps of food. . . . "

In 1949, Lowell Thomas, Jr., in a visit to Tibet (at the invitation of the Dalai Lama) wrote: "Nothing is known of modern plumbing. Refuse piles up on all corners . . . once a year these offal heaps are transferred to the fields to stimulate crops. The odors are not entirely pleasant. The nobles hold scented handkerchiefs to their noses as they ride along ... dead animals are tossed in refuse piles to be fought over and devoured by the city's scavengers—thousands of mangy dogs and ravens!"

This only some forty years ago. The feeling one has now is, I think, quite different. Just as the British brought, at the end of a bayonet, free trade to Lhasa, whether the Tibetans wanted it or not, the Chinese have brought, at the end of a bayonet, some of the trappings of modernity to Lhasa— including a much higher level of sanitation, whether the Tibetans want it or not: but at what a cost.

In its own way as remarkable as the Potala is the Holiday Inn in Lhasa. Here we were, four days without a hot shower, come dust-clad off the Tibetan desert, to find ourselves in front of a hypermodern structure claiming to have 486 twin-bedded guest rooms, each with a color TV, its own bathroom, with hot and cold running water; each room with its own key; two restaurants; a bar lounge with a string quartet whose limited but nicely played repertoire included Mozart and Beethoven; and enough oxygen to supply the needs of any guest having trouble breathing. It was almost too much to credit, especially when one was informed that the film to be shown that very evening on the TV would be *The Sound of Music* in English with Chinese subtitles. The hotel, I learned, was first built in 1985, and opened in September of that year, under the name Lhasa Hotel. The first six months were so disastrous, in terms of tourist complaints, that the Chinese decided to enter into a ten-year management agreement with Holiday Inns. The name was officially changed to the Lhasa Holiday Inn on August 8, 1987. The manager on my visit was Swiss, and apart from him there were three other Europeans who ran the hotel. The staff varied in size from 580 during the winter, which is the low season, to about a thousand in the summer, at the height of the tourist season. Forty-seven of the staff were from Beijing and the rest were local people. The two main problems are training and English. In a country where forty-eight percent of the people are nomadic, sleeping in a bed, Western-style—let alone making one—is exotic. All this must be taught.

English is a much deeper matter and goes to the heart of the question of what the Chinese occupation of Tibet is all about. Of all the countries I have ever visited, Tibet is the most linguistically alien. In Nepal, for example, one can get along quite well with English, which is why most frequent visitors, like myself, never really learn much more than trailside Nepali. In Tibet there is, at least among the Tibetans, little or no English. Kun, our Chinese guide, spoke no Tibetan, and if we had not had with us Tiger Mountain's Sonam Gyalpo, whose mother tongue is Tibetan, and several Sherpas whose mother tongue is a dialect of Tibetan, we would have been in a linguistic vacuum. On my own, trying to do things like asking for directions and drawing a blank if amiable look from my Tibetan conversational partner, I would find myself, idiotically, switching into French. Then the two of us—the Tibetan and I—would stand grinning helplessly at each other.

English is taught in the schools, but only if a Tibetan child is willing to accept instruction only in Chinese. All secondary education is presently given in Chinese. A child can have its primary education in Tibetan, but if he does not know Chinese, he cannot go further. This absurd and racist policy has resulted in the fact that a Tibetan who does not want to be educated in Chinese will also not be able to learn English, or any other foreign language, in school. A side effect of this is that, as far as I can make out, there are no Tibetan tour guides or hotel employees who work in jobs where a knowledge of foreign languages in essential. Another side effect, I was told, is that English-speaking people who want to learn Tibetan in Tibet have a very hard time finding English-speaking teachers. One has the impression that the Chinese are trying to wean the Tibetans away from their language—to increase the bonding of China and Tibet. Perhaps with the younger generation of Tibetans, who are being educated in Chinese, this will have an effect, and perhaps it won't.

For those visitors to Lhasa who stay there, the Lhasa Holiday Inn is like an island. Strangers tend to go out of their way to be friendly. Take the case of the parmesan cheese. After a couple of forays at the formal buffet in the main dining room of the hotel, I had taken to eating in the coffee shop, where the menu featured such items as "spaghetti Bolognese." The "spaghetti" was, I think, made out of barley, and had neither the consistency nor the taste of the "real" thing. I put "real" in quotation marks, because it may well have tasted like the item Marco Polo brought back from China when he introduced pasta to Europe. In any event, I grew quite fond of it and had it several nights for dinner. One night, while I was eating my spaghetti, I heard a female voice from a nearby table asking me if I would like some parmesan cheese. I said, "Certainly," and an attractive blond girl, who had finished eating and was in the process of leaving, stood up and fished out of an enormous cloth purse one of those little green cans of Kraft parmesan cheese with the small holes in the top of the can. She came over to my table, carefully shook a ration of cheese onto my spaghetti, and walked out with a smile. I never saw her again. Perhaps she was one of the people who answered a notice on the hotel bulletin board asking if anyone wanted to join an overland horseback trip to Chengdu—in Sichuan—a mere fourteen hundred miles from Lhasa. Or perhaps she joined one of the overland tours back to Kathmandu, or Everest, similarly advertised.

Kun, bless her heart, managed to come up with what she called "the Number One Bus in Tibet." It was a beautiful black Japanese-made bus that would trundle us around Lhasa as we visited the sights. She also taught us to chant in unison a Chinese phrase that sounds something like "toddley-ba," and means, she explained, "We are all here." Each morning we boarded the Number One Bus for our daily tour and chanted in unison, "Toddley-ba." The next few days went by in a haze of Buddhas, lamas, and yak butter. In every monastery there are rows of perpetually burning votive lamps—often the only source of illumination—filled with yak butter. Burning yak butter has a characteristic penetrating smell which permeates one's clothes. My down jacket still exudes a light miasma of yak butter, which, I think, it will have forever.

In visiting a monastery—or other historical building—one is sometimes not clear whether one is visiting a shrine or a museum. It is clear that the Dalai Lama's former summer palace, the Norbu Lingka, is a museum. It must have been lovely, with its gardens carefully tended, and people living there. Now the grounds look shabby and threadbare and the pitiful zoo with its huge and remorseful black bear is an eyesore. The buildings are well preserved, gaily decorated, but very cold. The only thing that moved me was the young fourteenth Dalai Lama's room, from which he must have heard the sound of the two Chinese shells that exploded near the palace in March 1959. One wonders whether he was listening to the Phillips victrola which still sits intact in the room. I noticed that there was an old RCA "His Master's Voice" record on it with the title *Tibetan Songs*. When he fled, the victrola and the records were left behind.

The Potala is more museum than shrine. The monks who attend it, if they are monks, seem more concerned that one pays one's photography fee than with anything else. The stupas—tombs—of the Dalai Lamas were to me very affecting. They are meant to overawe, with their tons of gold, but I kept thinking, where will the fourteenth Dalai Lama be buried? Will he return to Tibet only in death, or will death be a continuation of his exile?

The Jokhang, on the other hand, is definitely a shrine. It is at the Jokhang—the most sacred site in all of lamaistic Buddhism—that one sees, firsthand, the powerful, deeply profound attachment that Tibetans have to their religion. Thirty years of Chinese occupation does not seem to have made a dent in that. In front of the temple the Chinese have cleared away from the old Tibetan quarter, which used to surround the Jokhang on all sides, a sort of modern square— a sort of mall—lined with a few dreary Friendship Stores. But the pilgrims who come from all over Tibet to worship at the Jokhang have converted this into a kind of religious park. One reads about people prostrating themselves and locomoting on all fours, sometimes for days, to reach holy sites like the Jokhang. And, in front of the Jokhang, one finds groups of pilgrims prostrating themselves. When one makes the traditional clockwise tour of the exterior of the Jokhang through what is known as the Barkhor—the "Eight Corners," Lhasa's outdoor bazaar—one finds people circumnavigating the building on their hands and knees. One also sees pairs of Chinese soldiers, arms linked, walking ostentatiously around the Barkhor counterclockwise—the wrong way.

It is interesting to watch the course of one's own mind in the presence of so much nearly incomprehensible religious symbolism. Over the next few days we each, at various times, arrived at a state of saturation which we came to refer to—no disrespect—as being "Buddha'd out." I became Buddha'd out one afternoon in the Drepung Monastery, a few miles west of Lhasa. The Drepung, which was founded in 1416, was the largest and richest monastery in Tibet. In its heyday it housed ten thousand monks. It now has about four hundred, most of whom work the nearby orchard. It is a maze of chapels, festooned with Buddhas and labyrinthine murals. One does find the odd monk reading and chanting from one of the flat, often wood-bound, texts that fill the libraries of these monasteries. I had listened to one of the monks— a wonderfully serene-looking elderly man, whose mouth seemed largely untroubled by teeth—chant for about ten minutes when I realized that I was Buddha'd out. I decided that the only cure for this pitiable state of mind would be to find out the meaning of what this good man was actually chanting; even just a tiny bit of the meaning of what he was chanting. I enlisted the help of Sonam Gyalpo and one of the Sherpas and we approached the kindly-looking monk. I explained through my interpreters that I wanted to know just what a single page said. The monk studied me carefully and then said, through my interpreters, that I wouldn't be able to understand it. This was too much. In my Buddha'd-out state I heard myself saying, "Try me. I understand the quantum theory; Bell's theorem; the Everett many worlds' interpretation; Einstein, Podolsky, and Rosen. Just try me." I do not know how this was translated into Tibetan, but the monk did agree to chant a single page. Sonam and the Sherpa listened intently, their faces falling unhappily as the chant proceeded. At the end they had to confess that they had not understood a single word either. I decided that they were in the situation of a Reform Jew from a Manhattan congregation who goes to Brooklyn and asks one of the Hassidim to chant from the Talmud. I felt a great deal better about the whole thing and was prepared to visit our final monastery, the Sera.

On our way to the Sera Monastery, on the outskirts of Lhasa, we passed the new athletic field and stadium built by the Chinese. No one can recall the stadium's having actually been used for anything. Perhaps it can be used for the *lung-gom-pa*—the Tibetan mystics who used to put themselves into a kind of trance and run at high speed sixty miles or so at a clip across the Tibetan plateau. Alexandra Neel, in her walk to Lhasa, reports having encountered one from time to time. The Sera Monastery is noted as a site for what are called "sky burials." In Tibet, because of the shortage of fuel, cremation is for the rich. In the introduction of his translation of the Bardo Thodol—the Tibetan Book of the Dead—the text that is read to a dying Tibetan to prepare him or her for the forty-nine days of Bardol, the state after death when the next life is approached, W. Y. Evans-Wentz described the Tibetan attitude toward burial. He writes, ". . . Tibetans generally object to earth burial, for they believe that when a corpse is interred, the spirit of the deceased, upon seeing it, attempts to re-enter it, and that if the attempt is successful a vampire results, whereas cremation, or other methods of quickly dissipating the elements of the dead body, prevent vampirism." Since cremation is not commonly practiced, a low caste of Tibetans called *domden*s reduce the dead body into morsels, which are then eaten by birds of prey: vultures, ravens, and kites. There is an isolated rock formation close to the monastery, not open to visitors, where this ceremony is practiced at dawn. When

we got there it was midmorning, and the only trace of whatever ceremony might have taken place that morning was the
wheeling of a few isolated birds. It was an eerie sight. Then,
since we were leaving for Everest the next morning, we all
stood in line while a Sera lama touched our necks with a
heavy stone that was thought to ward off illness and injury—
good luck, perhaps, for a dangerous trip.

Early the next morning, I saw a Land Cruiser drive up to
the hotel. The young Chinese driver sped the car through the
parking lot, slammed on the brakes, and got out with a
satisfied swagger. He was wearing a kind of tight-fitting gray
teddyboy suit—common to the young Chinese one sees in
Lhasa—with a pair of what looked like high-heeled sandals,
apparently the latest rage. A cigarette dangled from the corner of his mouth; he was the king of the road. His Land
Cruiser seated six and baggage pretty comfortably. We divided up by generations. Dunaway, our British "iron man"
Garry Daintry, and I and two of the Sherpas got into one
machine with the Teddyboy driver, while the rest of the group
got into a second Land Cruiser. We left Lhasa by the northern
route, which connects to the Chinese heartland. This, after a
half hour's delay, while our driver stopped for a mysterious
errand. It later turned out that he was trying unsuccessfully
to talk another driver into taking his place; a measure of his
enthusiasm for the trip.

As we left Lhasa we encountered convoy after convoy of
soldiers. Lhasa had been alive with rumors about an impend-
ing border war between the Chinese and Indians over the
southern border of Tibet, the McMahon line. The putative
front was said to be two days' drive from Lhasa. People told
us that the local hospitals had been cleared, better to receive
the possible casualties. Travelers had said that the flight from
Chengdu was operating only on alternate days—the other
days being used to fly in military personnel. During our visit
to the Norbu Lingka we had encountered what we were told
was an entire squadron of fighter pilots who said they had
come to Lhasa for a "vacation." Each day, on Garry Daintry's

shortwave radio, we could listen to the Chinese and Indian "brotherly" conversations—in tones to make one's blood run cold. And now as we left Lhasa we encountered truckload after truckload of soldiers. For some reason, this seemed to unnerve our driver. He started passing cars with abandon. I heard Daintry say, "Don't even think of that." I looked up to see our driver pass a car, barely missing an oncoming truck. Daintry and I agreed that if the driver made one more dangerous maneuver we would stop the car. No sooner said than done. The driver made a lunatic passing maneuver on a blind hill and we stopped the car. The second Land Cruiser, which had been following us, also came to a stop. I went over to Kun and said that if the driver did not drive more carefully one of us was going to drive the car. "Unfortunately," Kun began, "the driver has been on vacation in China and is now suffering from the altitude." What luck! A million Tibetans to choose from and we have a Chinese driver with altitude sickness. Kun came into our car, trading places with one of the Sherpas. The petroleum engineers gave her a small stack of Joni Mitchell tapes to cheer her up. Kun spoke to the driver and informed us that he apologized and promised to do better. We drove on over the plateau with no further incidents.

After another dreary night in the Shigatse hotel we headed east in the direction of Nepal. Even though we were by now all of us Buddha'd out and eager to get into the mountains, Sonam Gyalpo said it would be a great mistake if we did not make a side trip to the monastery in Sakya. He was right. From a distance, the village of Sakya seems untouched by modern life. When one gets closer one notices that nearby is what appears to be a Chinese hydroelectric power plant with the unusual array of tin-roofed concrete-block houses. Despite the Chinese pressure, however, the monastery in Sakya is almost untouched—perhaps the most extraordinary of the remaining monasteries in Tibet. From the outside it does not look like a monastery at all, but like a fort. Inside the walls there is a courtyard—again with a medieval aura. It was with the monks of Sakya that the Khans made their alliance, and preserved in the monastery is the parchment with its gold seal—the seal of Kublai Khan—authorizing the monks of Sakya to rule all of Tibet. This eventually led to the institution of the Dalai Lamas. The statuary in the monastery has been beautifully preserved in the dry desert air, as has the fantastic library. Best of all, the monastery appears to be functioning. When we were there we saw a group of young novices at prayer in the great chanting hall, supported by its massive tree-trunk pillars. It is a beautiful and serene place and gives one a sense of what Tibet once was.

Our next stop was to be Xegar, the starting point of the road to the Everest base camp. At the town of Lhatse we passed the turnoff for the highway that leads west across Tibet, just north of the Himalayas, to Pakistan. It looked very inviting. Toward evening the Land Cruisers came to a bend in the road near a river. I looked out the window and saw a delightful tent camp. The rest of our Sherpas had commandeered a truck and had already set up camp and made tea. It was like coming home.

The next morning, our little caravan—two Land Cruisers and the truck with the tents and the food—headed for Everest. The road, which is a superannuated jeep track, appeared at first to climb aimlessly in the general direction of the Pang La—a pass at seventeen thousand feet. The terrain is bleak and fairly monotonous and nothing prepares one for the view from the top of the pass. I have spent a good deal of my life in and among mountains, but I have never seen anything like the panorama from the top of that pass. It may be the only place on earth where the ordinary traveler—as opposed to a mountain climber—can see four eight-thousand-meter mountains in one sweep. From left to right one sees, completely unobstructed, Makalu, Lhotse, Everest, and Cho Oyu. When one sees Everest from Nepal it is usually obscured by lesser and closer mountains. From the Pang La it dominates the horizon and it is absolutely clear that it is the king of that range. We could hardly tear ourselves away from the view.

The road then descended into a broad valley and the mountains disappeared. The main obstacle was a river, the Dzakar Chu, which can be impossible to cross. We managed to cross it with our caravan, but only after one of the four-wheel-drive Land Cruisers towed the truck through it, attached to a climbing rope. The road then became worse and worse, and one jounced along hoping the vehicles would stay on it. Suddenly, with almost no warning, one was at the Rongbuk Monastery, or what is left of it. The first thing one notices is the brightly colored stupa, and the second thing is, of course, Everest. Everest fills the skyline and one can make out all the features—such as the odd yellow bands that streak across the north face—that all climbers have written about since Mallory. It looks unclimbable, but we knew that there were several expeditions who were on the face, including a solo American, later killed. The road now all but disappeared and we made crude tracks through a bleak moraine until the vehicles could go no further, blocked by a rocky outcrop. This is the Everest base camp, at about seventeen thousand feet.

We set up our tents and the wind began to blow. The winds on Everest are notorious. The summit of the mountain is often in the jet stream and a characteristic plume of snow perpetually blows off the summit. The Sherpas got a fire going, and over tea we plotted our next move. The idea was to make a high camp in the snow at about 18,600 feet from which the fittest could spend a day trying to get to the Lho La, the high pass that leads into Nepal. (That was the place from which Mallory looked over to Nepal and claimed that Everest was unclimbable from the Nepalese side.) That was our plan. But everything rapidly became unstuck. Yaks were to carry all our gear up to the camp. But, it seemed, all the yaks in the Rongbuk were commandeered by a huge Swedish expedition whose neat tent camp was festooned by blue and yellow flags a few hundred yards from ours. Most of the Swedes were on the mountain, where they had rigged up some kind of satellite telecommunications system so that every night they could talk to their wives and girlfriends in Sweden. They had been on the mountain for weeks, and had taken all the yaks. So-nam Gyalpo made several forays among the three yak drivers and each time returned crestfallen. Just when we thought everything was lost, a remarkable compromise was reached. The yaks won't go, but the drivers will, and for a high price they can carry most of our stuff. We went back to our tents, the wind howling, and got ready for the next day.

The walk up to the high camp has an eerie beauty. The trail follows the moraine alongside the Rongbuk glacier. In my mind's eye I could see the map in Ullman's book—that map of Everest I looked at so often as a child. We are, for the time being, walking where Mallory must have walked. To our right, on the glacier, we could see the strange ice formations that look like monks at prayer—the French call them *"peni-tents."* From time to time we could catch a glimpse of the north face of Everest. Mallory's route branches off from ours and continues to the East Rongbuk Glacier while we continue up into the snow. I began to feel the altitude dramatically. Every-one had gotten ahead of me, and by the time I got to the camp, the Sherpas had set up our tents in the snow. I flopped into mine, too exhausted to move. The next day the weather was beautiful, but I was done for. The altitude had gotten me. While my co-expeditioners went off in the direction of the Lho La I made a few forays up to where I could see Everest and then came back and sank gasping into my tent. Late that afternoon they came back, exhausted but exhilarated. It was time to go home.

The next day we broke camp and made the long walk down to where we had left the vehicles. As much as I love the mountains, I was glad to see our base-camp tents and the rest of the group. Poor Kun spent three days in her tent. "Unfor-tunately," she said, "I do not feel well." We asked her if she planned to come back to Everest. "No," she said, "never."

Early the next morning we began to drive back to Nepal. The drive back was even more unreal than the one out. The weather was perfect, and while we had been gone the desert plateau had acquired a light tinge of green—green, turquoise blue, and brown—with the great white mountains hovering on the horizon. The road suddenly dove between the mountains and we were dropped into the lush tropical splendor of Nepal. Tibet, only a few miles away, had vanished like a dream.

Epilogue

The first of October is celebrated by the Chinese in Tibet as a national day. It is the anniversary of the Chinese Communist Revolution and coincidentally marks the Chinese takeover of Tibet, which began in October of 1950. The observance that took place in October 1987, some four months after we left Tibet, was different from the previous ones. In the first place, there were a large number of foreign tourists present. In the second place, the celebration turned violent. According to eyewitness accounts by the tourists, somewhere between three thousand and five thousand Tibetans in Lhasa took part in anti-Chinese demonstrations. Many of the demonstrators were monks from the nearby Sera and Drepung monasteries. The monks carried the outlawed Tibetan flag, which depicts a pair of lions beneath a snow-capped mountain, and led crowds of pilgrims in a traditional circuit of the Jokhang temple. As they marched, the crowds chanted, "This is Tibet—a free and independent nation!" Four days earlier, in a much smaller demonstration outside the Jokhang, two dozen monks had been beaten and arrested; now the crowds attacked a Chinese police station near the temple and burned it to the ground. The rioting continued over the next few days. At least fifteen people, nine of them Tibetans and the rest Chinese police, were killed, and thousands of additional Chinese security forces were flown into Tibet. The Chinese accused the Dalai Lama, who had just visited the United States and met with members of the Congressional Human Rights Caucus, of making remarks during that visit that had incited the Tibetans to riot. The Tibetans, however, said that the demonstrations had been sparked, at least in part, by the execution of two Tibetan nationalists a week earlier. Given the despair that many Tibetans feel about the occupation of their country, the proximate cause of these particular demonstrations could have been anything. What was new was that these demonstrations were acknowledged publicly by the Chinese, who consider all Tibetan matters to be a purely internal Chinese affair—a view that has, unfortunately, also been the official policy of the United States government. Apparently because of the strong reaction that the news reports of the clashes provoked in the West, the Chinese quickly reversed their policy of journalistic openness and expelled all foreign newspeople from Tibet. Tourism was also suspended until April 18, 1988, when the Chinese announced that they would allow tourists into Tibet on a restricted basis. No individual visas would be issued and all tourists would have to spend a minimum of one hundred yuan—twenty-seven dollars—a day. In addition, all these groups would be compelled to hire a Chinese tour guide. At this writing, with renewed riots in Tibet, foreign newspeople are still forbidden there.

All of this raises a deep moral question, namely, *should* travelers go to Tibet under the present circumstances? An impressive argument for the negative was presented on the op-ed page of the *Washington Post* by John Avedon, the author of *In Exile from the Land of Snows*, a powerful indictment of the Chinese in Tibet. Mr. Avedon wrote, "In 1986, almost thirty thousand tourists visited Tibet. They exulted in the most rarefied air on Earth, marveled at the Potala . . . , and enjoyed Tibetans' native kindness beside their nervous Chinese overlords. What most people failed to recognize was that the money they paid to see 160 rebuilt monasteries did not go to the Tibetans. Instead, it directly subsidized the purveyors of Tibet's destruction [the Han Chinese], 32,000 of whom are working in Lhasa's service sector."

He concluded, "So a Communist regime is selling the supposedly antique society that its creed has pledged to erase.

Another irony is Beijing's use of Tibetans to sponsor through the tourist trade their own demise."

Despite Mr. Avedon's strong arguments, and with a full awareness of what the Chinese are doing in Tibet, I would like to make the case that Western tourists *should* visit Tibet. Tourists are the only window that lets light into the country. It was tourists, after all, who informed us of the events in Lhasa in the fall of 1987 after the journalists were expelled. But let me give three personal examples of what I have in mind.

The first has to do with Tibetan artists. On the first of May, 1987, a new art gallery opened in Lhasa. A young Tibetan artist was given permission to use a large loftlike structure to create an art gallery in which he was going to try to sell mainly modern Tibetan art. There is a long history of Tibetan art, which has traditionally been purely religious. As Giuseppe Tucci writes in his book *Tibet*, "Tibetan art is essentially anonymous, and it is unusual for works of painting or sculpture to be signed. To paint or sculpt is an act of worship, and as such implies the negation of the person who performs it." Tucci would have been astounded at the art in this gallery. It is both personal and secular and represented the work of modern Tibetan artists. Its themes grow out of the natural austere beauty of Tibet. Only tourists can afford to buy this work. If they don't, the gallery will then disappear and who will see these paintings?

My second example involves children. It occurred on our trip back to Nepal after having seen Everest. We were camped out one night by a river in what seemed like an isolated spot. But one thing one learns while traveling in Tibet is that no matter how remote the site, people seem to materialize there. One has the sense that they emerge from the earth. No sooner had we pitched our tents than a small group of children appeared from somewhere. One young boy, who was carrying a book, spoke some English, meaning that he must have been doing his studies in Chinese rather than Tibetan. In fact the book he was carrying was his geology schoolbook, written in Chinese—and, like schoolchildren everywhere he wanted to show us what he had been learning, and so he recited his lessons to us.

The third example also involves a young Tibetan. It occurred just as we were leaving Tibet. We were at Zhangmu—waiting early in the morning for the border to open. Alongside us was a long line of porters looking for work. Most of them looked not much older than schoolchildren. One of them stepped slightly out of line and did not get back into line quickly enough to suit one of the Chinese soldiers who was supervising the lineup. The soldier went over and kicked the boy in the legs with his heavy boots. He was about to kick him again when he saw me watching him—and he walked away. What would have happened if I had *not* been there to watch?

The kindness and good humor of the Tibetan people in the face of the most terrible sort of adversity is grounded in their faith. The meanest object can, for a Tibetan, become an object of veneration. In her book *Magic and Mystery in Tibet*, Alexandra David-Neel tells a Tibetan folk story about a trader who every year went to India, where the Buddha was born. Each year he promised to bring back for his aged mother a relic from that holy land, and each year he forgot. But, "this time the merchant remembered his promise before reaching his home and was much troubled at the idea of once more disappointing his aged mother's eager expectation."

Just as he was having these thoughts he caught sight of a dog's jaw lying near the road. He got an idea.

"He broke off a tooth of the bleached jaw-bone, wiped away the earth which covered it and wrapped it in a piece of silk. Then, having reached his house, he offered the old bone to his mother, declaring that it was a most precious relic, a tooth of the great Sariputra.

"Overjoyed, her heart filled with veneration, the good woman placed the tooth in a casket on the altar of the family shrine. Each day she worshipped before it, lighting lamps and burning incense. Other devotees joined in the worship and after time rays of light shone from the dog's tooth, promoted [to a] holy relic."

Alexandra David Neel concludes, "A popular Tibetan saying is born from the story:

Mos gus yod na
Khyi so od tung

which means, 'If there is veneration, even a dog's tooth emits light.' "

PART III

Bhutan

9

Druk Yol: The Kingdom of the Thunder Dragon

On a horribly humid September afternoon in 1988, I found myself in a non-air-conditioned taxi cab in Calcutta trying to instruct the driver how to get to the South Park Street Cemetery. He seemed a very intelligent man with a lively command of English, but for some reason I was not able to get through to him the idea that I wanted to go to a place where dead bodies were buried. He seemed to think that I wanted to see a hospital like that of Mother Teresa—a common destination for visitors to Calcutta. It suddenly dawned on me what the problem was. There are no real cemeteries in Calcutta. The dead are burned and their ashes thrown in the Hooghly River. I then tried another tack and explained I wanted to go to a place that English visitors would go to visit their ancestors. The response was immediate and in short order, in a driving monsoon thunderburst, we pulled up in front of an ancient cemetery. The driver got out and spoke to the *chowkidar*—the watchman who apparently lived in the cemetery with five assistants, all of them huddled under the eaves of a crypt to get out of the rain. The negotiations completed, I was allowed into the cemetery and given a tour of it under an umbrella held by the taxi driver and the *chowkidar.*

It is a lovely cemetery as cemeteries go: an island of tranquillity in the Calcutta maelstrom. It was opened in 1767 and recently restored by the British Association for Cemeteries in Southern Asia. Some of the tombs are massive, some tiny. Some of the inscriptions appear newly carved and some are faded to illegibility. They collectively tell, implicitly, the history of British India. Charles Dickens's second son, Walter Landor Dickens, of the British Army, is buried there, as is Richmond Thackeray, William's father. The Scotsman George Bogle, the first British visitor to Tibet, is buried there. His monument contains the words IN SINCERE ATTACHMENT TO THE MEMORY OF MR. GEORGE BOGLE LATE AMBASSADOR TO TIBET WHO DIED THE 3RD OF APRIL, 1781. Soldiers, statesmen, women, and young children are all buried there, one of the last tangible reminders of the British raj. On the way back from the cemetery to my hotel, through the cloacal Calcutta traffic, made even worse by the intermittent cloudbursts which had turned the streets into a sort of malignant Venice, the driver asked me where I was going next. I told him, to Bhutan. "Bhutan," he said wistfully. "Bhutan is a nice place. You will like it there."

When told that one is going to Bhutan, most taxi drivers, like most people, tend to look at one blankly. But if one shot an arrow—archery is the national sport of Bhutan—north from Calcutta and slightly east about five hundred miles and got it up to about eight thousand feet above Calcutta's sea level, it would land in the Changlimithang Sports Grounds in Thimphu, the capital of Bhutan. Sixty miles or so farther north and it could hit the Kula Gangri, which at 24,784 feet is the highest mountain in Bhutan, and part of the Himalayan wall that separates the country from Tibet. To the west of Bhutan lies the tiny independent Indian protectorate of Sikkim, which received a certain amount of attention here when the then maharaja took as his consort the American socialite Hope Cooke. The rest of Bhutan, which is about the size of Switzerland, is bounded by India.

Bhutan, which its inhabitants actually call Druk Yol—the Thunder Dragon Land—is often regarded in the Indian subcontinent as a kind of Shangri-la—this is what my Calcutta taxi driver had in mind—and in many ways it is. With a population of only about 1.2 million, it is one of the few underpopulated countries in Asia. Indeed, like Switzerland, it imports a certain amount of "guest labor"—mostly Nepalese—who do things like road construction. It is one of the rare countries in Asia that actually *exports* food. Bhutanese fruit, grown mainly in the semitropical southern part of the country, is famous for its variety and quality. Bhutan is the only Himalayan country whose forests are basically intact. The Nepalese foothills, for example, are now so denuded that the land is being swept by erosion into the Bay of Bengal, and this deforestation is one of the principal causes of the periodic and often disastrous floods in Bengal and Bangladesh. (One of the ironies in the present dispute between India and Nepal is that as the Nepalese are forced to use more of their timber for fuel, the eroded hills exacerbate the floods in India.)

The conservation of Bhutan's forests is not an accident. Wood products, such as plywood, are the country's principal export. Trees are considered to be such a precious resource that any Bhutanese who wants to build a house made in whole, or in part, out of wood, must apply to the government for a permit that states how many trees may be cut down for that purpose. In Bhutan education and medical services are free. There are no known cases of AIDS in the country, and prostitution, if it exists at all, is invisible. There is hardly any begging in Bhutan, and visitors—the two thousand or so allowed by the government each year—are not allowed to tip anyone. Nor are they allowed to enter the Buddhist monasteries—Buddhism is the state religion of Bhutan—for fear of disturbing the contemplation of the monks, some of whom have taken vows of silence which can last for several years. This has kept the monasteries places of devotion, unlike those in Tibet, which are now largely tourist showplaces, or those in Nepal, which, because of the intrusion of tourists, often resemble film studios. Bhutan has a stable government—a constitutional monarch—presided over by thirty-four-year-old King Jigme Singye Wangchuk, the fourth hereditary monarch of the Wangchuk dynasty, who is immensely popular with his people. And it is a country where a high value is placed on simple honesty.

A perfect illustration of this was provided by an episode I witnessed on a recent visit. An acquaintance of mine was about to take the grueling seven-hour bus trip from Thimphu to the Indian border town of Phuntsholing. To fortify himself for the trip he stopped off first at the Swiss Bakery in Thimphu. It is so called because it is owned and operated by a Swiss who is married to a Bhutanese woman and has taken out Bhutanese citizenship. It features European-style pastries and Westernized sandwiches, such as yak burgers, which relieve the tedium—at least to Westerners—of the traditional Bhutanese diet, which features rice and dal—lentils—with an admixture of usually strongly spiced green vegetables or potatoes. (The only memorable local dish I had while in Bhutan was a melted Yak cheese concoction laced with bits of peppers.) The owner must have a certain nostalgia for his homeland, because near the front counter there is a faded poster of the Matterhorn. In any event, my friend finished his pastries and coffee and boarded the bus for Thimphu. Two hours later he noticed that he had left an extremely expensive camera on the table at the bakery. He explained this to the bus driver. The driver stopped the next northbound tourist bus to Thimphu and explained the situation to the driver of that bus, who said he would retrieve the camera and put it on the next southbound bus and that it would arrive in the hotel in Phuntsholing that evening, which it did. It never occurred to either of the drivers that someone might simply make off with the camera. As a Bhutanese said to me, "No one will touch a visitor's property except maybe children, who don't know what it is."

Despite its appeal one must never lose sight of the fact that, by Western standards, Bhutan is a very poor agrarian country. The life expectancy in the country is about forty-five years—lower than in neighboring India and Nepal. This is probably due to the uneven distribution of medical services in the country. People in Bhutan are dying from diseases like tuberculosis and—in the south—malaria, which could be eliminated by prevention and modern medical technology. No Westerner can, for example, drink untreated water anywhere in Bhutan, without running the risk of becoming seriously ill.

The Bhutanese people live with very little in the way of material comforts. I visited an apparently well-to-do farm family in eastern Bhutan and was struck by the austere quality of their lifestyle. There were very few glass windows in the house, which, even on a sunny afternoon in early fall, was very cold. Cooking was done on a smoky fire. It is a commonplace of these Himalayan communities that people smell of smoke. There was no running water and no plumbing facilities, no telephone and no electric light. But there was a simple room with mats on the wooden floor which had been set aside for monks in the event they needed a place to stay when passing through or performing rites for the family. There was—and this is what strikes everyone who visits Bhutan—a sense of harmonious lifestyle, of people in tune with themselves and their surroundings, people who have much to teach us about adapting to the world around us.

My own interest in Bhutan is relatively recent. This is just as well, since no tourists were allowed into the country prior to 1974, the year of the present king's coronation. Indeed, air travel into the country was only begun on a commercial basis in February of 1983. At the present time Druk Air operates two propeller-driven eighteen-seat Dornier aircraft that fly tourists, and others, between Calcutta, or Dacca in Bangladesh, and Paro, a town in eastern Bhutan located in one of the few valleys wide enough to provide space for a small airfield. Druk Air has just begun flying an eighty-passenger British Aerospace jet which will fly from New Delhi to Paro and carry most of the limited tourist traffic in and out of the country. My interest in Bhutan derives from one of those chance encounters with a historical figure who, for some reason or other, becomes something of an obsession.

In this case, the historical figure was that of the aforementioned George Bogle, whose tomb I had gone in search of in the South Park Street Cemetery in Calcutta. I first came across Bogle when I stumbled upon his *Narrative of the Mission of George Bogle to Tibet* first published in an edition edited by Clements R. Markham in 1879. As I mentioned earlier, I found this rare book in a private library in Kathmandu and had only a couple of days' access to it. I concentrated my reading on Bogle's account of his trip to Tibet, and skimmed over the parts on Bhutan, making a mental note to read them more carefully if I could ever get ahold of a copy of the book, which I did almost a year later, after I returned from Tibet. Here are a few more facts about Bogle, who was as far as anyone knows the first Westerner to visit Bhutan.

George Bogle was born on the twenty-sixth of November, 1746, in a place called Daldowie, Scotland, on the banks of the Clyde. He was the youngest of nine children, two of whom died in infancy. Throughout his adult life he expressed, especially in letters to his favorite sister Anne, known as Chuffles, his nostalgia for Daldowie, which, as it happened, he was never to see again once he left for India. It was decided early in his career that Bogle should become a merchant, and, after a desultory education, in June of 1765 he entered his brother's "counting-house" as a clerk. Here he remained for the next four years until, at age twenty-three, he received an appointment with the British East India Company in Calcutta. His arrival in Bengal coincided with a famine there which left a deep impression on him, and he reported to his father that "There were sometimes 150 dead bodies picked up in a day and thrown into the river." Bogle was placed on the so-called Select Committee of the Company, an entity that transacted all of the company's political business on the subcontinent. He also mastered Persian, which, as it happened, was the language of diplomacy on the subcontinent—treaties were often written in it—in somewhat the same sense that French, at the time, was the diplomatic language of Europe.

After Bogle had been in Calcutta for eighteen months, Warren Hastings arrived from Madras to become the governor of Bengal. Hastings was a remarkable and controversial man. It was he who decided that the British must assume full responsibility for the actual governance of India, while at the same time preserving what was best in traditional Indian life. He instituted a number of reforms in the administration of Indian affairs, which led to serious conflicts with the local British establishment and ultimately to an impeachment trial before the House of Lords which lasted from 1788 to 1795. He was eventually acquitted. Bogle's relationship with Hastings began in 1773, and the feeling of mutual admiration between the two men was established almost at once. To his father, Bogle wrote, "Mr. Hastings is a man who is every way fitted for the station which he holds. He possesses a steadiness, and at the same time a moderation of character; he is quick and assiduous in business, and has a fine style of language, a knowledge of the customs and dispositions of the natives, whose tongue he understands and, although not affable, yet of the most ready access to all the world." The feeling was mutual, so it was quite natural that when the next year, for reasons I will soon explain, a mission to Bhutan and then Tibet became desirable, Hastings turned to Bogle, who was only twenty-eight. His mission lasted an entire year, but on his return he found himself in the middle of the imbroglio which finally led to Hastings's impeachment. In addition he learned that his beloved Daldowie was in financial jeopardy, and much of his salary for the next few years went to help his father pay off his debts. In 1776 Hastings was restored as governor general, and Bogle's relationship with him was reestablished. At the time of his death, at the age of thirty-four in Calcutta, Bogle was engaged in the planning of a second mission to Bhutan which he did not live to carry out.

These are the essentials of Bogle's brief life, but before I turn to a description of Bogle's mission to Bhutan I would like to discuss the relation of Bogle, and other Englishmen of this period—the eighteenth century—to the native women of the subcontinent. This was to change radically in the next century, and many writers about the history of British India have speculated that the arrival of the memsahibs, with all their Victorian material and moral baggage, played a decisive role in the sharp class distinctions that developed between the British and the peoples of the subcontinent they governed. This, as we shall see, certainly played a very significant role in the nineteenth-century British attitude toward the Bhutanese.

During the period we are discussing it was a commonplace for a British man in India to take on a "bebee"—a native woman—with whom he would often have a family. In a fascinating memoir entitled "George Bogle and His Children," Hugh Richardson, who for nine years was head of the British mission in Lhasa (until the Chinese took over that country in the 1950s), describes the evidence that Bogle himself had such a family—indeed, that he had *two* such families. He apparently had sons with a subcontinental woman whose origins have not been identified, and it is certain that he had two daughters, Martha and Mary, by a woman whom Bogle family tradition identifies as a Tibetan princess— probably the sister of the Panchen Lama Bogle went to stay with in Tibet. In Markham's biographical sketch of Bogle, published in his edition of the *Narratives*, he writes only that "George Bogle left two daughters to mourn his loss, named Martha and Mary, who were sent to Scotland . . . " Of their mother there is no mention. It seems clear to me that Bogle's intimate connections with these native women is what made him such a sensitive observer of the subcontinental people he traveled among. Here for example is what he writes about the

Bhutanese in the *Narratives.* "The more I see of the Bhutanese, the more I am pleased with them. The common people are good-humored, downright, and, I think, thoroughly trusty. The statesmen have some of the art which belongs to their profession. They are the best built race of men I ever saw; many of them very handsome with complexions as fair as the French." Contrast this with the evaluation of Ashley Eden, a bishop's son and a pillar of Victorian society, who visited Bhutan on a similar mission in 1863. Here is Eden's commentary with approval on an appraisal of an earlier visitor to Bhutan. "As a race their failings are very correctly described by Captain [R. B.] Pemberton [who had visited the country in 1837] in the following words: 'I sometimes saw some few persons in whom the demoralizing influences of such a state of society had yet left a trace of the image in which they were originally created, and where the feelings of nature still exercised their accustomed influence, but the exceptions were indeed rare to universal demorality, and much as I have travelled and resided amongst savage tribes on our Frontiers, I have never yet known one so wholly degraded in morals as the Booteahs [Bhutanese]'." It is as if Bogle, Pembarton and Eden had visited different countries, having in common only a geography.

To understand the geography of Bhutan, one can imagine the level plains of Bengal and Assam as a sort of sea floor, which, in the recent floods, they very nearly have been. Following these plains north, one suddenly runs into an abruptly rising "coastline." These Himalayan foothills, which rise practically vertically some seven thousand feet out of the plains, constitute, apart from a narrow strip of flatland, the southern boundary of Bhutan. Not only are these foothills extremely steep, but they are covered by an all but impenetrable tropical rain forest. From the air one cannot see the ground through the dense carpet of foliage. However, at precisely eighteen places known as duars—a word akin to the English *door* and the Hindi *dwar,* or gate—river valleys cut through the mountains. All the motor roads from the south pass through the eighteen duars; anyone controlling the duars would control almost all the commerce in and out of the country. From time to time, invading bands of Bhutanese would sweep down through the duars to raid neighboring provinces such as that of the princely state of Cooch Behar. Indeed the first inkling the British had that there might be some kind of political entity, with possible hostile intent, on their newly created northern borders, seems to have occurred in 1772 when the Bhutanese invaded Cooch Behar through an adjacent duar and carried off both the maharaja and his brother. In describing this historical event, one must be a little careful when one uses the term *the Bhutanese* as if one were describing as early as 1772 the actions of a sovereign nation. Indeed, Bhutan was hardly a unified nation at all until the beginning of this century, but rather a collection of local fiefdoms located in isolated valleys, speaking their own languages and with their separate political systems. Even today there is a tribe in eastern Bhutan, the Bragpas, who wear animal skins and belong to a different race than the Tibetan-derivative race that inhabits western Bhutan. They speak their own language rather than the national language—Dzongkha—which is a dialect of Tibetan but sufficiently far removed from the original that a Dzongkha-speaking Bhutanese can understand Tibetans, but not vice-versa.

In any event, the Cooch Beharis appealed to the British to do something. The British in turn dispatched four companies of Sepoys with two cannon under one Captain Jones, who proceeded to administer a good lesson to the intruders. In fact it was such a good lesson that it thoroughly alarmed the Bhutanese. They, in turn, appealed to the Tibetans, who were at this juncture their patrons, to make peace. (The relation between Tibet and Bhutan, like that between Tibet and China, alternated between periods of armed hostility and patronage. At the present time there is an uneasy truce with the Chinese in Tibet, who have claimed a certain amount of the northern Bhutanese Himalayan frontier country as their own.) This prompted the Panchen Lama in Shigatse to write the letter to Warren Hastings that I mentioned earlier in describing the history of Tibet. It entreated the British to lay off the Bhutanese. The letter, which I quote in part here for its flavor, was a masterpiece of Asiatic diplomatic writing.

The lama begins by remarking that "The affairs of this quarter in every respect flourish. I am night and day employed in prayers for the increase of your happiness and prosperity. Having been informed by travellers from your quarter of your exalted fame and reputation, my heart, like the blossom of spring, abounds in gaiety, gladness, and joy; praise that the state of your fortune is in its ascension . . . " And on and on. That having been gotten out of the way, the lama gets down to business. It seems that the raid in question was the responsibility of a dubious character named Deb Judhur. During the next century, as the raids continued, finally culminating in the Duar Wars of 1865, the British would find it next to impossible to pin the responsibility for any given raid on someone they could actually lay their hands on. Deb Judhur was no exception—he was in Tibet—but the Panchen Lama assured Hastings that he had communicated with him. "I have reprimanded the Deb for his past conduct, and have admonished him to desist from his evil practices in future, and to be submissive to you in all matters," the lama assured Hastings, adding, "as to my part, I am but a Fakir, and it is the custom of my sect, with the rosary in our hands, to pray for the welfare of mankind, and for the peace and happiness of the inhabitants of this country; and I do now, with my head uncovered, entreat that you may cease all hostilities against the Deb in future."

If Hastings had been a different sort of person he might simply have left it at that. But he at once saw an opportunity to develop relations—commercial and otherwise—with a hitherto unknown area of the subcontinent: Tibet and Bhutan. To this end, as we saw, he commissioned young Bogle to lead such a mission. It is clear from Hastings's instructions to Bogle, quoted earlier, that while commerce was an important element—after all, the British East India Company was primarily a commercial enterprise—much of what motivated Hastings was simple curiosity. Take the matter of the potato.

As any traveler to Bhutan can testify, the potato is a common, if not relentless, part of one's diet. Indigenous to South America—Peru, Ecuador, Bolivia, and Chile—it was brought to Europe in the sixteenth century, and thence to Asia. The British, it would appear, are responsible for bringing the potato to the Himalayas. Indeed, as the anthropologist Christoph von Furer-Haimendorf argues in his book *The Sherpas of Nepal*, the potato was still being introduced to the Sherpa country near Mount Everest from the "English gardens" in Kathmandu as late as the middle of the nineteenth century. Be this as it may, there is no doubt that it was Bogle's mission that introduced the potato to Bhutan. Hastings instructed Bogle to plant potatoes anywhere the mission camped, simply to introduce a new crop into Bhutan, out of curiosity as to what would happen. As Peter Collister writes in his book *Bhutan and the British*, "At every halt Bogle carried out Warren Hastings' instructions to plant potatoes, the first batch of ten being at a place called Jaigugu which consisted only of three houses. At Maridzong which they reached after a journey including many descents and steep climbs, passing three waterfalls, he planted fifteen."

The route Bogle followed, as nearly as I can tell by studying the map, is essentially the same as the one taken by the remarkable Indian-engineered road that now leads from the border to Thimphu, a distance of about 150 miles of very difficult terrain. Bogle calls his destination Tassisudon, but the modern transliteration of the Bhutanese name would usually be rendered by Tashichodzong. The word *dzong* in Dzongkha refers to a fortresslike monastery, a structure that was usually placed at some strategic high point so that it dominated the surrounding countryside. Bhutan is dotted with such structures, many in ruins. The buildings that Bogle visited in the Tashichodzong are still standing. But they are a part of a reconstruction made by the present king's father in

1961. The Tashichodzong, on the outskirts of Thimphu, is the largest structure in Bhutan. It is also next to a nine-hole golf course, the only golf course in the country and probably the only one in the world which is also a cow pasture. The beasts appear to move obligingly so as not to interfere with play.

Half of the Tashichodzong is an active monastery to which non-Buddhist visitors are not allowed; as is true of all active monasteries in Bhutan, the rest of the *dzong* houses most of the present government. The king receives officially in a room on the second floor overlooking the magnificent courtyard. With special permission visitors can enter this courtyard after five P.M. when the government offices are closed. It is a lovely, tranquil place. Sitting in the courtyard I tried to imagine the feelings Bogle had about it when he entered the same courtyard. On my entry I was not regarded by "3000 spectators" nor presented with "several copper platters with rice, butter, treacle, tea, walnuts, Kashmirian dates, apricots, cucumbers, and other fruits . . . ," as was Bogle. But still.

There was, of course, no photography in Bogle's day, but there is a contemporary oil painting by one Tilly Kettle showing Bogle in what are described as "formal Bhutanese clothes." The hat he has on, which looks like an inverted flower pot, does not resemble anything I saw worn in Bhutan, but the long knee-length robe with its marsupial pockets known as a *khos*—pronounced "go"—is still the traditional male costume in Bhutan. They seem to come in two varieties, an oxford gray version for more formal occasions and a tartan version that is worn every day. Bogle is shown barefoot in his *khos*, while a traditionally dressed Bhutanese would wear high boots. It is more common now, however, to see men wearing a kind of knee-length argyle sock—like a Scottish golfing sock—and some sort of Western shoe, often sneakers or basketball shoes. Women wear usually dark-colored, ankle-length dresses called *kiras*. I never saw a Bhutanese woman in a short skirt or slacks, and Western women are advised that shorts or tight-fitting clothes are not appropriate in Bhutan. There is an effort by the government to discourage

Bhutanese from wearing Western clothes. Government officials, for example, are required to wear *khos* and *kira*s to work.

There was, of course, a political entity in what is now Bhutan—or Druk Yol—before the British "discovered" it. Although the identity of the original inhabitants of the territory is unclear, it is generally agreed that by the ninth century A.D. the country had two distinct populations. The eastern part of Bhutan was populated by what are known as Sharchops, people who, it appears, migrated north from Assam. The western part of the country was populated by Bhotias— hence *Bhutan*—people who had migrated south from Tibet. By the ninth century these people were practicing a kind of Tantric Buddhism that had been introduced into Tibet from India by the great eighth-century teacher Padma Sambhava and his disciples.

The Tibetans account for the fact that this guru's vehicle spread so rapidly by the notion that he was able to locomote from place to place on the back of a snow lion. In Bhutan, Padma Sambhava, so the legend goes, was able to make use of a winged tiger. The tiger landed in a place known as Taktsang, not far from the town of Paro, coincidentally the site of the country's only airfield. There is a nest of monastic structures—the Tiger's Nest—which cling impossibly to a cliff some three thousand feet above the valley floor. From below it is impossible to imagine how *anything* could be transported to the monastery short of using a flying tiger. In fact, a reasonably comfortable path leads first to a tea house established by the government for tourists—the Taktsang is one of the prime tourist attractions in the country—and then, above the tea house, to the monastery itself. Fortunately a wall of trees conceals from the pedestrian the fact that he or she has been navigating across the face of a sheer cliff with a drop of some three thousand feet. One can approach to within a few hundred feet of the lower monastery, which, like the upper one, is now off limits to non-Bhutanese visitors. It is not occupied full-time by the monks. (At the time of my visit there was a ceremony in progress involving, among other things, the eerie reverberations of conch horns and tambours. The monks waved cheerfully at us between rituals.) The upper monastery has about thirty monks in it who have taken a vow of silence of three years, three months, three weeks, and three days. The ban on visiting them has been imposed partly so as not to disturb their contemplation and partly because visitors were being sold antique artifacts from the monastery, a practice that has all but denuded the monasteries in Nepal of their great art treasures. Visitors who leave Bhutan are subject to a rigorous search of their baggage to make sure that no antiquities are being exported.

The only place in Bhutan where I saw even a hint of begging was at the base of the cliff leading to the monastery. Here children ask, timidly to be sure, for chewing gum, pens, and sometimes for money. I witnessed the progression from this kind of tentative begging in 1967, when I first visited Nepal, to the inferno of begging that now takes place in all the Nepalese villages where trekkers pass. It has rendered visiting these villages a nightmare, and the Bhutanese are determined to learn from this example. Tourists are asked not to give anything to children, especially candies, since there is a shortage of dentists in Bhutan.

The Buddhism that is practiced in Bhutan shows traces of Bon, the animistic religion that preceded it. Mountains and rivers embody living spirits. An interesting example is Chomo Lhari—pronounced "Jomolari"—a magnificent twenty-four-thousand-foot peak on the Tibeto-Bhutanese frontier. Chomo Lhari will never be climbed to the top because this would offend the spirit of the mountain. Climbing any peak in Bhutan requires permission from the king, and to get permission to climb Chomo Lhari, one must agree not to violate the summit. But this is not all. The spirit of the mountain is offended by the sight of fire. Hence one does not make an open fire within sight of the mountain. If one does, and one burns, say, refuse in it, there will surely be a terrible storm. I met a lovely young Bhutanese girl who had come from a small village in the east to take temporary work in the tourist hotel in Thimphu. She spoke a serviceable and delightful English and we spent several hours discussing various things. She told me that it was very dangerous to cook meat within the sight of Chomo Lhari. If one did one ran the risk of being taken off by a "gorilla." She told me that one of the girls in her village had been taken off by a gorilla and had become a gorilla bride. The men and boys in the village took their bows and arrows and spears and went looking for the girl. They found her in a cave and brought her back to the village. They got a lama from a nearby monastery to come to the village to exorcise the spell the gorilla had cast on the girl. Thereafter she was simply a girl. I asked my Bhutanese friend if she herself had talked to the girl. "No," she answered solemnly, "but my mummy did." When I went trekking to Chomo Lhari I made sure that I lit no fires in sight of the mountain.

To return to the history, in 1616, fleeing from persecution in Tibet, the lama Ngawang Namgyal, came to Bhutan. In the next thirty-five years, until his death in 1651, he succeeded in unifying all of western Bhutan, making Buddhism the state religion. He built the system of fortress *dzongs* whose ruins one sees today strategically placed in the valleys of Bhutan and which were used successfully to fend off invasions from both the Tibetans and the Mongols. When he died it is said that the secret of his death was kept for fifty years. It is the country he created that Bogle visited in 1774. Following Bogle's mission were several others, including one led by Captain Samuel Turner in 1783. What distinguished Turner's mission from its predecessors was the presence on it of the artist Samuel Davis. The watercolors done by Davis capture the sublime beauty of the Bhutanese countryside in a way that has never been excelled. Apart from a few roads and the odd telephone line, nothing much has changed in the countryside as Davis drew it.

None of these missions resolved the matter of the duars. Even the seizing of the seven Assam duars by the British in 1840 failed to stop raiding by the Bhutanese. A perfect microcosm of the whole can be found in the affair of Mr. Pyne's elephant. The incident is described in the "Report on State of Bootan [*sic*]," by Ashley Eden, whose mission in 1863–64 led to the Duar Wars. Eden writes: "Early in January 1861 the Bootan Frontier Office at Gopalgunge sent over men who stole a valuable elephant belonging to Mr. Pyne, the Manager of Messrs. Dear and Co. at Sillagooree. On Mr. Pyne's tracing the elephant and finding it to be in the Gopalgunge stockage, he asked the Booteah Officer to send it to him. The man acknowledged having it, but refused to deliver it up till he received a present of Rupees 300, a telescope, and a gun." A contemporary writer commented that the "Bootan people went on in their evil courses, stole an elephant from a Mr. Pyne, another from a native, and with much effrontery allowed them to be frequently seen from our side on the river bank, so that the owners were sorely tempted to recover them by force or stratagem. It is recorded that Mr. Pyne 'altogether bears his loss with less equanimity than the native as is natural to a man with English blood in his veins.' "

Whatever else one may say of Ashley Eden, he was certainly a man of remarkable courage. With twenty-five soldiers and four British officers and ten thousand rupees to be used to buy presents, he set out on the fourth of January, 1864, to compel some sort of treaty from the Bhutanese committing them to cease and desist from their hostile activities in the duars. After several weeks of marching through a variety of difficult terrain varying from the malarial lowlands to waist-deep snow in the high passes, Eden arrived in Punakah in central Bhutan in mid-March. Punakah was, until a few years ago, the winter capital of Bhutan—now it is Thimphu—and the magnificent *dzong* where Eden was received still stands. (In 1986 there was a fire that burned some of its interior, and at the time of my visit active restoration was under way.) Eden was received—if that is the word—by a local potentate known as the Tongsa Ponlop. This institution of ponlops—local regents—still exists, and before a king's son can claim the throne he must have been appointed either the Tongsa Ponlop or the Paro Ponlop. The ponlop did his best to humiliate Eden and his retinue. As Eden reported, "The Penlow [sic] took up a large piece of wet dough and began rubbing my face with it. He pulled my hair and slapped me on the back and generally conducted himself with great insolence. On my showing signs of impatience or remonstrating he smiled and deprecated my anger, pretending that it was the familiarity of friendship, much to the amusement of the large assemblage of bystanders." Eden was also compelled, under duress, to sign a treaty that gave the Bhutanese back the occupied duars before he and his party were allowed to return to India.

Eden was known to loathe the Bhutanese even before his mission, and his report is full of vitriolic comments about all aspects of Bhutanese life—for example, the betel nut. The betel nut is the fruit of the areca or the betel nut palm tree. It is chewed throughout Asia. It is a bright red—at least in the Bhutanese version—and it is chewed while keeping some sort of stone in the mouth that produces calcium carbonate which turns the betel nut into a mild narcotic. It also turns the chewer's mouth red. To Westerners, used to shiny white teeth as an aesthetic norm, the sight of red teeth is, to put it mildly, disconcerting. It is comforting to know that these stains are readily washed off. To Eden, chewing the betel nut was one more illustration of Bhutanese depravity. He writes, "The higher classes have their mouths filled with this disgusting stimulation: they almost live on it . . . " This gave him a brilliant idea for dealing with Bhutanese intransigence, ". . . The occupation of the Dooars [sic], if it affects them in no other way, will by stopping their supply of betel soon bring them to reason." More substantively, Eden's contempt for the Bhutanese caused him to underestimate their abilities as soldiers, and this soon cost the British dearly. Eden wrote, "Their chief arms are stones, a long knife, a shield, and bows and arrows; the latter they can scarcely use." And he concluded, "They admit themselves to be the most despicable soldiers on the face of the earth; they told us that if one man was killed there was a fight for his body, but if in that another was killed they always ran away."

It is not for nothing that archery is the national sport of Bhutan. It is the only sport in which Bhutan was represented in both the Los Angeles and Seoul Olympics. (No medals were won.) Villages have spirited competitions with each other and children of both sexes practice it from childhood. A Bhutanese specialty is long-distance archery. I watched a team of soldiers shoot from a distance that looked to me like the length of a football field, at a small target. Their bows, which they showed me, were made of bamboo and the bow strings were made of the vine of the stinging nettle. They said that if they could afford them, they would like to use American bows and arrows which, apparently, shoot even farther. In the national museum in Paro—a lovely place in which, like most of the historical places in Bhutan, no photography is allowed (for some reason, no motion-picture photography is allowed anywhere in the country except with special permission)—there is a display of the kinds of bows and arrows that were used by Bhutanese soldiers in the last century. They have long, sinister-looking metal barbs at the ends which were usually tipped with poison.

In December of 1865 a strong force of British mercenary Indian soldiers—Gurkhas, Assamis, and Punjabis—invaded the Bengal duars to settle, they hoped once and for all, the "outrages" that were being committed by the Bhutanese. They had six Armstrong mountain train guns, four eight-inch mortars, and several other heavy weapons. What then ensued was described by a Major Macgregor, who reported that "We have been accustomed to regard these Bhutias [*sic*] as a despicable, pusillanimous race, and yet we see them with stones and arrows offering no contemptible defence to some 500 to 600 men with Armstrong guns and inflicting on them a loss of 58 killed and wounded . . . I doubt . . . if we could have lost many more men if the enemy had been armed with muskets. The arrows are all sharp and pointed and fly with great precision, having penetration enough to go through a man's body."

The war continued with appalling losses on both sides—
the British suffered several hundred casualties to disease,
notably malaria—until the following fall, when the British
compelled whatever authorities in Bhutan they could make
contact with to sign the so-called Treaty of Sinchula (November 11, 1865). In this treaty the British got the right to annex all
the Assam and Bengal duars in return for which the Bhutanese were to receive a stipend that would eventually rise to
fifty thousand rupees a year. There then followed some
twenty years of uneasy peace with the Bhutanese in a state of
near civil war, often over which faction should control the
fifty-thousand-rupee stipend. This is where things stood until 1879, when Ugyen Wangchuk became the Tongsa Ponlop.
On December 17, 1907, he was appointed the first king of
Bhutan, hence founding the present hereditary Wangchuk
dynasty.

Contemporary photographs of Ugyen Wangchuk show
him to be a solidly built man with a broad, powerful face—
someone who gave off an aura of no-nonsense authority. It
took him some seven years prior to becoming king to consoli-
date his power within Bhutan—often by use of force—and
then he turned his attention to Bhutan's relations with its
neighbors. It is not clear how much was chance and how
much guile, but Wangchuk was able to take advantage of the
almost paranoid fear the British had of the Russians and
Chinese extending their influence south toward India. When
the British and the Tibetans had an armed skirmish in 1888,
Wangchuk very pointedly did not come to the aid of the
Tibetans.

By 1903 the British were, after some backing and filling,
able to enlist Wangchuk as a kind of diplomatic go-between
on the armed mission to Lhasa led by Francis Younghusband.
Collister, in his book on the British in Bhutan, reports that
Younghusband and his officers called Wangchuk "Alphonse"
"because of his rather Gallic appearance: short and well built
with a small 'imperial' beard, and usually sporting a grey
Homburg hat." In 1905, one of Younghusband's former offi-

cers, John Claude White, led an official mission to Bhutan, the high point of which occurred when the mission reached the ancient capital of Punakah and White was able to confer upon Wangchuk the insignia and warrant of Knight Companion of the Indian Empire, by means of which Wangchuk became Sir Ugyen. White later wrote, "It says a great deal for the change in conduct of affairs in Bhutan and the anxiety to show respect for the British government that they should have made the presentation of the decoration . . . the first occasion of so public and elaborate a ceremony."

On December 17, 1907, White was back in Bhutan to witness the signing of what has been called the "Magna Carta of Bhutan." The most significant part of the document read, "We, the undersigned abbots, lopons and the whole body of the Lamas, the state councillors, the chiolas of the different districts, with all the subjects, having discussed and unanimously agreed to elect Sir Ugyen Wangchuk, Tongsa Ponlop, prime minister of Bhutan, as hereditary Maharajah of this state, having installed him in open durbar on the golden throne on this thirteenth day of the eleventh month of Sa-Tel year, corresponding to the 17th of December 1907, at Punakah-phodey, we now declare our allegiance to him and his heirs and with the unchanging mind undertake to serve him and his heirs loyally and faithfully to the best of our ability. Should anyone not abide by this contract by saying this and that, he shall altogether be turned out of our company. In witness thereto we affix our seals . . ."

Now that the Bhutan was, in some sense, a princely state with a proper maharaja, the British had to decide how many "guns" it merited. In British India there were 565 princely states. These were divided by the British into three divisions. The first division consisted of the "salute states," the maharajas of which were entitled, on ceremonial occasions, to be saluted by the British army with the firing of a certain number of cannon. Two states got twenty-one guns, six had nineteen, thirteen had seventeen, and seventeen had fifteen. Bhutan was given fifteen.

King Ugyen Wangchuk ruled until 1926 when, on his death, he was succeeded by his son Jigme Wangchuk, who ruled until 1952. One of the most important things Jigme Wangchuk did was to preside over the transition of Bhutan's status when India gained its independence in 1947. The role of Bhutan in the British commonwealth had always been somewhat ambiguous. When it suited the British they treated Bhutan like any other princely state, which meant that they kept control over Bhutan's foreign policy. But when, for example, it was a matter of giving the Bhutanese large financial subsidies, the British tended to treat Bhutan as if it were an independent country. While this was frustrating to the Bhutanese, it probably saved the independence of Bhutan. In 1947 the British required the princely states to choose between India and Pakistan in the partition. Bhutan, because of its ambiguous status, never had to make the choice.

When India became independent it agreed to assume the British role, which meant, in particular, that it would guide Bhutan's foreign policy. On the other hand India has been the main benefactor of Bhutan. Among other things the Indians have engineered the road system, trained the army, and provided three out of the four pilots currently flying for Druk Air. My visit to Bhutan coincided with that of Rajiv Gandhi, the prime minister of India. On this visit Mr. Gandhi announced that he was donating one million nu—a nu is a Bhutanese rupee and it is tied in value to the Indian rupee—for the construction and restoration of religious structures in central Bhutan. But as a sort of declaration of their independence, the Bhutanese maintain their local time a half hour ahead of the national Indian time.

The present king's father, Jigme Dorji Wangchuk, took over from his father in 1952. As a young man he paid a visit to London. He was, according to an account I read of one visit, feeling a little nostalgic for home on Bhutan's national day (which is celebrated on various calendar dates depending on the augurs), and decided to shoot an arrow out of the window of the apartment where he was staying. It found its way into a neighbor's window and the future king then retrieved it by climbing like a cat burglar up a drainpipe and into the neighboring apartment. Fortunately for British-Bhutanese relations, he was not discovered. In any event, it is Jigme Dorji Wangchuk who is credited for initiating the process that is slowly bringing Bhutan into the modern world. In 1953, in a remarkable unilateral gesture, the king gave up the power of absolute veto over the legislature of Bhutan. There is now a national assembly made up of about 150 representatives. About two-thirds of them are elected directly by the people for three-year terms. Ten are from monastic orders, and the rest are appointed by the king. In 1968 the King gave the assembly the power to force any future king to abdicate if it felt that he no longer served the interests of the country.

Until 1960 there were no proper roads in Bhutan and the program was begun, in collaboration with India, that produced the remarkable network of vertiginous roads that links the country together. Until 1968 there were no banks in Bhutan—most transactions were by barter. That year the Bank of Bhutan was established, along with a monetary system that has replaced barter exchanges. Until 1962 there was no postal system in Bhutan. That year stamps were issued and in 1969 Bhutan joined the Universal Postal Union. Like many small countries, Bhutan has realized that there is hard currency to be made if only one can convince foreign stamp collectors to buy one's stamps. The Bhutanese have made a successful effort to design unusual stamps. I saw a full display in the museum in Paro. They included a three-dimensional stamp, a series in which the stamp is also a small playable record, five triangular stamps which portray the yeti, and the world's first steel stamp printed on a thousandth-of-an-inch-thick steel foil. It is not clear why anyone needs a steel stamp, but it certainly is pretty. In 1971, the year before the king died, by a unanimous decision of the General Assembly, Bhutan became a member of the United Nations and opened up the Permanent Mission of the Kingdom of Bhutan to the United Nations in New York.

The affection and respect that the Bhutanese have for their present King Jigme Singye Wangchuk is evident to anyone who visits the country. It clearly goes beyond any sort of pro forma gesture. I learned that the king, who was born on November 11, 1955, the Wood-Sheep year in the Bhutanese calendar, is both a sports fan and sportsman. At the moment his favorite sport seems to be basketball. He plays every day with players from the army. (The Royal Bhutan Army was founded by the present king's father in 1959 and has about six thousand men in it. One of their missions is to control the smuggling that takes place across the Tibetan borders.) The king, who is a Boston Celtics fan, plays forward. He used to play a good deal of soccer. His position was goalie. I asked a Bhutanese, who seemed to be knowledgeable about these matters, if other players were hesitant about scoring goals off of the king. He said no, and he told me that in one game a player scored a particularly brilliant winning goal off of the king in the last minute of the game. The king was so impressed that he asked the player after the game to show him how he had done it. When the king left the field, the player was approached by one of the king's aides carrying a small envelope. Inside the envelope were five hundred rupees—a gift from the king.

One of the mysteries about the king of Bhutan that I was not able to resolve fully while I was there is the matter of the succession. I was shown, from a considerable distance, the modest wooden bungalow which is the king's residence. It is in a little forest just outside of Thimphu. He appeared to live alone. However, I was told in strict confidence that he had been privately married to four sisters for nine years and that he had had children with each of them. Moreover an eight-year-old son of the oldest sister, who is, I was told, twenty-nine, had been selected as the future king. All of this seemed to be common knowledge to many Bhutanese I spoke to, but, for whatever reason, they impressed upon me the fact that this was a kind of state secret. However, on October 30, 1988, the king announced it publicly and a formal marriage celebration was scheduled for the twenty-second day of the ninth month of the Earth-Dragon year—that is, for October 31, 1988—and, in the same ceremony, Prince Jigme Gesar Namgyal Wangchuk was named crown prince. At age eighteen the young man will be designated the Tongsa Ponlop, the essential prior step to his being able to succeed his father. As far as I can determine there is no stigma in general attached to a child's being born out of wedlock in Bhutan. There are, however, I was told, strict rules about the support, financial and otherwise, that must be given to the child's mother during and after her pregnancy. There appears to be a fair amount of divorce in Bhutan, where first marriages, which are voluntary and not arranged, take place at about the age of eighteen.

The present king was first tutored privately in Bhutan, then sent to India and then Oxford to complete his education. He has been especially concerned about education in Bhutan. A survey done in 1979 showed that there were 124 schools—104 primary schools, fourteen junior high schools, and six high schools. A university to be named after Ugyen Wangchuk is being planned. Many Bhutanese who have gone through the high-school system go abroad for higher education. Nontraditional—Western-style—doctors, for example, are now trained in India. Traditional doctors, who practice herbal medicine, are trained in Bhutan. All education in Bhutan is free and the instruction is in English. However, the study of Dzonkha, the national language, is compulsory at all levels. The use of English in this pervasive way has provoked a certain amount of conservative reaction in the country. I came across the following letter in the *Kuensel* (*Enlightenment,*) a weekly national newspaper that was started a year or so ago with the help of a ninety-three-thousand-dollar grant from the United Nations Development Program, which has a large presence in Bhutan. It appears in three editions: Dzongkha, Nepali, and English. I quote the letter as it appeared in the

English edition of Saturday, September 24, 1988. It is signed by Chen Chen of the Dzongkha Development Advisory Committee and reads,

> Although our country has her own rich culture, tradition and language as a sign of her sovereign independence it is observed that many people are accustomed to western language and style.
>
> They are more familiar with speaking English than dzongkha and even their babies are first taught to speak English, making them forget their mother tongue or the national language dzongkha.
>
> Due to this influence, even in the remote villages, the villagers try to teach their children to say uncle, aunty and mummy instead of the beautiful words ashang, ahni and aai.
>
> It is the responsibility of every citizen to keep in mind their national language. I would rather say that a language has not merely a distinctive idiom but it also embodies distinctive patterns of thought and feeling. It is this idiom of the thought and feeling, if we can use such an expression, that often defies translation. It is the vehicle through which people can exchange their views, idea and opinions and react with one another thus fostering a greater understanding that is responsible for peace, harmony and unity and side by side, increase economic development in the country.
>
> Therefore, I would request all concerned to afford their self interest in learning dzongkha which is the identity of our peaceful and religious kingdom.

A perfect illustration of the many Bhutanese attitudes toward outside influence is the matter of tourism. Until 1974 there was essentially no tourism in the country. That year, in connection with the coronation of the present king, a number of hotels, guesthouses, and cottages were built to accommodate visitors. They now accommodate tourists. The large hotels in places like Paro and Thimphu are built in traditional Bhutanese style: wood and stone, one or two stories, and without nails. They are very comfortable, but not, by Western standards, luxurious. They are built far enough away from the community they serve so as not to interfere with people's daily lives. The one near Thimphu—the Motithang Hotel—has in its lobby a small shrine dedicated to the eleventh-century Buddhist poet-saint Milarepa. Next to the shrine is a quotation from his verse that reflects the tranquil atmosphere of the hotel:

The non-arising Mind Essence cannot
Be described by metaphors or signs;
Be extinguished is oft described
By fools, but those who realize
It, explain by itself
Devoid of symbolized and symbolizer,
It is a realm beyond all words and thought
How wondrous is the blessing of my Lineage!

Since 1974 a couple of thousand tourists a year have been admitted to Bhutan. (In 1987 the number was about twenty-three hundred, mostly American and Japanese.) It is all but impossible for a tourist to enter Bhutan unless he or she is a member of an organized tour arranged through the Bhutan Tourism Corporation either directly or through an overseas tour operator which in turn deals with the Bhutan Tourism Corporation. One simply does not find tourists, as one does in Nepal and as one used to in Tibet, wandering at random around the country. The corporation sets the daily rates for these tours, which, in 1988, were about $100 a day if one was trekking outside the cities and about $130 a day in the cities. The typical tourist stays about nine days. In 1989 these rates will practically double.

I had the opportunity to discuss this with Karchung Wangchuk—no relation as far as I know to the king—who is the manager of trekking and mountaineering for the Tourism Corporation. He said that the feeling among the Bhutanese was that even twenty-three hundred tourists were too many. He was especially concerned about the fifteen hundred tourists who trek, something that has been possible only in the last few years. He felt that fifteen-hundred trekkers were too many and planned to cut the number to about six hundred. (There are well over thirty thousand a year in Nepal.) He would like to see a situation in which, even on the more popular treks like the eight-day Chomo Lhari trek which I took, there would never be more than one trekking party at a time on the route. (On the popular Nepal treks some of the camping sites now resemble tent cities.) He wants every trekker to have a wilderness experience, to be able to see the people and the animals, such as the magnificent herds of wild blue sheep near the mountains, in their primitive simplicity. Because of this planned reduction in tourism, the Bhutanese have closed the tourist offices they had in New York and elsewhere. All tourist queries will now be handled through the embassies and consular offices. The two thousand permits to visit Bhutan will be granted on a first-come, first-served basis with word of mouth the only advertising. After forestry and agricultural exports, tourism is the third major earner of hard currency. I estimate it earns a few million dollars a year. While the Bhutanese economy can certainly make good use of this money, I am quite certain that if the government ever felt that the integrity of the society was being threatened by tourism, they would not hesitate to end it.

Because there are so few trekkers, even if one is trekking with a small group, one often has the feeling that one is alone. This struck me forcibly one day when I was hiking by myself not far from Chomo Lhari. In the distance I saw a small caravan approaching: men in red robes, some walking and some riding the surefooted Bhutanese ponies that Bogle wrote about with such affection. The ponies had bells on them and their tinkling echoed across the valley. When they came closer I could see that each man was armed with the very long knife Bhutanese men in the countryside use for everything from peeling fruit to trimming tree limbs. In some other country I might have felt a sense of menace. But not here. I had no idea where these men came from or where they were going. The parade might have been something out of the Middle Ages. When they approached me they smiled and briefly waved. They did not seem to have any particular curiosity as to who this rucksack-carrying, eyeglasses-wearing Westerner was. They, and I, were simply well-intentioned, friendly travelers going our own ways. They seemed in perfect harmony with their surroundings and at peace with themselves. I thought of a sort of summary statement Bogle wrote about the Bhutanese people two hundred years ago. He wrote, "The resources of a light heart and a sound constitution are infinite."

Selected Bibliography

Nepal

Anderson, John, ed. *Nepal: Insight Guides.* Singapore: Kok Wah Press, 1986.

Bista, Dor Bahadur. *People of Nepal.* Kathmandu: Government of Nepal, Department of Publicity, 1967.

Buhler, Jean. *Nepal.* Lausanne: Editions Rencenive, 1964.

Chevalley, Gabriel, et al. *Avant-Premiéres à l'Everest.* Paris: Arthaud, 1953.

Furer-Haimendorf, Christoph von. *The Sherpas of Nepal.* London: J. Murray, 1964.

_____. *The Sherpas Transformed.* New Delhi: Sterling, 1984.

Hagen, Tony. *Nepal.* Berne: Kummerly & Frey, 1961.

Hornbein, Thomas F. *Everest: The West Ridge.* London: Allen & Unwin, 1967.

Houston, Charles S. *Going High.* New York: American Alpine Club, 1980.

Hunt, Sir John. *The Ascent of Everest*. London: Hodder & Stoughton, 1953.

Joshi, Bhuwan L., and Rose, Leo. *Democratic Innovations in Nepal*. Los Angeles: University of California Press, 1966.

Landon, Percival. *Nepal*. London: Constable, 1928.

Levi, Sylvain D. *Dans l'Inde*. Paris: F. Reider & Co., 1925.

Majupuria, T. C., and Majupuria, I. *The Complete Guide to Nepal*. Bangkok: Craftsman Press, 1983.

Maraini, Fosco. *Where Four Worlds Meet*. London: H. Hamilton, 1964.

Mihaly, Eugene Bramer. *Foreign Aid and Politics in Nepal*. London: Oxford University Press, 1965.

Morris, John. *A Winter in Nepal*. London: Hart-Davis, 1963.

————. *Nepal and the Gurkhas*. London: Her Majesty's Stationery Office, 1965.

Peissel, Michel. *Tiger for Breakfast*. London: Hodder & Stoughton, 1967.

————. *Mustang: A Lost Tibetan Kingdom*. London: Collins, 1968.

Regmi, D. R. *A Century of Family Autocracy in Nepal*. Benares: Commercial Printing Works, 1950.

Rieffel, Robert. *Nepal: Namaste*. Kathmandu: Sahayagi Prakhashan, 1978.

Snellgrove, David L. *Buddhist Himalaya*. Oxford, England: Cassirer, 1957.

Tucci, Giuseppe. *Nepal: In Search of the Malla*. New York: E. P. Dutton, 1952.

Ullman, James Ramsey. *Man of Everest: Tenzing*. London: George Harrap, 1956.

Unsworth, Walt. *Everest*. Boston: Houghton Mifflin, 1981.

Tibet

Avedon, John F. *In Exile from the Land of Snows*. London: Michael Joseph, 1984.

Booz, Elisabeth B. *Tibet*. Lincolnwood: Passport Books, 1986.

Buckley, M., and Strauss, R. *Tibet: A Travel Survival Kit*. Berkeley: Lonely Planet Publications, 1986.

David-Neel, Alexandra. *Magic and Mystery in Tibet*. New York: Dover, 1971.

————. *My Journey to Lhasa* (1927). Boston: Beacon Press, 1983.

Fleming, Peter. *Bayonets to Lhasa.* New York: Oxford University Press, 1985.

Foster, B., and Foster, M. *Forbidden Journey.* San Francisco: Harper and Row, 1987.

Harrer, Heinrich. *Seven Years in Tibet.* New York: Granada, 1984.

_____. *Return to Tibet.* New York: Penguin, 1986.

Hopkirk, Peter. *Trespassers on the Top of the World.* Los Angeles: J. P. Tarcher, 1983.

Markham, Clements R., ed. *Narratives of the Mission of George Bogle to Tibet* (1774, 1879). Facsimile edition. New Delhi: Manjusri Publishing House, 1971.

Miller, Luree. *On Top of the World.* Seattle: The Mountaineers, 1985.

Richardson, Hugh M. *Tibet and Its History.* Boulder: Shambhala, 1984.

Shakabpa, Tsepon W. D. *Tibet: A Political History.* New York: Potala Publications, 1984.

Snellgrove, D., and Richardson, H. *A Cultural History of Tibet.* Boulder: Shambhala, 1984.

Thubten, T., and Turnbull, C. *Tibet.* New York: Penguin, 1987.

Tucci, Giuseppe. *Tibet: Land of Snows.* New York: Stein & Day, 1967.

Wentz, W. Y. Evans, ed. *The Tibetan Book of the Dead.* New York: Oxford University Press, 1985.

Bhutan

Collister, Peter. *Bhutan and the British.* London: Serindia Publications, 1987.

Eden, Ashley. *Political Missions to Bootan.* Facsimile edition. New Delhi: Manjusri, 1972.

Edmunds, Tom Owen. *Bhutan.* London: Elm Tree Books, 1988.

Hickman, Katie. *Dreams of the Peaceful Dragon.* London: Victor Gollancz, 1987.

Steele, Peter. *Two and Two Halves to Bhutan.* London: Quality Book Club, 1970.